W9-BBS-148

5117

JIMMY BUFFETT

A GOOD LIFE ALL THE WAY

RYAN WHITE

TOUCHSTONE

NEW YORK   LONDON   TORONTO   SYDNEY   NEW DELHI

Touchstone
An Imprint of Simon & Schuster, Inc.
1230 Avenue of the Americas
New York, NY 10020

First Touchstone hardcover edition May 2017

TOUCHSTONE and colophon are registered trademarks
of Simon & Schuster, Inc.

For information about special discounts for bulk purchases,
please contact Simon & Schuster Special Sales at 1-866-506-1949
or business@simonandschuster.com.

The Simon & Schuster Speakers Bureau can bring authors to your live event.
For more information or to book an event, contact the Simon & Schuster Speakers
Bureau at 1-866-248-3049 or visit our website at www.simonspeakers.com.

Interior design by Kyle Kabel

Manufactured in the United States of America

10 9 8 7 6 5 4 3 2 1

Library of Congress Cataloging-in-Publication Data
Names: White, Ryan (Journalist) author.
Title: Jimmy Buffett : a good life all the way / by Ryan White.
Description: New York : Touchstone, [2017]
Identifiers: LCCN 2016052808| ISBN 9781501132551 (hardcover) |
ISBN 9781501132568 (pbk.)
Subjects: LCSH: Buffett, Jimmy. | Rock musicians—United States—Biography. |
LCGFT: Biographies.
Classification: LCC ML420.B874 W55 2017 | DDC 782.42164092 [B]—dc23 LC
record available at https://lccn.loc.gov/2016052808

ISBN 978-1-5011-3255-1
ISBN 978-1-5011-3257-5 (ebook)

For Stella.
Dream big.

Contents

MEMBER BURNETT: How many planes do you own right now?

MR. BUFFETT: Four. A couple of—one for business. Two for business. And the others just for kind of fun.

MEMBER REID: Do you fly all those?

MR. BUFFETT: I fly a seaplane. I fly the jet. I fly a Pilatus. We don't have the big plane anymore. The plane that was involved in the Jamaica thing is on a static display in Orlando at our restaurant.

MEMBER BURNETT: My last question for you, sir, looking at your corporate chart and the success that you have had with Margaritaville, and it clearly is extensive, I think you mentioned or your attorney mentioned that you wrote the song in 1977. When you wrote that song did you have any idea what it would become?

MR. BUFFETT: It's been a pretty good song. No, it was written in five minutes about a hot day in Austin, Texas, with a margarita and with a beautiful woman. I finished it in Key West. I had no idea.

— *From the testimony of James William Buffett, chairman of the board, Margaritaville Holdings, before the Nevada Gaming Control Board, March 7, 2012*

JIMMY BUFFETT

Chapter 1

Once Upon a Time
in Key West

Captain Tony's Saloon, at 428 Greene St., Key West, Florida, was once an icehouse, and then a morgue. Actually, it was an icehouse and a morgue simultaneously, because that's a smart use of resources on a little island.

By the time the U.S.S. *Maine* exploded in Havana Harbor in 1898, the building had become a telegraph station—the first to receive the news, and from there it moved to the rest of the nation. They say the tree growing up through the bar these days was the hanging tree, from which sixteen pirates and one murderous woman (in a blue dress) met their end—but they say a lot of things in the tropics. "It was the base of the mast for the DeForest Wireless Telegraph install in 1905–1906," Monroe County historian Tom Hambright says. Captain Tony Terracino, who died in 2008 at the age of 92, did enjoy mixing his facts and his fictions.

For a while, the building was a cigar factory. But for the most part, 428 Greene has been home to bars—a whole bunch of bars: legal and illegal, gay and not specifically, and all manner in between. Now, as it was in the beginning, Captain Tony's is a place to cool off.

Sloppy Joe Russell opened Sloppy Joe's there in 1933. Hemingway drank there back before where Hemingway drank meant much to the bottom line. Aside from his tab, anyway. No one had thought to put him on a T-shirt. And T-shirts in general, while popular on the shrimp docks and in the bars, hadn't been turned into a business plan because there weren't enough tourists to keep a T-shirt operation in the black.

In 1937, the building's owner tried to raise Joe's rent from $3 a week to $4 a week. Disinclined to pay such an outlandish amount, he moved Sloppy Joe's a block up the street to the corner of Greene and Duval.

Anthony Terracino arrived in Key West in 1948 and for the same reason so many have landed in Key West over the years. He was running away. Specifically, he needed to put some distance between himself and the gangsters who'd left him for dead in a New Jersey dump. In 1958, he bought 428 Greene from David Wolkowsky, whose grandfather had opened a store in Key West in the 1880s and begun collecting properties David would spend much of his life managing, renovating, and enjoying.

Author's photo

Captain Tony would, over the years, build a résumé like a Dos Equis ad—the most interesting man in his world: saloon proprietor, bootlegger, gunrunner, raconteur, lothario. "All you need in life is a tremendous sex drive and a great ego; brains don't mean a shit," he liked to say. And so when people figured out you *could* move a lot of T-shirts, they put that slogan on Captain Tony's T-shirts. Then they put it on posters. The beer koozies say "Oldest Bar in Florida."

Captain Tony's was *the* hangout at the dawn of the seventies, one of them at least. Novelist and poet Jim Harrison was there, working out alongside friend and fellow writer Tom McGuane. They'd gone to Michigan State University together and so Harrison would hit town from up north and crash at McGuane's place on Ann Street.

Tom Corcoran was a kid from Shaker Heights, Ohio, just out of the navy, six-feet-five, fit, fresh-faced, and not as innocent as he looked working a taco cart on the street.

"What are you doing?" Harrison said to Corcoran one night, giving him a good look over.

"Selling tacos," Corcoran said.

"I can see that. Are you a poet or something?"

Corcoran said he was indeed a writer, and he eventually showed Harrison some poems and lyrics. Harrison asked Corcoran to send six of his pieces up to Michigan, where Harrison was planning on publishing a journal of poems. Corcoran never sent them. He still has them marked in a folder and kicks at the memory, but he had a taco cart in Key West back then. He was busy.

The navy sent Corcoran to Key West in 1968. Not long after he left the service in 1969, he headed north to Montreal for a few days, and then south until he ran out of money around Fort Lauderdale. He got a job digging ditches and slept on the floor of an ex-girlfriend's apartment. He'd hoped for more than the floor, but ditch diggers can't be choosers. As soon as he got his first paycheck, he dropped the shovel and pointed himself farther south to where U.S. 1 runs out near the ocean. It was winter 1969. It was cold as hell in Ohio when he walked into Captain Tony's. "And I thought, *Shit, this is exactly what I need*," Corcoran says.

He eventually landed in a second-floor apartment in a former cigar factory that's now the Simonton Court Hotel. He kicked around and weighed his options for a couple of weeks before he called Boston and told his girlfriend Judy she should quit her perfectly good job at an advertising agency and join him on an island closer to Cuba than Miami. And she did just that. Before long, she was working at Captain Tony's and Tom had the taco cart and Harrison had a little piece of a novel.

"When the blond one whose name was Judy bent over the cooler to get our beer we were cleanly mooned," Harrison wrote in 1973's *A Good Day to Die*. "Polka-dot panties. But I knew she was hopeless because she lived with a rather affable freak who sold tacos from a pushcart."

Harrison's narrator was sitting at the bar in Captain Tony's, and that was Judy and Tom, and that is how the southernmost city in the continental United States collected people to play together and inspire one another in the shadow of Hemingway's mythology.

Most of the crowd was literary; some were painters or potters. But there weren't a lot of people, period, and no musicians to speak of. Sometimes Jerry Jeff Walker, who was living on Summerland Key, would roar into town drunk at the wheel of a red Corvette convertible he bought with "Mr. Bojangles" money—maybe most of the "Mr. Bojangles" money at that point. The Nitty Gritty Dirt Band had only recently made it a top-ten hit.

Short on pocket change, Jerry Jeff would play the song for cash in the bar to people who probably didn't even know he'd written it. "And he'd sit there and sing it and I'd go, 'Mother of God, I'm sitting here listening to Jerry Jeff Walker sing 'Mr. Bojangles,'" Corcoran says. "So I introduced myself. And of course everyone liked to hang around with Judy." (See also: panties, polka-dot.)

Sometime around the spring of 1970, and allegedly at the request of Sheriff Bobby Brown, Walker relocated near Miami, to the bohemian enclave of Coconut Grove. Teresa Clark—a bartender at Sloppy Joe's everyone called Murphy—joined him. Corcoran visited once. He remembers a lot of sangria and a terrible hangover.

Up in America, the story was unease. Peace and love were history. The headlines read Vietnam—and then into Cambodia we went. Charles Manson and his family went on trial. Four were killed and nine wounded at Kent State. The Beatles broke up.

But down in the tropics, the living was easy for all the right people who had found the right place at the right time. In Key West, there were sentences to craft, and brush strokes to perfect. There were tarpon and bonefish to hunt. The drugs were plentiful, and the sex wouldn't kill you. America's malaise hadn't made it to the end of U.S. 1 and neither had the tourists. Much to the dismay of civic leaders.

On May 7, 1971, the *Key West Citizen* relayed the news from the Monroe County Advertising Commission's meeting at a restaurant in Marathon: "The commission has contracted for a billboard at Disney World which will be located between the exhibition gate and main gate . . . This brings the total of Monroe County advertising billboards throughout the state to 40."

The cost of the billboards was $140 per month, 12-month lease with an option to renew. In February 1971, peak season, Homestead, Florida, had registered 7,204 visitors heading south toward the Overseas Highway. The Florida Keys needed to bump that number. They were running out of viable—or at least legal—business options.

Not a week after that story, the front page of the *Citizen* announced cuts to city services in the name of austerity. For ninety days, the only purchases Key West could make would be emergency purchases.

Not that civic austerity was much of concern in the Old Anchor Inn (aka the Snake Pit). Nor in Captain Tony's, or Crazy Ophelia's, or Howie's Lounge, or anywhere else where the locals, scraping by anyway, could always scrape together enough for the emergency purchase of another round.

Tom and Judy got married and moved to Grinnell Street. They had a son, Sebastian. Tom went to work bartending at the Chart Room, where the sheriff who ran Jerry Jeff to Coconut Grove would drink alongside treasure hunters who hung out with dope smugglers who knew the shrimpers who didn't kick the shit out of the artists.

Spring gave way to summer. Hurricane season arrived and, before it came to an end, was joined by election season. Key West needed to pick a mayor. The sewer system was one issue. The Conch Train, the rattling choo choo—a "tourist toy," as Shel Silverstein would later describe it—that roams the streets of Key West guiding visitors through island lore, was another. Should the city buy the tour company? Shouldn't the city fix any number of other problems first? Like maybe the streets the Conch Train runs on? Didn't matter in the end. The city couldn't get the $300,000 in necessary financing. The Conch Train wasn't an emergency.

Charles "Sonny" McCoy won the election. The Chamber of Commerce's cruise ship committee launched a fundraising drive to pay for entertainment at Mallory Square when the M.S. *Seaward* would arrive. "Hippies are not welcome in Mexico now," an Associated Press story in the *Citizen* announced. At the Sands Restaurant and Cocktail Lounge, "the one and only" Billy Nine Fingers was playing ragtime, pop, and classics. Over at the American Legion on Stock Island, Decca recording artists Bill and Betty Howard offered country music, "the Nashville Sound," an ad promised. Life on the little island went on weird and wild.

Then one day Jerry Jeff and Murphy rode back into town aboard the Flying Lady—Jerry Jeff's 1947 Packard—and they brought a friend, another singer who'd thought he'd had a gig at the Flick, a famous Coral Gables folk club. When he got to the club, the club told him he was a week early. With time to kill, Jerry Jeff and Murphy brought him straight to Corcoran and the Chart Room, with its low capacity, dark wood, scuffed floors, thumbtacked navigational charts, and Mos Eisley charm.

"And of course the story goes they stopped at every bar down the Keys," Corcoran says. "They didn't. They couldn't have made it."

Maybe yes, maybe no, but they did charge into the Chart Room and Jerry Jeff did announce their arrival in a style befitting the local custom: "We need a drink!" he boomed. Off in the corner, a washboard player scrubbed along to an autoharp. Vic Latham, who'd been sitting at the bar, rose to greet Jerry Jeff. They knew each other from New Orleans in sixties. It was Latham, in fact, who bailed Jerry Jeff from jail the night he wrote "Mr. Bojangles."

Latham had been good for a couch and a little pocket change when he found a musician in need. Thanks to New Orleans, Latham knew the third member of the traveling party, too.

Jerry Jeff shook hands with Corcoran, who gave Murphy a hug and was then introduced to the new guy, Jimmy Something. Jerry Jeff mumbled (or slurred) the last name unrecognizable.

"Hey, Jimmy," Corcoran said. "Whatcha drinking?"

"Heineken," Jimmy Something said.

"First one's free," Corcoran said.

Someone mentioned Jimmy was a singer, too. From Nashville. They drank some more. Did his busted marriage come up? Who remembers? There was more drinking. The edges blurred into lights and laughter. Night grabbed hold of the island. Jimmy Something found a warm welcome.

"I think he must have hooked up with a young woman," Corcoran says.

He did.

"I woke up, and I didn't know where I was," Jimmy Buffett said forty-four years later, looking out from a stage on a beach on the other side of the island. "And that was okay, because there was a young lady who said, 'That's okay. Let's go ride the Conch Train.' So we got a jug of wine and sat on the back of the Conch Train—facing backwards."

Kierkegaard said something about life being understood backward, but lived forward. What Buffett saw from a miniature train moving in one direction, in a seat facing the other, was exactly what he needed.

Nashville had turned cold and gray. The weather sucked, too. He hadn't conquered "Music City." "Music City" barely noticed he was there.

Key West felt like a dream born of favorite books and old television shows, of family history come to life along rutted roads in a town with a budget deficit and a surplus of charm. He'd gone searching for elsewhere and found it at the last American exit. Key West looked like a good place to lick some wounds and catch his breath.

Bouncing along on the back of the Conch Train with a jug of wine and a new friend, Buffett saw a future where "the smilin' eyes match the smilin' faces." He saw . . . a song—unlike any he'd written. He scribbled it down: "I Have Found Me a Home."

He'd quickly meet McGuane, who'd introduce him to everyone, including Harrison. He'd perfect his "'bar singer goes wild on the rebound' routine"—as Buffett phrased it in a remembrance of Harrison after he died in March 2016. "Many generations of misfits have claimed Key West as their town," Buffett continued, "but I would have to argue that, in the early 70s, it truly was our town."

But only he would figure out how to package and sell it.

Chapter 2

The Mythical, Mystical, Poetic, Romantic, and Artistic History of Jimmy Buffett

The *Chiquimula* lies somewhere beneath the black water where the Blakely River flows into Mobile Bay. She burned to the waterline in 1953—a "fire of undetermined origin," the paper said the next day—but for years she remained visible at low tide, fading away, little by little, until she was more memory than roadside curiosity.

By the time the *Chiquimula* burned, she'd been sitting next to the causeway for thirteen years. Storms had robbed her of three of her four towering masts, but none of her mysteriousness. To Gulf Coast tourists armed with cameras, and to artists who'd sit on the riverbank and put brush to canvas, she was a beautifully decrepit hulk—176 feet of "what's her story?"

"And like a lady who has been around a bit—her presence has inspired a world of gossip," the *Mobile Press-Register* wrote on March 10, 1946.

If the gang in Key West wondered where the new guy had come from, the *Chiquimula* held a few clues. Jimmy Buffett wasn't the first Buffett to set out for adventure—that would have been his grandfather, the *Chiquimula*'s former captain.

9

"Skipper Draws Back Pages On History of Sailing Ship," read the headline striped across page 1-B that long ago Sunday. "Schooner Deserted in Mobile Bay Skirted World Before Taking Rest." Captain James Buffett, then residing at 316 McKinley St., Pascagoula, Mississippi, shared a little of his history, too.

He'd been aboard another windjammer, running oil and ammunition to Europe during World War I. Before that, he'd "hustled case oil" to Japan for the Standard Oil Company and taken a stab at seal hunting in the Indian Ocean.

When he made call in Mobile in 1946, he was delivering the 440-foot aircraft repair ship *Maj. Gen. Robert Olds* to the Mobile Air Technical Service Command for decommissioning. A year earlier, he'd guided the *Olds* through a typhoon off Okinawa, riding out 60-foot seas and 142-mile-an-hour winds.

"From windjammers to B-29s is the story of Capt. Buffett," the *Press-Register* wrote, "and while he admits he would rather have the rolling quarterdeck under his feet, he had to concede the airplane was here to stay after making a round trip from Guam to Oklahoma City via Superfortress."

Built in Seattle for United Fruit Company, the *Chiquimula* launched in 1917 hauling railroad and steel parts to the company's Central American plantations. When Captain Buffett took command in February 1924, she was carrying lumber, salt, and coal between the West Indies and the Unites States. He sailed her until 1927, long enough to put a fast end to one rumor. Had the old ship been part of the rum-running fleet off New Orleans during the nation's "dry spell"? "No, sir," the captain said. "I don't believe it. She's far too slow!"

He recalled pushing her through a hurricane north of Cuba en route to the Canary Islands. "The gallant ship weathered the blow," the paper said, "although she strained her timbers to such an extent that she has leaked from that day to this."

Then there was the time the wind stopped. Running salt from

the British West Indies to New York, the *Chiquimula* was stranded for three days off Atlantic City. "For a while," the *New York Daily News* reported on page two of its Sunday, September 20, 1925, edition, "the outlook was black . . . Helpless in a dead calm, she finally signaled a coast guard cutter and got a scanty supply of food to bring her to New York." When the *Daily News* reporter visited the *Chiquimula* in quarantine, Captain Buffett had gone ashore to "clear his ship," but his wife and two children, Jimmy and Patricia, were among those aboard. "Mrs. Buffett," as Hilda was identified, said it was her second time to sea with her husband, and likely her last. The ship's first mate—"taciturn and short of speech"—shrugged while reading a paper. "You have to expect calms and short rations now and then," he said.

Captain Buffett shared his first mate's nonchalance. Something as elemental as a lack of wind wasn't going to keep him from the sea. In 1961, when the *Press-Register* attempted another story on the remains of the *Chiquimula*, writer Ed Lee was left to fall back on earlier reporting. "We tried to contact Capt. Buffett," Lee wrote, "but he is still going to sea. At present he is master of the *Tiny Tim*, a pogey boat operated by Smith Fish Meal Co. of Pascagoula and he was away from port every time we tried to reach him. However, according to our records, the good captain, who told us he began his career as a mariner at fifteen, has been sailing for forty-nine years."

Fifteen. Other versions of the story put James Delaney Buffett Sr. to sea at thirteen, fourteen, or sixteen. In all of them, he was *young* when he jumped out the window of his family's home in Sydney, Nova Scotia, hopped a ship, and set out into the world, putting oceans between himself and the dark, cramped coal mines dotting the landscape back home.

The thought of a life confined in those mines, huffing dust and dirt with every breath, might have been enough to push him and his younger brother (William) out that window toward whatever unknown sat waiting beyond the horizon. More than a leap from a window, it was a leap of almost unimaginable faith in what *could* be.

From Nova Scotia, James Buffett worked his way to Pascagoula, Mississippi, and back out of Pascagoula, and back to Pascagoula. Returning again and again to Horn Island, one of a string of barrier islands in the Gulf of Mexico where ships hauling lumber would moor and unload. While the ships were emptied, sailors waited and wandered and crashed in boarding houses.

Mrs. Seymour's place was on the Pascagoula River, but its nickname, the Singing River, is more poetic. Legend holds that the Pascagoula tribe worshipped a mermaid and when the first Catholic missionary arrived in the 1500s, the mermaid, not particularly interested in competition, rose from the water and called the Pascagoula to her with a song. They followed her voice into the river's waters and were never seen again. But they are heard—in a low hum over the river that builds to a crescendo and continues to this day. No one's been able to explain it, but in an 1890 story written for *Popular Science Monthly*, Pascagoula resident Charles E. Chidsey did identify the song's single note. It's an F.

A more peaceful (if no less alluring) siren's song drew Captain Buffett to Pascagoula on a more semipermanent basis. The oldest of Mrs. Seymour's seven children was Hilda, who was seventeen in 1916 when James Buffett walked into the boarding house.

The best telling of the story belongs not to the captain's famous storytelling grandson, but to Mary Loraine "Peets" Buffett. In "A Sailor's Life," written in 1986 for *Mobile Bay Monthly Magazine*, Captain Buffett's daughter-in-law recalled the night she met her boyfriend's father for the first time. It was 1941. They were at a restaurant called Pelham's. The captain was running a cargo ship named *Delmundo* between New Orleans and South America for the Mississippi Shipping Company. When he was at sea, life in Pascagoula moved on whims; when the captain returned home, so too did order. Catherine, the third-born, didn't date. The youngest—and wildest—Billy, didn't delay on his way home from school. Patricia, the second oldest, married and living next door, was at the ready for whatever the captain might want or need. As for the captain's oldest child, "J. D. was in early each evening," Peets wrote. Everyone was well behaved.

Peets was nineteen then, working at Ingalls shipyard and living in Gulfport. She was her own woman, curious, nervous, and a touch apprehensive as she walked into the restaurant. She'd heard plenty about the captain, and figured him "demanding" in that way that keeps a ship sailing but doesn't make for a particularly entertaining dinner companion. But she also sensed J. D. was a potentially serious proposition. "Besides," she wrote, "we planned to sneak off after dinner and go for a moonlight sail."

First, the captain chastised J. D. for being late (her own fault, Peets wrote). Next, he asked Peets what kind of name Peets was for a girl. Then he offered a sturdy handshake and invited her to sit down and have a beer. "Help yourself to some of this seafood, too," he said. "It's mighty damn good."

To the question of her name, Peets noted it was her last name, and it was Welsh. The captain agreed he'd call her Peets, adding that his family* also came from Wales. By the time dinner broke, she was enthralled by his stories of life at sea. She wanted to know more. Like how he landed in Pascagoula.

Hilda was how. The captain came and went from Mrs. Seymour's boarding house without noticing that one of the daughters had

---

* It is possible Captain Buffett's English ancestors include John Buffett, a sailor who, upon arriving in the Pitcairn Islands in 1823, married the daughter of one of the H.M.S. *Bounty*'s mutineers. This was a point of emphasis in a 2005 *Wall Street Journal* story about the long-suspected family connection between Jimmy and billionaire investor Warren Buffett. In 1983, the two traveled to Norfolk Island, between Australia and New Zealand in the Tasman Sea, to meet all the many descendants, "legitimate and otherwise," of John. How many were actual descendants was tough to say. As Warren Buffett's sister told the *Journal*, "There are plenty of miscellaneous Buffetts."

taken an interest in him. Eventually, Hilda took matters into her own hands and slipped a note into a book he was reading. They were married in 1918. James Delaney Jr. (J. D.) was born in 1919 and would celebrate his first birthday in Cuba.

The Buffetts had set sail from Pascagoula to New Orleans aboard the *Monfalcone*,* a 372-foot, five-masted barkentine. At St. Andrews Dock, they picked up three million feet of lumber and set out for Havana. A storm delayed their arrival. By the time they made port, there was no money to pay for the lumber, and so the ship waited for a deal to be cut.

It was there, on the deck of the *Monfalcone*, where J. D. took his first unsteady steps—on his first birthday. Captain Buffett celebrated by hoisting the ship's signal flags, and each skipper followed suit until all the flags on all the ships in Havana harbor were flying in celebration.

Soon the *Chiquimula* would be the ship to take the captain away and bring him home again. Sailing ships would give way to steamships, and then steam to diesel, and Captain James Buffett would master them all and carry licenses as proof. Life would loosen when he was gone, and tidy up when he returned. He was the moon controlling the tides. To his grandkids, he was the key to the universe. They called him Foo Foo.

With his father's discipline and eye for detail, J. D. Buffett enlisted in the Army Corps of Engineers on his twenty-second

---

* In 1923, the *Monfalcone* set out from New Orleans to Los Angeles, where she was to begin running lumber along the West Coast. Instead, she hit a storm three days out, had her masts ripped free, and barely made Panama. Eventually she was towed to Los Angeles. By 1925, steamships and market conditions made most sailing ships obsolete, and so, in 1928, she was purchased and refitted for duty as a gambling barge. Anchored in international waters off Los Angeles, the *Monfalcone* regularly ran afoul of the law, and occasionally, other gambling ships. In 1930, she caught fire with nearly three hundred passengers aboard and burned to the water line. A United Press story noted the orchestra "played lively music until all the passengers had been removed" to water taxis for the six-mile ride back to Seal Beach. What didn't burn sank, including a safe containing $50,000.

birthday and flew around the world with stops in Maine, Montana, Africa, and India. He and Peets married on May 6, 1942, and he was a master sergeant by the time he was discharged in February 1946—a month before his father guided the *Olds* into Mobile.

On December 25, 1946, J. D. and Peets welcomed their first child, James William Buffett. This was the same day W. C. Fields died. The same W. C. Fields who could juggle anything he could lift. W. C. Fields, who said, "'Twas a woman drove me to drink. I never had the courtesy to thank her." W. C. Fields, who also said, "If you can't dazzle them with brilliance, baffle them with bull."

"I think this only goes to prove God does have a sense of humor," Jimmy would write nearly fifty years later, marking his half-century milestone with a Christmas album named *Christmas Island*.

Buffett was born in Pascagoula, but he grew up in Mobile, thirty-six miles east on U.S. 90. They call Mobile the Mother of Mystics. It's home to the country's first carnival societies. It's where each year the Order of Myths (the Double-O Ms), founded in 1867 (and first parading in 1868), punctuate Fat Tuesday with Folly chasing Death around a single broken Greek column atop a float pulled by mules and flanked by flambeaux men—their kerosene-fueled lanterns flickering dancing light about one last night of sin before Ash Wednesday's salvation.

The Order of Myths qualifies as the oldest mystic society in America, and its founding the beginning of Mobile's modern carnival era. But the first celebration dates to 1703—fifteen years before New Orleans began throwing its more famous bacchanal. Mardi Gras continued in Mobile until the Civil War put an end to the party. The story of carnival's return stars a Confederate soldier named Joe Cain, who came home to find Mobile occupied by Union troops uninterested in letting the good times roll.

On Fat Tuesday, 1866, Cain decided it was finally time to have a little fun. He and some friends dressed as a Chickasaw Indian tribe, with Joe masked as the fictional Chief Slacabamarinico. He was said to be from Wragg Swamp, "which is west of midtown Mobile," L. Craig Roberts wrote in *Mardi Gras in Mobile*, "now filled in and the site of Mobile's major malls and shopping centers." The group paraded through town—past Union troops—with Confederate uniforms under their costumes.

The next year, Cain and company rode again. This time in the company of a bass drum, on the side of which was written, "The Lost Cause Minstrels." That was 1867. In 1868, Cain and his group paraded with the Double-O Ms, marching straight into history. Some of the story is even true.

Steve Joynt is the editor and publisher of *Mobile Mask* magazine. In the 2015 edition of his "Reveler's Guide to Mardi Gras," Joynt dug into the Joe Cain story. In a History Museum of Mobile file titled "Myths and Mardi Gras" he found a 298-word article with the byline of Joseph S. Cain. The date and publication are missing. But the story puts Joe in New Orleans in 1866, with Mobile's Washington Fire Company No. 8. "Even in Joe's account there are factual errors," Joynt wrote. Washington No. 8 traveled to New Orleans in 1867. Whenever exactly Cain visited New Orleans, he did write the event was "so pleasurable that I determined on my return home, that Mobile should have its own Mardi Gras celebration . . ."

Joynt found more than enough evidence to suggest Joe Cain didn't lead parades in 1866 or 1867. There's no mention anywhere of revelry that would have been noticed and noted as it was in 1868 when Mobilians opening the *Mobile Daily Register* on Ash Wednesday would have read, "Yesterday was a new era in the mythical, mystical, poetic, romantic, and artistic history of Mobile." Carnival had returned. Joe Cain and his Lost Cause Minstrels likely did lead the way, even if they were maybe only a few steps ahead of the Order of Myths, and his legend only grew.

Folly and death in the Church Street Graveyard, Mobile, Alabama.

In the Church Street Graveyard, cheap plastic beads decorate Joe's gravestone, which reads: "Here Lies Old Joe Cain. The Heart and Soul of Mardi Gras in Mobile." Joe Cain Day is celebrated each year on the Sunday before Fat Tuesday and features the Joe Cain Procession, also known as the People's Parade. It's preceded by Cain's Merry Widows, a mystic society founded in 1974 whose members, veiled and dressed in black, wail and moan on their march to Joe's grave before moving on to his former home for a toast or two (or many more).

"Down in Mobile they're all crazy," Eugene Walter wrote in his 1953 novel, *The Untidy Pilgrim*, about a man from central Alabama who goes to the coast—below the salt line—and settles among the offbeat. "Because the Gulf Coast is the kingdom of monkeys, the land of clowns, ghosts and musicians and Mobile is sweet lunacy's county seat."

Lunacy's is but one flag Mobile's flown. Spanish explorer Alonso Álvarez de Pineda, who charted most of the Gulf Coast, arrived in 1519. Twenty years later, Hernando de Soto followed in search of gold. In 1559, a third Spanish explorer set up shop and was blown away by a hurricane.

The French arrived in the late 1600s, setting up first at the western tip of Mobile Bay on what is now Dauphin Island. Finding bodies strewn about (likely a Native American burial ground washed out by the weather), they called it Massacre Island.

Brothers Jean-Baptiste Le Moyne de Bienville and Pierre Le Moyne d'Iberville established the first permanent residence in 1702, miles upriver from Mobile Bay. It must have appeared inviting, though an invitation accepted mostly by disease, natural disaster, and an angry Native population. Mobile moved to its current site in 1711. The French held the area until 1763, the English until 1780, and then the Spanish got their shot. The United States took over in 1813 when General James Wilkinson marched American troops from New Orleans and Mobile became part of the Mississippi Territory.

Mobile grew into the second-largest seaport on the Gulf Coast and is home to two wrecks more notable than the *Chiquimula*. In 1860, the *Clotilde*, thought to be the last slave ship to arrive from Africa, was abandoned nearby.

The U.S.S. *Tecumseh*, sunk by a Confederate mine in 1864, rests at the bottom of Mobile Bay. It was aboard the *Tecumseh* that Adm. David Farragut is said to have made famous the phrase, "Damn the torpedoes! Full speed ahead!"

They say if you weren't born in Mobile, you'll never be a Mobilian. "Been here fifty years and I'll never be a native," says one local. "They used to say, 'Unless you're conceived under an azalea bush in Mobile, you're not a Mobilian,'" says another. And inside the centuries-old mansions on Government Street, power and prestige are passed down through the generations and codified in carnival's royal courts. And if you weren't a native, and if you lived outside the power structure, you stood on the sidewalk and shouted yourself hoarse hoping for a box of Cracker Jacks to come flying from a float and then scrapped for the loot when it landed. Jimmy Buffett fought for the Cracker Jacks like everyone else.

J. D. and Peets got jobs at the Alabama Dry Dock and Ship-building Company. J. D. worked his way from the estimating de-partment to managing government contracts, a job that demanded an attention to detail that came naturally to the son of a sailor. Each job had a checklist, and each box on that list had better be checked. Slip up, miss something—anything—and maybe the next job goes to another company. Lose enough contracts and people lose jobs. Best to get things right the first time, and if you're over-seeing the entire operation, best to know the job inside out and from every angle.

"Our dad was, to say the least, 'old school,'" Buffett wrote in the foreword to his sister Lucy's cookbook, *LuLu's Kitchen: A Taste of the Gulf Coast Good Life*. Old school is strict, but it isn't without style. He recalled his father's grill, a sturdy, after-hours project "constructed out of titanium plates designed as armor for warships and smuggled in pieces from the welding shop." He loved to cook, a glass of Cutty Sark in his hand, and that grill, built to survive hurricanes, did just that and would follow him from house to house, from one side of Mobile Bay to the other, until Lucy one day put it to work in the kitchen of a restaurant.

Peets Buffett remained her own woman—a sledgehammer against glass ceilings and conventions. She was the Alabama Dry Dock and Shipbuilding Company's first equal-employment coordinator. When she retired in 1979, she was the company's first female director of industrial relations. *After* she retired, she went back to school. At the age of 64, she graduated cum laude from the University of South Alabama. If she loved one thing, it was learning. If she loved two things, they were learning and a good party.

When she died in September 2003, not six months after J. D. succumbed to Alzheimer's, *60 Minutes'* Ed Bradley gave the eulogy.

He recalled a wheelchair-bound Peets at the foot of a New Orleans staircase that led to a French Quarter soiree.

"Ed," she said, "I'm going to trust you to get me up those stairs."

As friends and family arrived at the funeral mass, they were handed a card. Peets's eight-point guide to life (which Lucy reprinted in her cookbook):

1. Read often, even the classics.
2. Accept everyone for who they are, not what they do.
3. Be well traveled.
4. Learn to be a listener. Shhhh!
5. Live by the sea.
6. Listen to your spirit and find joy.
7. Education, like money, doesn't make you happy or successful, but it sure helps.
8. Love AND family are the best things we have.

Peets was, Bradley said, a lot like Jimmy's song "One Particular Harbour," a warm, inviting, protecting presence where children play and "all are safe within." Corcoran knew her well and calls her the ultimate rock-and-roll mom. "A lot of Jimmy's sensibilities came from her," he says. "She was just everybody's coach and best friend."

J. D. and Peets added two daughters, Loraine Marie (Laurie) and Lucy Anne (LuLu), to the family, and Jimmy endured a traditional Southern parochial education in Mobile, first at St. Ignatius and then at the McGill Institute, an all-boys school (until it merged with the Bishop Toolen High School for Girls in 1972, long after Jimmy's shadow had become a ghost). He was an altar boy. He played trombone in the band. He was even a cheerleader, the perfect extracurricular for the relentlessly upbeat. He worked as a lifeguard. He kept his hair short and his smile wide. He idolized Huck Finn and Jim Hawkins. He could have been any kid, anywhere, starring in a middle-class American story. He *was* that kid, and might have followed that kid's path into law or finance or some other middle-management outpost in a cubicle culture—but for the captain.

The captain and Hilda lived on Parsley Avenue in Pascagoula, and from their backyard, a path cut through brambles of reeds and blackberry bushes to the edge of Baptiste Bayou, where there was a little crab pier.

One day, the captain pulled a nautical chart of North and South America from a cedar chest in his workshop and led his grandson to the pier.

"Where are we?" the captain said.

"On the crab pier."

"Look again," the captain said, pointing to the chart.

Slowly, his point came into focus. They were at the beginning, of everything. Jimmy could trace a path with his finger down Baptiste Bayou to Mississippi Sound and past the barrier islands—the Cajun Bahamas—to the Gulf of Mexico. From there, the only thing standing between Jimmy and the world would be a lack of imagination or an overabundance of caution. At the bottom of the map, Captain Buffett had written two words: Start Here.

All he had to do was leap and the world would be his, and that turned out pretty well for Huck and Jim and Foo Foo, didn't it?

In Buffett's father's later years, as Alzheimer's left him "chasing false echoes," as Buffett would write so poignantly in song, they'd travel together in search of a little truth and beauty and peace of mind. They took a trip to Nova Scotia to see again where it all began for the captain, and, therefore, where it all began for the kids.

"We were in Sydney and we had an aunt there and she took us to the house," Buffett said onstage in Key West in April 2015. *The house*, the one the captain left behind.

Later, Buffett asked his dad what he thought of the day. "He just said, 'Well, I'm just glad he jumped out of that window or we'd all have been goddamn coal miners,'" Buffett said. "So thanks for jumping out that window, Foo Foo."

* *Chapter 3* *

The *Nashville Telegraph*

Sometime in 1969, Milton Brown got a call from a panicked Jimmy Buffett. "Milton," he said. "Buzz isn't going to sign me unless you'll tear up that agreement." Milton was, and is, a songwriter in Mobile perhaps best known as the guy who wrote the theme song for Clint Eastwood's *Every Which Way but Loose*. Buzz was, and is, Buzz Cason, founder of Nashville's first rock-and-roll band, writer of hits, vocalist, producer, and doer of music business. "That agreement" made Brown something like Buffett's first manager, a complicating contractual hang up for Cason as he worked to sign Buffett to a publishing deal in Nashville.

"I said, 'Jimmy, consider it torn up,' and I forgot about it," Brown says.

He sat at his desk in his office—a small house where he operates a real estate and music production business. There was an old reel-to-reel recorder behind him on a shelf full of books that includes a copy of Buffett's *A Pirate Looks at Fifty*. On a wall, above a comfortably worn couch, hangs a framed and autographed late-1970s photo of Jimmy. Laughing and wrapped in his sailboat's furled mainsail like it was a hammock, Buffett wrote: "Milton, Would you buy a used car from this man? Love Jimmy."

"Isn't that funny?" Brown says.

True to his word, Brown forgot about Buffett's old contract, but he didn't tear it up. It went into a file, and that file was filled with other papers and then filed alongside more files in filing cabinets. The agreement was buried in the stacks and forgotten for thirty years until it finally worked its way back to the surface. It's now neatly matted and framed and hangs above a filing cabinet stacked with phone books and papers and topped like a cake by a Betty Boop figurine.

"My wife is going through old files and shredding stuff and throwing things away and lo and behold, she comes upon this contract that Jimmy and I signed," Brown says. "And I'm reading it, and it says, ten percent of everything."

Well, it says ten percent of everything for a three-year period beginning May 28, 1969, and the artist could terminate the contract with fifteen days written notice should the agent not arrange for at least one release or a master recording in a twelve-month period. "It wasn't like what the Colonel had with Elvis," Brown says.

But it's a neat piece of history on the wall and makes for a good story. Brown was talking to Jimmy's mother one day, and he said, "Peets, let me tell you what I found."

"What?" she said.

"I found a contract that says Jimmy owes me ten percent of everything he earns."

Brown did the math and figured Jimmy had probably made $800 million. "This goes back," he says. "He's probably made a whole lot more now."

Ten percent of his guesstimate was a lot of money then (and a lot of money now). Brown remembers that Peets looked at him and said, "Milton, please don't tell him that. He'll have a heart attack."

"Fast forward now to fairly recently," Brown says. "He was at the Grand Hotel and I had breakfast with him and I told him that story of my conversation with Peets, and he said, 'I wouldn't have had a heart attack. My *lawyers* would have had a heart attack.'

"So, anyway, there have been a whole lot of good times and he's been a good friend for a lot of years."

He and Buffett met because a beauty queen walked into Brown's recording studio in the late 1960s. When Margie Washichek won Miss U.S.S. *Alabama* in 1967, the *Panama City News* put the story on its July 17 front page and described her as a "pert" Spring Hill College coed. Her father owned a marine junkyard in Mobile, and the recording studio Brown built above a dentist's office with friends was partially operated by scraps salvaged from Marina Junk. When Margie came to see Brown, it was to ask a favor. Her fiancé was a singer. Would Brown maybe give him a listen?

"The first thing I noticed when Jimmy walked in the room was that persona," Brown says. "The Jimmy persona. The smile lit up the entire room. Even though he wasn't the Caribbean Cowboy yet—way before the sand-between-the-toes days—it was that glow. Even before I heard him sing, there was that presence."

After Buffett graduated from the McGill Institute in 1964, he left the coast for the first time in his life, heading north to Auburn University because after graduation you went to college, and because college looked a whole lot safer than getting tangled in the increasingly complicated turmoil in Southeast Asia. Auburn it was, and if he was to follow the all-American template, college would be followed by a stable job to pay for a house, a nice wife with which to begin a family, a family to amuse on those two weeks of paid vacation every year, and good health care to help keep the household humming.

"When I discovered the guitar I went in an opposite direction," Buffett said at the American Library in Paris in 2015, "which led me to New Orleans, because the French Quarter was there. Because I wanted to be a bohemian and I wanted to do that stuff."

At Auburn, he met a few Sigma Pi guys he liked during rush week and they had rooms available; he rushed the fraternity and moved in. At one of their parties he saw a guy named Johnny Youngblood surrounded by girls. He was playing guitar and singing songs by the Drifters, the Tams, and Sam Cooke.

"It was black music sung by a bunch of drunken white college kids," Buffett wrote in *A Pirate Looks at Fifty*. And everyone loved it. Buffett interrogated Youngblood about the guitar. Youngblood pulled a pint of Scotch, more than happy to answer Buffett's questions but admitting he only knew three chords.

"Teach me those chords."

He learned D, and then C, and once you get there, you're two-thirds of the way to freedom, fun, and popularity with members of the opposite sex. Buffett quickly flunked out of Auburn, but he took those chords and that spark of inspiration when he left campus. How he came to attend Pearl River Junior College is, if not the stuff of legend, at least the stuff of halftime shows.

Narrating a 2013 Jimmy Buffett–themed football halftime show by Pearl River Community College's* marching band, Buffett claimed to have found the school by accident on a return trip from Baton Rouge, Louisiana, where he'd been attempting to get into Louisiana State University. He was in the redneck Louisiana and Mississippi of his deepest, darkest fears—above the salt line—and stopped at a light in Poplarville wondering how he might redeem an academic career in tatters. Maybe he could fly helicopters in Vietnam. His father would respect that, and then . . . *hello*. He saw a woman walking to class, followed her onto campus, and registered.

It's about seventy-five miles from Poplarville to New Orleans, and Buffett made that drive most every weekend in an oil-guzzling,

---

* In 1960, Pearl River Junior College and Agricultural High School changed its name to Pearl River Junior College. It became Pearl River Community College in 1988.

smoke-belching Ford Falcon nicknamed the "Tan Hopper." It's almost twice as far from Hattiesburg, Mississippi, to New Orleans. Hattiesburg, home to the University of Southern Mississippi, was stop number three on Jimmy Buffett's sixties Southern college tour.

"Hattiesburg: Where tomorrow is yesterday," Buffett said to big laughs during a 1992 taping of Jerry Jeff Walker's television show *The Texas Connection*. "It's not on the sign as you go into town."

"I was really taking two night classes a week and living in New Orleans," Buffett said, smirking. "Commuting to school."

"That's not a heavy load you were carrying," Walker said.

"It was not a heavy load. I think it was photography and use of the library."

Like Pearl River, Southern Miss wasn't much more than an alibi. The action was in New Orleans and its scrappier Gulf Coast neighbor—Biloxi. There was open gambling in Biloxi long before gambling was legalized. There were bars with cheap drinks and liberal definitions of who should be allowed to consume them. Biloxi is where Elvis vacationed. It's where Jayne Mansfield, on her way to New Orleans, died in a car crash in 1967 after leaving Gus Stevens' Seafood Restaurant and Buccaneer Supper Club. Biloxi had scars and a temper and ill-considered tattoos.

Buffett began playing a pizza joint in Hattiesburg, and then bars in Biloxi. At the pizza joint, the Vietnam vets who held down the backroom reassured him his choice of a guitar over a gun or a pilot's seat was the right decision. New Orleans took care of the rest.

New Orleans was voodoo and hoodoo and Elvis singing out to the Crawfish Lady from a balcony above French Quarter streets in the opening moments of *King Creole*.

Pirates haunted New Orleans. It's where Jean Lafitte did business in a blacksmith's shop full of dark corners and fire. And where, down Bourbon Street, rumor says Lafitte met with Andrew Jackson on the second floor of a bar (where Oscar Wilde and Mark Twain would later drink) to plan the same Battle of New Orleans that Buffett, his cousins, and their friends would one day reenact on the banks of Baptiste Bayou in Pascagoula.

New Orleans is where Huck's river made its last mighty push toward the gulf, Buffett's grandfather's ships working north against the current coming home at the end of another adventure. The Buffetts would meet the captain when he'd arrive at the Governor Nicholls Street Wharf and then head to dinner at Tujague's.

New Orleans is where, on one of those rendezvous, Buffett spied a banana palm in a French Quarter courtyard. Surrounded by slash pine and live oak, the palm was faintly out of sorts. It was a suggestion—of some exotic elsewhere out there on the wind. "It was a discovery as fascinating to a ten year old boy as the Galapagos must have been to Darwin," Buffett would write in the notes to his 1996 album *Banana Wind*. "It was not the tree itself, but the place from which it had come that set me to daydreaming and thinking about the tropics." After all, he noted, the night sky in Pascagoula isn't much different than the night sky in Martinique.

In the New Orleans of 1967, the Bayou Room, surrounded by Bourbon Street strip joints, was Carnegie Hall for the Gulf Coast's bohemians, hippies, and freaks. The Gunga Den, a nearby burlesque club was pretty great, too. Both had stages Buffett aspired to play.

New Orleans was school. He studied the way musicians and friends like Bob Cook, Brent Webster, and Gene Marshall worked the French Quarter crowds. Buffett dreamed of a Martin D-28 like Marshall's and would take his not-a-Martin, set up on a street corner and do what musicians have been doing in New Orleans since the beginning of time. He worked for tips along that fine line between Big Easy work and Big Easy play.

"Well, we've been having a good time for a long time," Allen Toussaint told me a few months before his death in 2015. "It took us longer to see the big picture than anywhere in else in America. We were just so localized. We were having a good time with each other, and whoever came to town saw what was going on.

"And Jimmy, of course, he'd view something like that and he'd see it for all it is, whereas some would just see circuses, he'd see all there is, the ingredients."

The recipe included stand-up basses, long after the rest of the world was plugging in, acoustic guitars, pianos, second lines and brass bands. *Laissez le bon temps roulez*.

Trends, Mr. Toussaint noted, move east and west in America. New York makes something hip and then Chicago jumps on board and by the time it lands in Los Angeles, New York has moved on with a backward glance, smirking at the beach bums. Or Los Angeles develops a little laid-back cool and off it heads toward the Big Apple.

"You have to take a left turn to come down to this boot and there we are," Toussaint said. "So geographically, as well as soulfully, we have been sort of off the beaten path of a certain kind of progress. And whenever you find that, I don't care how primitive or how modern it is, you kind of like that."

Buffett put together a band, the Upstairs Alliance, which included friends from his new fraternity at Southern Miss, Kappa Sigma. They played campus; they played parties; they auditioned at the Bayou Room and actually got the gig. They had Upstairs Alliance business cards made. Address: 616 Ursulines Street, Apt. 6C. Slogan: The Sound at the Top. Contact: Jim Buffett or Rick Bennett.

At the Gunga Den, a red curtain with gold tassels framed the stage. At the Bayou Room, hats woven from palm fronds hung on a bare brick wall behind the band as they played hits like the Byrds' "I'll Feel a Whole Lot Better,"* and Stones and Beatles covers.

Author's photo

Buffett's first home base in the French Quarter. It was as easy a walk to the Café du Monde as it was to the Bayou Room.

When their set was done, Jim Buffett might swing by the Preservation Hall to hear Sweet Emma Barrett hammer on the piano out in front of her band. Then he'd hit the street corners, playing all night. He'd watch the sun rise from the bank of the Mississippi River then get coffee and beignets. He'd wanted to be a bohemian and do all that *stuff*, and he did. As detailed in *A Pirate Looks at Fifty*, Buffett got into Eskatrol, an amphetamine marketed for weight loss. He had a high-priced call girl girlfriend.

---

* Audio of this is available on YouTube. They did right by the Byrds.

The apartment on Ursulines, in a townhouse built in the 1830s, was rumored to be the "House of the Rising Sun"—making it one of dozens of houses of rising suns in and around New Orleans. Whatever its past, it was a perfectly located clubhouse, a place to while away an oppressively hot afternoon with a nap before the sun set, the temperature cooled, and the night glowed bright.

The Upstairs Alliance didn't last. First bands never do. But Buffett learned a few stage tricks and got a feel for working a crowd, be it at the Bayou Room or on the corner of Conti and Chartres Streets, where he'd work out songs like the Toussaint-penned Benny Spellman hit, "Fortune Teller," about a guy falling in love with the woman who tells him he'll fall in love. Is it magic? Is it about being in the right place at the right time and recognizing an opportunity? Is there much of a difference between the two?

Buffett had lucked into his encounter with Johnny Youngblood *and* the unnamed Siren of Pearl River Community College. He was bold enough to aim for the Bayou Room and brave enough to dream beyond the business world his peers were zeroing in on. And Buffett was smart enough to see a street corner and a Bourbon Street bar as but another departure point with as much potential as the old crab pier on Baptiste Bayou. Start there.

Buffett caught his next break in 1969 after graduating from Southern Mississippi on May 24 with a Bachelor of Science in history and, fittingly, public address. He flunked his draft physical. Free to chase a career in music, he pointed himself farther north.

He had a PA system (because he'd been the Upstairs Alliance member able to get a line of credit), and a few contacts, including Brent Webster. Buffett set out alone—a one-man touring operation handling booking, transportation, setup, set lists, and payout.

He was doing fine until the sight of a tornado ripping up a trailer park in South Dakota pointed him back toward the Gulf Coast. "I had been behaving rather badly for several years," he wrote in *A Pirate Looks at Fifty*. The pangs he felt could have been good old-fashioned Catholic guilt programmed by years of parochial school. Or it could have been fear, a moment's hesitation at the window.

Buffett turned the car around, asked his girlfriend Margie to marry him, and they moved back to Mobile. He stuck a toe in the mainstream, but didn't dive in. He didn't quit music. Instead, he got a gig in the bar in the corner of a hotel named after Raphael Semmes, who'd commanded the U.S.S. *Somers* in the Gulf of Mexico during the Mexican-American War, moved to Mobile, and during the Civil War, captained the CSS *Alabama*.

The Admiral's Corner, in the Admiral Semmes Hotel, sat on the edge of the town's 1711 city limit, and it was there Buffett developed his first dedicated audience. Then, with Margie's introduction, he went to see Milton Brown.

By then, Brown had heard some singers and seen some stars. Near as he can figure, his family settled in the Mobile area in the 1860s—1870s at the latest. He probably wasn't conceived under an azalea tree, but he's the one who made that joke.

Brown's mother was into show tunes, and so he was into show tunes. When he got to the University of Alabama—like Buffett at Auburn—he discovered black music in a white environment. "Like Odetta, like Josh White," Brown says. "But they couldn't come play here because of segregation."

However, Eastern Air Lines was running nonstop weekend flights from Alabama to Chicago. Tickets were cheap. Brown would fly up and hit the Rush Street clubs. He saw Odetta. He saw Josh White. "Goose-bump time," he says.

Then he got into bluegrass. After that, he got into the army, heading to Germany around the same time as Elvis. Brown came home, went to work for his dad, but held on to a tenor guitar he bought overseas.

Once a week, Brown would play a folk song on the television morning show *Alabama Jubilee*. Don Davis hosted; he would eventually run Harlan Howard's publishing operation, Wilderness Music. Davis was married to Anita Carter—of *those* Carters, the only Carters who matter in country music.

The youngest daughter of Ezra and Mother Maybelle, Anita would sing background for Brown. "And I'm so ignorant of it, I don't even realize who I've got singing backup when I'm singing these folk songs," he says.

Every week he'd gather the band for about fifteen minutes before they went on the air, teach them the song, and then they'd go live. No overdubs. No do-overs. He'd ask the viewers for requests, and they'd mail the titles of songs they'd like to hear. He'd learn those and play them. He aimed to please.

"I'd begun to write country music by then, and one of the people I really liked was Ernest Tubb," Brown says. Davis knew Tubb and said he'd pitch a song Brown had written with "E. T." in mind. Tubb passed.

Disheartened but undeterred, Brown took a shot writing a duet for Tubb and Loretta Lynn. Brown cut the demo and, right before his wedding, sent Tubb a song titled "I Won't Cheat Again on You (If You Won't Cheat on Me)."

Brown and his new wife honeymooned in Nashville, and when they returned to Brown's 660-square-foot former bachelor pad, the phone rang. His wife picked up the phone. "It was the first time she'd answered the phone as Mrs. Milton Brown," Brown says. "And she said, 'Milton, it's someone who says she's Mrs. Ernest Tubb.'"

If "E. T." could have the publishing, he'd record Milton's we-each-done-each-other-wrong song. "E. T." was in luck. Publishing was open. On February 18, 1969, at Bradley's Barn in Mt. Juliet, Tennessee, Ernest Tubb and Loretta Lynn cut "I Won't Cheat Again on You (If You Won't Cheat on Me)" with Brown watching from behind the board.

Brown's own studio in Mobile, Product Sound Studio, opened in 1967. A *Billboard* item from July 1, 1967, announced Honeycomb

Records, "a label featuring country music product." Sound Investment Inc. owned Honeycomb and had been formed in January 1967. Travis Turk, a sound engineer and DJ, was president. John Edd Thompson, a songwriter and soon-to-be beloved TV meteorologist, was vice president. Brown was secretary. Nick Panayiotou, who dabbled in radio and whose father owned a Greek restaurant called Constantine's, rounded out the team.

Brown was sufficiently impressed with Buffett to invite him to record. Working the soundboard at Product Sound—a board he'd rigged from scrap—Turk helped Buffett get both sides of a 45 to tape. The A-side, "Abandoned on Tuesday," seemed as incongruous to the soon-to-be-married Buffett as "I Won't Cheat Again on You (If You Won't Cheat On Me)" was to the recently married Brown. There's no happy ending in "Abandoned on Tuesday," just a guy left standing glum and alone "with a dream in my hand"—and that's just the first verse.

The B-side, "Don't Bring Me Candy," would prefer its romantic partner bring herself instead, and not play games, not even Monopoly, because someone is going to land on Boardwalk, and "the one who lands on Boardwalk has to pay." In love, life, and real estate, location has always been everything. Be honest and true is all the singer asks.

They were standard-for-the-late-sixties folk tunes. Simple song structures and straightforward sentiments. They weren't complicated, and there were plenty more where those came from—with more arriving all the time—and so Brown invited Buffett to join him up in Nashville for a session at Spar Recording Studios.

Brown could get Spar at a discounted late-night price, and the players hanging around the studio were ace. Junior Huskey might be on bass. Lloyd Green could be on pedal steel. Brown could polish the production of his songs better in Nashville than he could in Mobile, and the market was right outside the door.

Nashville was where you went to do business if you weren't

going to Los Angeles or New York. Whenever Brown had ten songs ready, he'd drive north and knock them out in three hours at Spar—almost always first takes. Then came the day he only had seven songs, but studio time booked. He asked Buffett if he'd like to cut a few of his songs. Buffett recorded three and then raced back to Mobile for his regular Admiral's Corner gig. He could have stayed and spent a night in Nashville, but he wouldn't.

"He didn't want to lose that job," Brown says. "And he asked me, 'Would you run these songs, would you pitch them for me?'"

The first to bite was Jack Grady, who ran the Nashville office of CBS's publishing wing, April-Blackwood. "I forget, it was a nominal amount, something like a hundred dollars per week," Brown says. Plus an album and a single, and all Grady needed was approval from his boss—who was in Europe. He'd call the next day.

"I go back the next day, he keeps me waiting an hour," Brown says. "Never a good sign." When Grady finally emerged, it was with half the deal. If it had been $100 per week, the new one was $50. They'd do an album, but no single. Brown explained to Grady that Buffett had just gotten married. He wanted to move to Nashville and give songwriting a serious shot. He needed more than they were offering. There wasn't any more, Grady said. "Well I'll get back to him," Brown told Grady, "but I just don't think he can take that."

Brown went back to the Holiday Inn where he always stayed— even on his honeymoon—the one nearest Music Row, which is Nashville's Wall Street. The guest elevator was broken so he took the service elevator to his room and arrived to another ringing phone. It was Buzz Cason, the aforementioned musician, songwriter, producer, and East Nashville native. Cason was assembling his own publishing company and he'd heard Buffett's April-Blackwood deal had fallen through. It hadn't been an hour, and Brown hadn't even had time to call Buffett, much less anyone else.

"You remember when Jimmy wrote that song called 'Coconut Telegraph'?" Brown says. That was after his feet had found the sand, but it was recorded in Muscle Shoals, Alabama, and captured the free-and-easy flow of information on a tiny island. "I've thought of it many times over the years. It must have been the *Nashville Telegraph*," Brown says.

Cason was willing to make the deal Grady couldn't, or wouldn't. It wasn't fame and piles of cash, but it was a job in a town that, with a little luck, could give you both. It was better than no deal. For the second time in his life, Jimmy Buffett packed his bags and headed north from sweet lunacy's county seat.

* *Chapter 4* *

"I Guess They'll Get Us Started"

Spar Recording Studios, in a basement near Vanderbilt University, was home to a little sleight of hand.

Hit Records made hit records, but not *the* hit records. It was a sound-alike operation. Each week they'd check the charts, record covers of the two most popular songs (cuts from Elvis and Dion, for example), package the 45s, rush them to the racks, and undercut the competition—the actual hit makers—by as much as half.

"And they had salesmen all over the country," Cason says, his leg up and an ice pack on his knee—one of those injuries that results from nothing more than time. He'd limped into Creative Workshop, the first studio in Berry Hill, a neighborhood south of downtown Nashville that had been a bedroom community when he built in 1970. Now it's a swarm of music studios and publishing houses (usually both in the same building). House of Blues has a studio up the street. Past that, Brent Maher, who helped Cason build Creative Workshop and then discovered the Judds, has his own shop with gold and platinum records on the walls. Next door to Creative, another studio Cason built and then sold has been turned into a recording palace, a complex of nine studios called Blackbird that's owned by Martina McBride and her husband John.

Creative Workshop was the first, though. Travis Turk, who'd help Milton Brown build the studio in Mobile, came to Nashville to help Cason and became the new studio's chief engineer. Turk had the technical chops. Cason had music business experience.

He grew up in East Nashville—trendy now, not then—and formed the town's first rock band, the Casuals. The Casuals became Brenda Lee's backing band and Cason can pepper a story with the big names: Elvis, Sammy Davis Jr., Ricky Nelson.

Hanging on a wall in Creative Workshop's lobby is a red, white, and blue show poster from July 5, 2014. The Country Music Hall of Fame and Museum presented Poets and Prophets, a salute to "legendary" songwriter Buzz Cason. Writer of "Everlasting Love" and "Soldier of Love." Producer of "She Shot a Hole in My Soul."

Robert Knight's take on "Everlasting Love," cowritten with Mac Gayden, hit number thirteen on *Billboard*'s Hot 100 in 1967 and featured the rhythm section of drummer Kenneth Buttrey and, on bass, Norbert Putnam, a studio player with a growing reputation who'd come up from Muscle Shoals just as that small north Alabama town was beginning to grow its reputation as "The Hit Recording Capital of the World."

Framed on another wall are the cover of Cason's 2012 autobiography, *Everlasting Love*, and the first page of a chapter titled "Jimmy Buffett, Down to Earth." Next to a photo of Buffett sitting on a suitcase in an empty Union Station in New York in 1971, and written in Buffett's CAPS-LOCK scrawl, are two endorsements: "Buzz, I love reliving my past. You got it right," and "This book makes me want to quit my day gig and go off and join a rock 'n' roll band."

Other signs point to the blurb's redundancy. Above the door heading to the studio, still wrapped in cellophane, is a street sign announcing JIMMY BUFFETT DRIVE. On the opposite wall, a platinum award for Buffett's 1992 box set, *Boats, Beaches, Bars & Ballads*.

There has, over the years, been some small controversy as to whether or not Buffett sang on any of those Hit Records knockoff sessions at Spar. Cason says no. Turk says no. Buffett appeared on a cover, because he was hanging out and they were shooting a cover. That's it. Nothing more. Spar was, however, where Buffett cut what became his first album, *Down to Earth*—as apropos a title as that box set's would later prove.

Nashville might have been the land of possibility, but opportunity was a harder proposition than hope. They made records, and hits, and hit records in Nashville, but there weren't a lot of places to play live music in those days. The stage tricks Buffett picked up in New Orleans weren't much help in Tennessee, because there weren't many stages. Compounding the problem, he wasn't selling his songs to other singers and producers, because his songs weren't Nashville songs. He'd probably have been better served working alongside the folkies in New York's Greenwich Village, or falling into the Laurel Canyon scene in Southern California. But he and his new wife had a Nashville budget, and so Nashville it was.

Buffett signed with Russell-Cason Music Co. in July 1969, a moment marked by the *Mobile Press-Register* on July 21. Buffett told his hometown paper his music was "contemporary," citing John Hartford and Joni Mitchell. "I would like to project a message people would listen to and think about," he said. Margie, the story said, was Buffett's biggest fan.

"With Jimmy's talent and Margie's enthusiasm, it's hard to doubt that some day soon Mobile will see his face and name on record album covers and perhaps even watch him perform on television." He and Margie buttressed the future's promise by posing for a photo that looked exactly like happily ever after in the making.

In Tennessee, however, it cost more than his wife's enthusiasm to pay the bills. Margie got a job with ASCAP,* but that wasn't enough, either. "So I had to get a real job," Buffett said in Paris in 2015.

He found it in the Help Wanted section of the *Nashville Banner*. *Billboard* needed a writer. "I went from one week knocking on doors getting rejection after rejection for songs I was trying to pitch, to working for *Billboard* magazine where people sent me free records and I had an expense account," he said.

His real job was covering Nashville's bold-faced comings and goings.

> **Kris Kristofferson** has written three songs which will be featured in the new movie by the **Rolling Stones**. He also has his first album out which is on Monument . . . **David Allen Coe**'s long awaited Penitentiary Blues on the SSS label has just been released. Coe wrote all of the songs while in prison . . . **Al Mair**, general manager of **Gordon Lightfoot**'s Early Morning Productions was in town for several days from Toronto . . .

So read the scoop from Nashville in *Billboard*'s May 30, 1970, edition. Buffett, under various spellings of his name, wrote reviews, too. In that same May 30 issue, Jimmy Buffet declared Ronnie Millsaps's set at Roger Miller's King of the Road Motor Inn to be "professionally tight." Presumably that was Ronnie Milsap.

---

* The American Society of Composers, Authors and Publishers protects (and collects on behalf of) the people who write the songs. Margie didn't stay there long. By October 1970, she'd moved to assistant director of talent and tickets for *The Johnny Cash Show*. In 1974, she was hired by Capitol Records as national artist relations coordinator in Los Angeles.

Earlier that year, on January 17, Jim Buffett raved about Tony Joe White's performance at Municipal Auditorium, saying he "showed the crowd what 'swamp rock' was all about," and with minimalist flair—just Tony Joe's electric guitar and a drummer, "Sammy Creasy." (Sammy Creason, probably.)

"I kind of looked for little stories around town . . . and I had a great time doing it," Buffett told Dave Hoekstra on WGN Radio in 2015. "Plus, it opened a number of doors."

Doors to executive offices, studio floors, and publishing houses. Buffett would run into Chet Atkins or Jerry Jeff Walker. He might kill a few minutes chatting up musicians between sessions. Or he could shoot the shit with his boss.

Bill Williams was *Billboard*'s Nashville editor. He knew the town and the business that turned its gears. A hit song was nice, but owning the publishing on a hit song was even better. At night over beers, Williams would impart wisdom. Foremost: take care of your end of the deal, because all anyone else cares about is their end.

"Artists are a disposable commodity," Buffett told Hoekstra. There's always another kid who can sing. They roll into Nashville every day. And they know—every one of them *knows*—that all they need is a shot, someone to offer a stage, or listen to a song. All they need is someone to believe enough to pass a contract across a desk.

Buffett wasn't any different. He wanted was his name in lights, his photo on an album cover, exactly as had been foretold in the *Mobile Press-Register*. Once that album became a hit, and he became a star, the second record would take care of itself. The money spigot would open. Eventually he wouldn't have to pull his albums from the Misc. B section to the front of a record store's "B" bin. He'd have his own section. After a couple number ones, maybe they'd even spell his name right. Two T's, always, and everyone who'd ever laughed would look up at him onstage "spellbound, with lumps caught in their throats," exactly as he imagined in one of his "contemporary" folk songs, "Ain't He a Genius."

"So I'm working at *Billboard*," Buffett told Hoekstra, "but I'm singing at anti-Vietnam rallies in my fringe jacket in Nashville, and that was risky business in those days." It was antiestablishment, and Nashville liked establishment. Establishment meant order. Order meant money. A lot of people were making money in Nashville, and they'd prefer to continue making at least as much money, and more if at all possible.

Buffett didn't write to script. He wasn't really writing country music. He was, as he said, trying to make people think. Tucked in his ode to the all-American superhero "Captain America," Buffett took a poke at Spiro Agnew and a swipe at Merle Haggard's anti-anti-Vietnam protest hit. Buffett's Captain America, "hip" as he is, "just can't dig the Okie from Muskogee," Buffett sang.

"Ellis Dee (He Ain't Free)" took up the cause of a poor black man who got nothing but grief from a world that never tried to see things through his eyes. "There's Nothing Soft About Hard Times" gave voice to the hopeless, its dirt-poor narrator separated from his family and whiling away his days on a bench in New Orleans's Jackson Square, drinking wine and waiting to "bum another dime."

In "Richard Frost," a singer leaves Alabama, changes his name, and instead of bright lights, finds himself frustrated, stuck in a roadhouse bar in Oklahoma. "Is every song a routine chore?" Buffett wondered.

On January 2, 1970, Captain James Delaney Buffett died. Jimmy and his cousin Baxter were among the pallbearers at his funeral, and a few weeks later, Buffett wrote "The Captain and the Kid," capturing his grandfather's restlessness on land, and Jimmy's eternal admiration. "He's somewhere on the ocean now, that's where he ought to be," Buffett sang. "One hand on the starboard rail, he's waving back at me."

At Spar, with Turk producing, Buffett recorded most everything he'd written. Twenty or thirty songs* knocked out and punched up with the band, Buffett's voice arriving upright, like he was trying to sound older than he was, and as much like Gordon Lightfoot and Fred Neil as he could. He sounded . . . serious. And it was serious business, this topical folk music of the times.

Consider "The Missionary," about a true believer, a far-away salesman pitching the virtues of home: peace and prosperity and goodness. "I told them how we'd learn to change our sword blades into plows," and doesn't that sound like something you'd want, too, folks? Who wouldn't? Upon closer inspection, however, he discovers his country at war, its "brave and strong" leaders murdered. Disillusioned, he realizes he'd been preaching a lie.

Buffett and Brown teamed up to write "The Christian?"—a protest song about religion and hypocrisy. "That was the era," Brown says, "and it basically was: Mom and Dad, you messed it up and it's going to be our generation that has to fix it." Buffett and Brown built a lyric simple enough to connect, yet clever enough to catch your ear: "You picked a hell of a time to be thinking about Heaven."

Country music has always done better business with faith than crisis of faith, and without question the question mark on the song's title—"The Christian?"—came with enough power to unnerve radio programmers, and that was enough to terrify executives, neither of which were sure what to make of the singer or his songs. Nashville didn't line up outside Cason's door to bid on the new kid in town.

---

* Many of those early songs remain unreleased through no fault of Turk's. He has been working for years to get them out, and been close a few times before Jimmy's interest waned and the project fell from favor. Cason said one idea was a collection titled *Uncovered Treasure*. Another plan called for Jimmy to pen extensive liner notes. Turk holds out hope something will happen.

But Cason and Buffett played tennis in nearby Oak Hill with a guy named Mike Shepherd and a DJ named Roger Schutt. Schutt was best known as Captain Midnight. When he died in 2005, his CMT.com obituary pegged him as "confidant, guru and pinball-playing partner" to Waylon Jennings, Jessi Colter, Tompall Glaser, and the rest of what became country music's outlaw wing. Kinky Friedman called Schutt the "patron saint of sleepless nights."

Shepherd ran Andy Williams's Barnaby Records and was the only one who was any good at tennis. "The rest of us couldn't play for nothing," Cason says.

"I've been hitting balls for seventy years," Shepherd says. Since he was nine years old. He still plays tennis every Tuesday night. Cason remembers mentioning Buffett's work to Shepherd while they were playing. Shepherd remembers Buffett coming to see him to pitch songs.

"Barnaby was owned by Andy and distributed by Columbia Records," Shepherd says. He was running the label with Ray Stevens from an office on Seventeenth Avenue in Nashville. Most of what they did was manage the catalog Williams had purchased from Archie Bleyer's Cadence Records. Cadence had released Williams's early hits, as well as the Everly Brothers, the Chordettes, and others. A jazz and blues subsidiary, Candid Records, worked with Lightnin' Hopkins and Charles Mingus.

The back catalog was nice, but in Nashville everyone wanted publishing on what was, and a hand in discovering what will be next. "Guys started to come in," Shepherd says. Pitching songs and singers. "Guy comes in with a dub. He worked for *Billboard*. He came up from Alabama. He was running around Nashville trying to get songs published."

The guy played Shepherd a song called "The Christian?" Shepherd thought it was great. Told the guy, "You know what, we'll put this out." Shepherd took Buffett to New York, made the introductions, and the deal was signed.

"I said, 'Man, Mike let us recut it. It's at that funky Spar studio over there,'" Cason says. He hadn't built Creative Workshop yet, but he was sure they could get into a better studio than Spar. They'd handed him demos, after all. Nothing more. Shepherd thought the record was fine as it was. Cason took the proposition to Buffett.

"Do you want to let them put out those demos?" Cason asked.

"I guess they'll get us started," Buffett said.

In the June 6, 1970, edition of *Billboard*, instead of a byline, Jimmy Buffett was himself a bold name, one of twenty-eight songwriters elected to ASCAP membership. Among the new singles *Billboard* felt deserving of attention from the commercial gatekeepers were the latest from Frankie Valli ("Circles in the Sand") and Perry Como ("Love Is Spreading Over the World"), Sam & Dave ("Knock It Out the Park"), and Buffett.

Of "The Christian?" Buffett's employer wrote: "Strong debut out of the Nashville scene is a potent piece of material with a biting lyric and a top vocal workout. Could make it big!" A week later, *Billboard*'s next Jimmy Buffett mention included the news he'd left *Billboard*—along with a reminder "The Christian?" was widely available.

"And it didn't do anything," Cason says. "The album didn't do anything either, much."

"Nothing happened," Shepherd says. "Completely stiffed."

Down to Earth was about people who had nothing but a belief about how things should be. It was idealistic and certain and hard-edged. It was, as its title suggests, grounded in day-to-day struggles. Even the album cover—"The cover!" Shepherd says, laughing—was a weather vane. The sixties were over and the hippies had been dispatched to the backseat of a rusted car buried in Cumberland River silt and shale.

Gerry Wood, who worked at ASCAP with Margie Buffett (and later also wrote for *Billboard*), took the photo as he and Jimmy cruised the river in Wood's ten-foot rowboat. For *Island Life*, in September 1992, Wood wrote they were looking for the cover of an album that was going to be titled *Jimmy Buffett Drives Religion and Politics into the Ground*.

That junked-out automobile was almost too perfect. Buffett climbed in the back, and Wood said, "If you feel or hear anything slithering in there, it's probably just a water moccasin."

Wood worked fast to capture Buffett in a faded floral shirt, his lips pursed and his hands folded and resting on the seat in front of him. The photo rightly sighs. The title changed, but the photo fit all the same.

Cason remembers (and Shepherd confirms) a $2,500 advance for *Down to Earth*. They scored $4,000 for the next Jimmy Buffett record, because they needed Bergen White to arrange strings. "We thought we really had pulled something off," Cason says.

High Cumberland Jubilee was cut at Creative Workshop and picked up where *Down to Earth* left off. Specifically, *Down to Earth* ended with "Truck Stop Salvation," the story of a rock star ripping through an ultraconservative backwater, the kind of place where the sheriff comes armed with "self-inflicted grammar" and the locals are whipped into a frenzy by a guy "who's not weird, just a man who's bein' free."

Cason cowrote six of the *High Cumberland Jubilee*'s eleven songs. Most of the album was about loners and losers and outcasts out on the road. Like "Ace," out in the street, "never knowing what he's going to find." Like the woman "In the Shelter" of New Orleans, "the city where she knows she might lose it all," and probably will. So she sits by the river and cries, wondering what life means.

The tears in "Livingston's Gone to Texas" are Holly's, cried for her man who just had to leave and see the world. "It's crazy and it's different, but it's really being free," remarks the song's narrator (while putting the moves on Holly in her time of sorrow).

"Rockefeller Square" sneered at another kind of freedom—to play the outcast—enjoyed by the rich kid safe in the knowledge "there'll still be a piece of Daddy's kingdom" when he's ready to come home.

A young professional couple, Buffett and Margie weren't immune to a little acting of their own. They'd leveraged themselves and bought a Mercedes, crafting German engineering into a symbol of American adulthood.

The finer things were nice, but Buffett's sympathies were clear. He stood with the hippies wearing dime-store clothes and driving beat-up trucks.

Two years into Nixon's America, Buffett had aligned his songs and their characters with the outsiders. And on the second side of *High Cumberland Jubilee*, he took a few of them out of town and put them in a cabin in the Tennessee hills. He called them the Hang-Out Gang and, showing off on the album closing "High Cumberland Jubilee/Comin' Down Slow," they could swing from a Beatlesesque piano ballad to a wild blue grass stomp quicker than any program director could say "We won't play that."

So Buffett wanted his star to shine bright and wide, but he continued to want it with *his* songs, no one else's. The sheriff's lousy grammar was the sheriff's problem, not Buffett's.

In his 2009 memoir, *Moon River and Me*, Andy Williams wrote, "Barnaby was never more than a sideline for me." Others referred to it as a vanity label. The difference between the descriptions is slight. Williams had enough interest in its business, however, to want it closer to his home. Shepherd says he was told he needed to move to Los Angeles, a move he didn't want to make because he'd gotten married the year before and had an eight-month-old child.

Of course, when you're married and have a baby, you also don't want to lose a perfectly good job, and so Shepherd moved to Los Angeles and Jimmy Buffett's career got lost along the way. Literally, according to Barnaby, which never released *High Cumberland Jubilee* and claimed the master tapes had gone missing. Cason, shaking his head, still calls it "the Barnaby fiasco." As for Shepherd, his concerns regarding his move west were prescient. A year after he and his family arrived in Los Angeles, Shepherd was divorced and his wife had moved back to Nashville.

Cason took Buffett to New York to try to get him a new record deal. "And we got turned down by every label in New York," Cason says. "Paul Colby at the Bitter End was one of the only people who liked him."

Colby, who died in 2014 at the age of 96, managed the Greenwich Village club for a decade before he bought it in 1974. The Bitter End was, in the words of Kris Kristofferson, speaking to the *New York Times* in 1992, a place where "people like me and Bob Dylan didn't just perform, we came to hang out." It was a songwriters' room, and its tables were reserved for people who liked songs.

Cason took Jimmy to see Colby and Colby tossed him onstage. "After he made it, I remember Colby telling me, 'I knew that kid was going to make it,'" Cason says. "And there were several people who later regretted it, labels that turned me down."

Even Buffett's biggest fan, Margie, had something of a change of heart. They both did. They were young and it was hard, money was tight and nothing was going right. The world is full of couples in love, couples with good and true reasons to get married. Those reasons don't always hold against pressure and time. Jimmy and Margie split, and it was enough to sour even a generally good-natured guy.

"I hated Nashville," Buffett told *Rolling Stone* in 1975. "It's too closed and incompetent, and there's a lot of nepotism. I was sick of it, so I moved to Key West."

Chapter 5

Regattas, Regrettas, and Adventures at the End of the Road

The Original Tequila Regatta, later rechristened a Regretta after unsuccessful attempts to replicate, took off from the Chart Room in the fading days of 1971. "We three were in the bar," Tom Corcoran says, meaning himself, Buffett, and Phil Clark, another sometimes–Chart Room bartender. Sometimes Clark did other things. Sometimes he was the bartender and still managed to do other stuff—like charge the locals' drinks to tourists' rooms at the Pier House hotel. It was the perfect crime.

"You could see the beach from the Chart Room in those days," Corcoran says. "There was no vegetation whatsoever. There was a swimming pool, and sand, and that's it."

That was more than enough for an obstacle course, of sorts. The first obstacle was a shot of tequila at the bar. Then they were to race to the pool and swim across to the second shot of tequila. Next, a sprint down the beach to a waiting catamaran—and a third shot of tequila. Aboard each catamaran, a teammate awaited. Corcoran was paired with Judy—in life and in competition. Clark teamed up with his girlfriend, an artist named Sonia. Buffett was with a third woman, Mason. From shore they'd race around two buoys and back to the beach, the winner to be named King of Key West forever or until everyone forgot about it, whichever came first.

The catamarans had been rented from a businessman named Wendell, but everyone called him Swindle Wendell. "Nobody knew his last name," Corcoran says. Wendell was from Georgia, his boats were licensed in Alabama, and he was renting them for $8 an hour in Florida. "Totally illegal," Corcoran says. But Wendell was on time with his rent to the Pier House, and so who really cared about something as minor as a few registration stickers?

Wendell had six or eight catamarans. They all sucked, and he knew it. That was part of his charm, or his con, depending on your point of view. The current off the Pier House beach headed out to sea, and so Wendell would rent these "unseaworthy pieces of crap," as Corcoran recalls them, to tourists who'd get out in the channel and break down. In the small print of the rental contract was a clause that said Wendell would happily rescue you if you were in trouble—for an extra $35.

On this particular day, however, Wendell didn't hang out on the beach to wait and see if the drunken locals needed saving. Neither did anyone else. After Buffett and crew threw back their shots and set sail toward glory, everyone on the beach went back to the Chart Room. "They don't give a shit," Corcoran says.

Which wouldn't have mattered, but Clark had a head-on collision with the first buoy and popped his sail. Buffett lost his rudder and it sank to the bottom. "I was the only operational boat, and so they declared me the winner and said, 'Alright, we gotta get our asses back,'" Corcoran says. Then his mainsheet tore. Oh shit.

They lashed the catamarans together. The women stretched out on the third with a joint. Corcoran, Buffett, and Clark grabbed the line from the first and began to swim toward the now-deserted beach. It was *work*—exhausting and pointless. They couldn't beat the current. They paused to try to figure a way to make the current work *for* them. They couldn't. It wouldn't. "We were being drawn out to sea," Corcoran says. "This was bad."

From behind them, then, came the sound of . . . *laughter*? Laughter. Who was laughing? Mason, Judy, and Sonia were laughing. Their boat had broken free from the flotilla, but they were too high to say anything. The guys looped back around, reconnected the boats—this time with the passengers in front—but were still being swept to sea, to the Gulf Stream, to a bad night. They kept swimming. Finally, they perceived some progress, but not enough. That's when a black motor yacht appeared. Corcoran remembers forty, maybe forty-five feet of boat. Jet black. No one had seen it before. No one saw it after.

"Could have been military for all I know," Corcoran says. "CIA. It just doesn't see us." Or didn't care—until Mason took matters into her own hands. She was wearing a long, flowing gossamer swimsuit cover and in one gracefully stoned motion launched herself from the boat, winged her arms like a butterfly and got the yacht's attention.

No less mysteriously, the yacht adjusted and made for the group.

They shouted and waved and pointed toward the beach. They saw no one aboard the yacht. They saw an open window. That's all. Then a big, heavy hawser unfurled over the stern and in their direction. They didn't see who threw it. They grabbed hold and the yacht towed them to the beach and then disappeared for good.

"And that's 'I'm hanging on to a line from a sailboat, oh nautical wheelers save me,'" Corcoran says. "That's what it's all about." That, as another song would one day say, was living your life like a song.

Solares Hill was a newspaper in Key West named after the highest point on the island, geographically speaking. Three months before Jerry Jeff and Murphy packed their house guest in the Flying Lady and drove Jimmy Buffett to Key West, *Solares Hill* republished William Adee Whitehead's "Notices of Key West."

Whitehead was indispensable in Key West's early years: fire chief, city councilman, school board member, and eventually, mayor. He was also the island's first historian. In 1829, he assembled a survey of life on Key West. A year later, as the island's first collector of customs, he "helped bring 'law and order' to the marine wrecking frontier on the reefs." So said *Solares Hill*.

Whitehead wrote "Notices of Key West" in 1835 for a gentleman in St. Augustine who had requested a description of the island. Whitehead led with the good stuff. "That the harbor of Key West was the resort of Pirates, occasionally, has been proved by the evidence of many who were connected with them in their lawless depridations [*sic*]," Whitehead wrote, "and by the discovery of hidden articles that could only have been secreted by them."

Ponce de Leon first visited in the early 1500s, and for many years after, the Keys were home mostly to those pirates, fisherman supplying Havana, and Native Americans. The mainland tribes and the island tribes don't appear to have gotten along. Battles between the two pushed the islanders farther and farther southwest along the Keys until they ran out of islands and, backs to the ocean, were slaughtered. What non-Natives found when they finally began to kick Key West's tires was an island strewn with the losers' remains.

It became known as Cayo Hueso—Bone Island—"which the English, with the same ease that they transformed the wine Xeres Seco into 'Sherry Sack,' corrupted into 'Key West,'" *Solares Hill* explained. Not that history could entirely wipe out as cool a name as Bone Island. Today there's a Bone Island Brewing, a Bone Island Haunted Pub Crawl, and one Bone Island Chiropractic among Google's "Bone Island" listings.

In August 1815, in exchange for "military services rendered," the Spanish governor of Florida, Don Juan de Estrado, gifted Key West to Juan P. Salas. Salas was so unimpressed that for seven years he didn't touch his patch of scrub and palms and limestone marl. What Salas saw when he took a look at his island wasn't opportunity, it was malaria, yellow fever, and not much else. So he went to Cuba.

John Simonton had a better imagination. A businessman from Mobile, Simonton met Salas in Havana, purchased Key West for $2,000, and was handed the keys to the island in January 1822. John Whitehead (William's brother), John Fleeming, and Pardon Greene signed on as partners.

A General John Geddes arrived from Charleston, South Carolina, claiming he owned Key West, having purchased it from a man named John Strong who had bought it from . . . Salas, who'd sold the island twice. Strong did the same, selling Key West to Geddes and another man. A good grift has always been in fashion in Key West.

Simonton's claim won out, and he and his partners set about taking advantage of the deepest port between New Orleans and Norfolk, Virginia. Dedicating a new city hall on July 4, 1876, Walter C. Maloney quoted Whitehead's "Notices of Key West" at length in a speech he lamented he'd had but fifteen days to write. Woe the poor citizenry had Maloney more time to prepare what was eventually published under the title A Sketch of the History of Key West, Florida. As it was, he went on (and on, and on)—about the history of mail delivery to Key West, the history of its newspapers, its annual mortality rates, its religious affiliations, its taxes paid. No detail was too inconsequential. In 1832, the year Key West was incorporated, the value of all real estate was $65,923.75. There were 81 buildings—including sheds.

"The original proprietors and first settlers of Key West considered the manufacture of salt as the most probable means of making it known to the commercial world," Maloney told the assembled crowd.

"The first fire of any consequence was in 1843," he said, "when the large wooden warehouse of F. A. Browne, standing on the south side of Simonton Street, near the water, was destroyed."

Coincidentally, in the middle of his speech, and much to the relief of all in attendance, a bar caught fire. It might have been a cherished bar, and any bar burning down is sad, but watching it burn beat listening to Maloney. Most of the crowd left.

Maloney might have been better off following William Whitehead's lead. He should have talked pirates. In 1819, during James Monroe's administration, Congress authorized a small naval force to combat piracy. In 1822, with piracy still on the rise, the secretary of the navy sent Captain David Porter to Key West to set up shop. Porter ordered enough firepower for the job and arrived in Key West in 1823 to launch what turned out to be an effective antipiracy campaign.

(If pirates were hanged, they weren't hanged from that tree on Greene Street, where Captain Tony's is today. They'd have been hanged outside the Monroe County Courthouse, on Fleming Street, where chickens scratch in the shade of a towering kapok tree.)

From its founding, Key West has been more closely associated with Cuba and the Bahamas than the United States. During the Civil War, Key West was the southernmost northern outpost. It was the Union, not the Confederacy that held Fort Zachary Taylor. In 1982, in response to a U.S. Border Patrol blockade on U.S. 1 south of Miami, the Keys announced their succession from the Union and formed the Conch Republic. They continue to celebrate each year on April 23 and describe it as Independence Day, Bastille Day, and Cinco de Mayo rolled into one.

Key West was and is for dreamers, schemers, and contradictions. It's boom or bust and always has been. Sometimes it's boom *and* bust. Even today, as cruise ships spit out tourists, the tourists pass by the homeless and the desperate. As the hotel prices go up and rents increase, the people who serve the meals, clean the rooms, and sling the drinks increasingly can't afford to live where they work.

Wrecking, sponging, cigars, and shrimping drove the earliest fortunes. Wreckers, in an effort to better business, would set false signal lights to draw ships to the reefs. Between salvage operations, they'd sponge. By the 1890s, the man known as Key West's Sponge King was making $500,000 a year.

The chief competitor to prosperity has been hurricanes. In 1846, all but six of the eight hundred homes on the island were damaged or destroyed. In 1912, Standard Oil founder Henry Flagler's crews drove the final nails into a rail line from the mainland, connecting Key West to the United States. In 1919, as the Casa Marina hotel was being built, a hurricane caused $2 million worth damage to Key West. In 1924, the La Concha hotel opened on Duval Street. In 1926, another hurricane strafed the Keys. In 1928, an early version of the Overseas Highway was completed (though ferries were still necessary to get all the way to Key West).

Then the stock market tanked and the Depression arrived. Key West was bankrupt by 1934. New Deal projects resulted in the construction of the Key West Aquarium and Mallory Dock. The Works Progress Administration brought artists to Key West to begin selling the island to tourists. In 1935, a hurricane washed out forty miles of railroad and killed hundreds. By 1938, with the help of what was left of the railroad, the highway was completed and you could drive from the mainland straight through to Key West.

Hemingway arrived in 1928 to write and fish and drink, to be the guy all the other guys would aspire to be. He based his barkeep in *To Have and Have Not* on Sloppy Joe, and the La Concha was the first landmark to come over the horizon as Harry Morgan made his way back from Cuba. Even then tourism was part opportunity, part specter, Harry telling another he was convinced they were being starved out "so they can burn down the shacks and put up apartments and make this a tourist town."

And later in a bar, a visitor says to his wife: "Let's get out of here, dear . . . Everybody is either insulting or nuts."

"It's a strange place," a Professor MacWalsey replies. "They call it the Gibraltar of America and it's three hundred and seventy-five miles south of Cairo, Egypt."

It's hot, and that heat breeds its own sweet lunacy. Writers, artists, outcasts, they found their way. They led the way, as they usually do. Tennessee Williams, Truman Capote, Tom McGuane, Jim Harrison and, eventually, James William Buffett—who, after kicking around on couches and in spare rooms, rented an apartment at 1911 Seidenberg Ave.* for $150 per month and began making himself a Chart Room regular.

Buffett fell in easy with that crowd. He was fun and funny. The Chart Room was generous, serving free hot dogs and popcorn. For starving artists, starving treasure hunters, anyone with the munchies, the Chart Room was good economics. If you only had money to eat or drink, there you could do both.

Buffett asked Corcoran if he could set up and play for tips. Corcoran took the proposal to David Wolkowsky, the man who'd opened the Pier House† hotel and the Chart Room Bar in 1968 as a retreat for artists and writers. Wolkowsky kicked the decision back to Corcoran. *You know the guy. You know the bar. You make the call.*

Corcoran told Buffett he could play for drinks and tips and asked him again what he was drinking. "Crown Royal," Buffett said, upgrading from his initial Heineken. It wasn't much of a business decision, but it was undeniably a business decision.

He began to work that "bar singer goes wild on the rebound" angle playing at the Chart Room, at Captain Tony's, at Crazy Ophelia's and Howie's Lounge. One version of the Captain Tony's story says Buffett had the same deal there as the Chart Room—drinks and tips—until Tony did the math and figured it'd be cheaper to pay the guy, and more profitable to charge him for beer.

Buffett became a member in good standing of Club Mandible, a roaming social club possibly wished into existence when McGuane earned entry into *Who's Who in America* and was asked to list his club memberships. He didn't have any, so he made one up. Club

---

* "Don't bother to Google the street view," Corcoran wrote in an email after stumbling upon the address in an old file. "Too overgrown to see anything at all." That's true.

† Now the Pier House Resort and Spa, the Chart Room is billed online as the place "Jimmy Buffet" played his first Key West show.

Mandible took its name from the lower jaw of a mythical creature that ate the Conch Train. Members wore matching purple shirts and were dedicated in the twin pursuits of inebriation and fornication.

McGuane became Captain Berserko, a character Jim Harrison described as taking on "Tolstoyan grandeur" over the years. In Tom Bissell's *Magic Hours: Essays on Creators and Creation*, Harrison recalled dropping a straw into a large aspirin bottle full of cocaine. When he got home to Michigan he couldn't remember his cat's name. In his own *The Raw and the Cooked: Adventures of a Roving Gourmand*, Harrison wrote: "Of course, there was a period in the early seventies when one might fly-fish for tarpon on three hits of windowpane acid backed up by a megaphone bomber of Colombian buds that required nine papers and an hour to roll."

Being a book about food, and more specifically, about good food, Harrison noted that after such a day, you never gave a damn about the quality of the meal. "Now when I hunt or fish with Buffett we talk about what we're going to cook for dinner," Harrison wrote. "He doesn't even sing 'The Way We Were,' the reality of which no one can accurately remember."

Author's photo

In the winter of 1972, another newcomer arrived. Chris Robinson grew up in St. Augustine—unless you ask him where he grew up. "I didn't grow up," he says. "I was raised in St. Augustine. But, god, I don't want to grow up." He was raised next door to Vaughn Cochran (no relation to Tom), an artist and the washboard player who was scrubbing away in the Chart Room the day Buffett first arrived. Robinson had been planning to aim himself toward the West Coast when Vaughn convinced him to swing by Key West first.

"So I came down here to visit and got a job at the Chart Room, taking Phil Clark's place while he went up to St. Augustine with Sonia, who was his girlfriend, who became my first wife," Robinson says.

Phil and Sonia were headed to an art show, and so Robinson took the job for a week. "That was a pretty eye-opening experience," he says, "because Key West was kind of run out of that bar in those days. The mayor was there, the police chief, the sheriff, the fire chief, the city attorney, state attorney. You could get arrested, bonded, tried, get a building permit."

About the only one who wasn't there when Robinson arrived was Buffett. He was . . . somewhere else in February 1972, but when he returned, he stepped off the plane to his friends waving a banner that read "Welcome Home Mr. Entertainer."

"And he hadn't really done anything," Robinson says. "He had one album out that hadn't done anything."

No one cared. In Key West, what was possible was as real as what was. Vaughn Cochran and his wife, Cydall, had come down from St. Augustine after college. He had a degree in ceramics and loved to fish. They rented a house on Stock Island, one that had been relocated from downtown Key West and had a pool its previous occupants had allowed to go native and fill with wildlife.

Stock Island, a few steps east across the Cow Key Channel Bridge, was gritty and industrial, its characters sketchier, their intentions not always as sunny and the place was open all night. Or at least the Boca Chica Lounge was. Some things are called infamous because people misuse the word. A few places are actually infamous. Local authorities called the Boca Chica the Gun and Knife Club. "We used to say you never worked a shift on the road until you rolled in the mud and the blood at the Boca Chica Lounge," former sheriff Bob Peryam told the *Citizen* in 2013. "We were always the least-armed people when we went in there."

The front and back of the bar were separated by a chain-link fence intended to a) catch beer bottles turned projectiles, b) separate the shrimpers from the rest of the crowd, or c) all of the above.

"A redneck island bar, and if you were in the Boca Chica you were probably in trouble," Vaughn Cochran says. "You had had way too much to drink and it probably wasn't going to be a happy ending. If you were on a roll you could walk out the door and it's ten or eleven in the morning."

Aside from its rusted-out backcountry charm, Stock Island's best feature, as far as Cochran was concerned, was the two-car garage at his house. He turned it into an art studio. Soon enough he met another guy with a degree in ceramics (Key West was lousy with ceramics grads in 1972, apparently), and they rented space at the corner of Greene and Duval Streets.

That wasn't as difficult as it would be today. Storefronts were empty. Lots were plentiful. Parking was easy. For $125 a month they got the lot, built a shack, and opened the Key West Pottery Company. Cydall Cochran, skilled with a needle and thread, began making muslin shirts that Vaughn would hand-paint. When the shirts began to sell better than the pottery, a new business they called Bahama Mama's was born.

Cydall remembers Bahama Mama's being open from 11 a.m. to 2 p.m., then closed for siesta, and then open again from 4 p.m. to 6 p.m. After that, everyone moved to the Chart Room. "It was like a meeting of the minds, there was an energy there I've rarely experienced in my life," Vaughn says.

Winter gave way to spring, which drifted into what Chris Robinson says became known as "the Classless Summer of '72." Buffett came and went, Mr. Entertainer on the move and on the rebound, and another songwriter landed in Key West for a visit. Keith Sykes was friends with Jerry Jeff Walker (who wasn't?). They'd been on tour together in Canada, Jerry Jeff talking about the Keys and telling road stories.

"In those days, every place they played they had these marquee signs on trailer wheels with an arrow on top of it," Sykes says.

Everyone got their name in lights, right there under that arrow and, if you were lucky, next to a good drink special that might help draw a crowd. Jerry Jeff told Sykes about this guy whose name was Buffett but how every time he would play, regardless of how his name was spelled out front, someone would come in asking, "Where's the food?"

"The way Jerry Jeff told me that was pretty funny," Sykes says. With a break in his schedule and Jerry Jeff's stories on the brain, Sykes decided to pay a visit to Key West, landing right on time for a field trip.

The plan the next morning was for a small armada of pleasure craft to set out for the islands west of Key West. Sykes remembers Man Key. Robinson remembers Ballast Key. Could have been either. Might have been both.

"It was just sort of dumb luck to get there at that time," Sykes says. To prepare, they made sangria the night before, dumping in oranges, apples, lemons, limes, wine, and bottles of 151-proof rum. "We had it there marinating overnight in a garbage can," Robinson says.

At 6 a.m. the next morning, Sam the Cleanup Man arrived at the Chart Room, took a look in the garbage can, and couldn't believe it hadn't been cleaned up the night before. He emptied the can, scrubbed it up, and when Robinson arrived said, "You guys must have had one hell of a party in here last night."

"It killed the palm tree he poured it out on," Robinson says. "I swear to God."

Sam might well have saved some lives that day, but he created a problem: the hangout gang was out of booze. Everyone chipped in what they had left and bought some watermelons and pure grain alcohol. "It was hard to drink," Sykes says, "but we managed."

Boats began shuttling people out to the island. Robinson remembers McGuane making a couple of runs to get everyone to the party. "By noon there were girls waterskiing naked in the ocean," Sykes says.

"A big, flat, white sandy beach and you'd have drinks on your belly, just floating down the current," Robinson says. "Everybody was half naked or naked, playing around."

Sykes decided he liked Key West. One other musician was there that day, a harmonica player Buffett had met during a sparsely attended gig at his alma mater, Southern Miss. Fingers Taylor was a skinny kid from Jackson, Miss., who could drink all night and wore the same pallor as Sykes, what's commonly known as a motel tan. Sykes says he and Taylor huddled in the slim shade of a palm tree to keep from frying. "And we were just sort of laughing to ourselves," Sykes says, "saying, 'Look at those people.'"

It was another world. The navy's presence was waning. The dope trade was real, and no big deal. A cruise ship came by every once in a while, and that was about it. The weirdoes, the shrimpers, and the Conchs—the natives whose families had roots in the Bahamas—had the run of the place.

Nixon was on his way to reelection. There was a break-in at the Watergate Hotel. Vietnam was winding down. A recession and an energy crisis were on the horizon. But to absorb the news from the real world you had to be home and in front of the TV at six o'clock, and the Chart Room was open at six o'clock. You could catch the eleven o'clock news, but the Chart Room was still open at eleven o'clock.

In the summer, there were barely any cars. All anyone needed was a bicycle. "It was one of the first gay-friendly towns," Cydall Cochran says, the kind of place where a drag queen at night could work in a bank during the day and everyone would know about both performances. "So the mix of people was a perfect blend of madness." It reminded her of another West, *The Great Gatsby*'s West Egg.

"We mostly hung out in the Chart Room and hit Duval most nights," Cydall says. "Jimmy always had his guitar, so we traveled in a group and drank more rum than was good. Of course, years later you would recognize a night or two in Jimmy's songs."

It's little wonder Robinson stayed. After, Phil Clark and Sonia returned from St. Augustine, Vic Latham—the Chart Room bartender with the New Orleans roots—decided *he* needed a vacation. Robinson filled in for him and by then a month had passed since he first stopped for a short visit. Phil and Sonia announced they were sailing to the Bahamas on a forty-one-foot Cheoy Lee. Clark told Robinson, "I'm not going to bartend when I get back. Just take my job."

Robinson did—for the next two years. Sonia returned early (and alone) from the Bahamas. Then a car hit her dog in front of Sloppy Joe's, and in the process of providing comfort in her time of need, Chris and Sonia became an item and got married.

Robinson rented a first-floor apartment on Waddell Avenue, next door to Louie's Backyard, a restaurant that opened in 1971 with a cigar box for a cash register and a $1 million view of the Atlantic Ocean (that didn't cost anything close to $1 million in 1971).

Robinson first had a musician for a roommate. A navy lieutenant lived above him on the second floor. He was paying $200 a month and everyone thought he was crazy for spending that much, but he had his own beach. He could swim out twenty yards and find lobster. Dinner and a swim; what wasn't to love?

So in that Classless Summer of '72, they partied while the world came and went. Club Mandible organized assault after assault on

Duval Street. They polished off tequila gimlets from twelve-ounce brandy snifters at the Chart Room and tequila shots in the Snake Pit. There were no frozen margaritas because there wasn't a blender to be found in any of the island's bars.

Author's photo

No front porch swing, but there was a hammock on the private beach behind the Waddell Avenue apartment Jimmy Buffett made famous. He had the second floor. Chris and Sonia Robinson had the first. Fun was had by all.

Eventually Sonia moved in with Robinson and, when the navy lieutenant moved out from the apartment upstairs, Buffett took his place. Chris and Sonia had a kid. Vaughn and Cydall would come over. Tom and Judy Corcoran would join the party with their son, Sebastian, in tow. The kids could play and swim. The grown-ups could duck through a fence to Louie's. Buffett's cat, Radar, would play with Robinson's dog, Sir Raleigh Ten Speed, who had a fondness for Kahlúa and cream.

Hanging out one night, they spiked the punch with LSD. Only to see the mayor, the city attorney, and other civic power brokers arrive with the hope of hearing Buffett sing—and got away with it.

Corcoran recalled a night—a morning, really—at the Boca Chica Lounge when he was being held up by the bar and felt a tap on his shoulder.

"You look like you could use a ride home, Tom."

It was the sheriff.

"Yeah, I guess so."

"C'mon."

They walked into a bright morning, each wobbly step crunching the graveled parking lot. When they got to the sheriff's car, he reached into his pocket, removed his keys, and handed them to Corcoran, who wasn't too drunk to be confused.

"Remember," the sheriff told him, "I can get you out of trouble, but you can't get me out of trouble."

"If you want to know what Key West was like back then," Corcoran says, "there you go."

Comparatively, what's a little psychedelic punch at home in the evening?

"Mango daiquiris were our daytime beverage," Cydall says. "With dark *añejo* rum and on a raft floating out in front of Louie's. We could fit maybe five, so someone had to swim in to make the next batch."

It wasn't all fun and games, but there were plenty of both. And what of Mr. Entertainer? The sign was a joke, but part of why he fell in so easily with the crowd was because Buffett was entertaining. He was easygoing. Had he left Nashville for New York or Los Angeles, he'd have been just another folk singer working the song mines, but Key West didn't have a Jimmy Buffett. And Key West gave Buffett a canvas no other songwriter had. All that and a hammock from which to work. A place in the shade to think.

"Most of his first big hits were from the hammock, but you never saw him actually writing anything down," Cydall Cochran says. "But a few days later, a new song would be heard."

Chapter 6

There's No Substitute
for Experience

Where did Jimmy Buffett go when he left Key West? With the freedom to go anywhere, he seemed to be everywhere at once and nowhere very long.

He was at the Bistro, in Atlanta. Deborah McColl sang and played Wurlitzer piano in a group there called Silverman and remembers him sitting in with them sometime in 1972. "Jimmy actually hitchhiked up from Florida," she says.

He was in Chicago, at the Quiet Knight, where the janitor was so much more than a janitor; he was a poet, a mentor, a painter, a one-armed piano player and natural storyteller who'd fought with the Abraham Lincoln Brigade in the Spanish Civil War.

He was working New Orleans or Biloxi. He was playing colleges across the South. He was in Texas—Dallas or Houston or lighting up a night in Austin with a new scene of songwriters developing, in part, on the strength of Jerry Jeff's personality (and constitution).

He was on the highways, the railways, and the airways in between. He was here there and even back in Nashville, because however closed, incompetent, and nepotistic it *felt*—Nashville mattered. He might have found himself a home in Key West, but the people willing to assist in his anything-but-laid-back ambitions were in Tennessee.

"Jimmy came to me and he said, 'Man, I've got to get booked,'" Buzz Cason says. Buffett had spent countless hours honing his chops in the sweltering attic of the cabin he and Margie had rented in East Nashville. He still had the old Bourbon Street arrows in his stage quiver. Songs were stacking up. He needed to play live. He needed to hit the road. He needed to perform. He could earn enough of a living doing that. He was sure of that.

"I said, 'The only guy I know who books the kind of stuff you do is Don Light,'" Cason says. "And so I called Don. There are a couple different stories about that."

When Light died in June 2014, the *Tennessean* newspaper's celebration of his life leaned on a few of Light's favorite aphorisms: "If you can find a need and fill it," Light liked to say, "you've got a job," and, "There's no substitute for experience, and only one way to get it."

He was quotable, yes, but neither of those were things Don Light *just* said. He embodied those ideas. His was a well-earned wisdom. After leaving the marines in 1961, Light worked as a DJ and played drums at the Grand Ole Opry. When he began writing at *Billboard* in 1962, covering the gospel music industry, he discovered there wasn't a gospel music industry. So in 1965, he cofounded the Gospel Music Association and opened Don Light Talent. He had no experience booking acts, but he saw a need and so he learned to book gospel acts. Light built a gospel music business that had previously been based on handshake deals. Let there be contracts, he said. And there were.

He had his own style, too. For example, he also liked to keep a can of Budweiser in his shirt pocket. Just in case.

"He had this unique eye for talent, unlike anyone else in this town," Buffett told the *Tennessean*. "Don Light was an honest guy that took an interest in me . . . I was lucky to have him in my life."

In 2006, when the Nashville Songwriters Association inducted Buffett into its Hall of Fame, Light gave a speech and said it was his *Billboard* successor, Bill Williams, who sent Buffett his way. The chart-topping, millions-selling country duo Big & Rich sang "Margaritaville" and Cason, also onstage that night, says while they were all posing for photos, he leaned over to Light and said, "Man, I sent Jimmy Buffett to you. It wasn't Bill Williams."

"It's funny at this age," Cason says. "You go and get three, four different stories. You just gotta average them out." No matter the exact equation, the sum is always going to be equal to Don Light joining the small but committed group of People Who Believed In Jimmy Buffett.

"He was a guy I felt could do this," Light told writer Peter Cooper in 2013. "I've been right about that more than I've been wrong. Early in our relationship, he went to visit Jerry Jeff Walker. He went for a week and stayed three."

When Buffett returned to Nashville, he put some of his stuff in storage, left a guitar at Light's office, and headed right back to the island. Before fax machines, before email, before Buffett had a phone of his own, Light would call the Chart Room. "That's where we did business," Light said. "I'd call, leave word for Buffett to call. He'd be there in the afternoon."

Cooper wrote for the *Tennessean* at the time he interviewed Light. He works for the Country Music Hall of Fame now, teaches at Vanderbilt, and writes and records excellent songs, often alongside pal Eric Brace. Cooper's conversation with Light reinforces Bill Williams's importance without diminishing Cason's.

Williams asked Light if he'd listen to Buffett and sent him to Light's office that night. "A little frame house," Light said. Not far from Vanderbilt's campus, just off Chet Atkins Place on the edge of Music Row. Buffett brought over a demo tape, 7½-inch reel-to-reel, and punched Play.

Good humor and petty crime filled the air as "The Great Filling

Station Holdup" introduced a couple of not-too-bright good ol'
boys who pull a pellet gun on a gas station attendant and speed off
with $15, a can of oil, "a big ole jar of cashew nuts and a Japanese
TV." They'd have gotten away with it, too, if not for beer. They
were drunk in a burger joint when the sheriff put an end to the
crime spree before it could pick up any real momentum, leaving
them with nothing but regrets: "No picture on a poster, no reward
and no bail."

"Pencil Thin Mustache" introduced itself with nostalgic wordplay
about how "now they make new movies in old black and white."
Buffett had constructed a collection of memories from his favorite
television shows of the fifties. He tapped his adolescent crush on
Sky King's niece Penny. He successfully coupled "bawana" (attach-
ing it to *Ramar of the Jungle*) with "marijuana" (smoked only by
jazz musicians). He wished he had the same pencil thin mustache
that defined detective Boston Blackie's cool. Buffett was only in
his mid-twenties and already had a well-developed sense of what
used to be.

Light remembered "a couple of the slower songs" on the tape.
"Railroad Lady" could have been written by then. In the spring of
1971, months before they'd blitzed Key West, Buffett and Jerry
Jeff hopped a train from New Orleans to Nashville and wrote a
song inspired by a woman they encountered in the dining car
along the way.

"She saved our life," Buffett said in 1974, pausing for a beat.
"She read us the menu."

He was at the Record Plant in Sausalito, California, recording
a set for radio station KSAN. The singers had worked up quite
an appetite, Buffett said, by opening windows between railcars
and howling into the Southern night. On 1999's *Gypsy Songman:
A Life in Song*, Jerry Jeff pegged the ride as the final run of the
L&N's *Pan American*, a contemporary of the Illinois Central's *City
of New Orleans*.

"Riding through the night," Jerry Jeff said, "was one Jimmy Buffett, one Jerry Jeff Walker and one bottle of Wild Turkey"—if you're wondering why howling into the night from a speeding train seemed like a good idea.

"Railroad Lady" wasn't about any of that, however. It was about the slow, inevitable decay of what once was elegant and romantic. Of a woman, "just a little bit shady," who'd lived high on the generosity of men, and of the railroad itself, both done in by progress and by time. The rails are left rusting. The dining car is covered in dust. And the woman, she's on a bus, headed home to Kentucky.

The tape spun from one reel to the other while Light listened and wondered what to make of the shaggy-haired, good-humored, in-need-of-a-break singer Bill Williams and/or Buzz Cason had sent his way.

Light must have seen the spark Milton Brown first saw, the spotlight smile and easy charm. He saw Buffett was smart. He'd soon witness a lifestyle that would assure Buffett never ran out of songs, but he also recognized the work ethic to get them written. "I told him, 'I think I can get you a record deal, and if I do, I'd like to be your manager,'" Light said. Had Light managed anyone before? Not really. There's only one way to get experience, and Don Light saw another job no one else was doing.

"I believe in separation from the pack," Light told Cooper. When Buffett signed his publishing deal with Cason, that was more than a lot of other songwriters had. It wasn't a big deal, but it was bigger than no deal. Now he had a manager. The next step was a record deal and that . . . that took a while.

The thing about Nashville that was absolutely true is that it was conservative. It was careful. The cultural upheaval of the sixties, the tension between the Baby Boomers and their Greatest Generation parents, mostly missed Music Row. Chet Atkins earned his name on a street sign as not only an artist, but as a producer and a businessman. He perfected, polished, and sold what became known as the Nashville Sound.

Glossy and lush, carefully orchestrated—calculated—for cross-over appeal, the formula, executed perfectly by million-dollar voices like George Jones and Patsy Cline, proved so profitable that when interviewers asked Atkins to define the Nashville Sound, he'd jingle the change in his pocket.

Light took Buffett's songs for a walk along Music Row, to Atkins and those who would be him. He was met by polite rejection. *I like him, but I'm not sure I can get him on the radio.* Light would wait a few months, there'd be turnover at this label or that label, and he'd take the songs out again. *I like him, but . . .*

Radio was what record executives knew. To establish an artist, to build a fan base and sell records, you had to get airplay. Goofball pellet-gun holdups, and songs with lines like "now I'm getting old, I don't wear underwear" were . . . different, and different was a risk. Risk was a hard sell.

In 1972, country radio liked Dolly Parton's duets with Por-ter Wagoner, and Merle Haggard (recently pardoned by Califor-nia governor Ronald Reagan). Tammy Wynette, Conway Twitty, Buck Owens, Charley Pride, Loretta Lynn, and Ray Price all had number-one country hits. Buffett wasn't like any of them. He wasn't any more like Neil Young, who released *Harvest*. He didn't have Chicago's horns or hooks. Jimmy Buffett certainly wasn't going to be confused for Mick and Keith in *Exile on Main Street*. Buffett couldn't even be pegged a Next Dylan; that albatross was waiting on a kid named Bruce Springsteen, who'd release *Greetings from Asbury Park, N.J.* in January 1973.

Light collected "no thanks" after "no thanks," and then another label would play a new round of executive come-and-go, and Light would go knock on that door again. *I like him, but I'm not sure I can get him on the radio.* "They weren't off base on that," Light said.

No, but they were wrong just the same. They were wrong even

when Light showed them how to be right, when he took them to *see* Buffett at the Exit/In in Nashville, or the time he talked Macon, Georgia–based Capricorn Records cofounder Phil Walden into checking out a gig at Mercer University. Walden and Capricorn helped make Southern rock a genre by signing the Allman Brothers Band and the Marshall Tucker Band.

Walden called Light the morning after Buffett's show and said he thought Buffett was great, but that he already had enough artist/writers who weren't selling any records. Walden needed more hit records. Radio made those. *I like him, but . . .*

"I ran into that a lot," Light said.

Labels looked to the past, and to what had worked. Light was pretty sure he was watching the future take shape. Kids were sitting in front of Buffett in increasing numbers. The receipts were adding up.

"The people liked *him*," Light said. Not just the songs, they liked the singer. Onstage, Buffett wasn't beholden to a set list. He was barely beholden to *songs*. "If it was him and a guitar, he could talk all evening," Light said. He sent Buffett to a booking showcase one time, a matchmaking event where colleges and coffeehouses gathered to meet talent and send out offers. If an act was good, an act got jobs. Buffett opened with an apology. "My manager said we had to sing and play more, but I've only got twenty minutes," he said.

It worked. He got jobs, and if Light could book Buffett somewhere once, he'd play there twice. After that, he might play multiple nights. Eventually he'd move to a bigger room.

Buffett could feel out a crowd and win it over. At the Quiet Knight, he might spend a month opening shows. "And the headliners would change every week," he said onstage in Key West in November 2015. "In the space of one month, the first person I opened for was Jerry Jeff. The second was Dan Hicks and His Hot Licks. The third was the Siegel-Schwall blues band out of Chicago. And the fourth was Neil Sedaka making a comeback tour.

"Let's say the first three were cool."

Buffett knew Sedaka's work—classic Brill Building, Tin Pan Alley stuff. His set was one more thing unlike anything Buffett was playing. "I'm folk-singing away up there going, Holy Mother of God, what am I going to do?" he said. "So, they booed me sufficiently for the first thirty minutes and then Neil came on and he did his first set and this place exploded."

From the other side of the room, Buffett watched and thought they'd kill him when he returned to open the second set. Between shows, a woman who worked at the Quiet Knight grabbed Buffett's arm and said, "C'mon." They threw back a couple of drinks, ran down to a thrift shop and found him some quality fifties wear. They slicked his hair back and then had a few more drinks. "Got real drunk," Buffett said, "and I did Elvis impersonations and had them on the tables."

At the end of the night, Buffett told Dave Hoekstra on WGN Radio, Quiet Knight owner Richard Harding pulled him aside and said, "See? You found a way."

A few miles south of the Quiet Knight was another folk club, the Earl of Old Town. Steve Goodman and John Prine were sharpening their songs there. Goodman caught Buffett at the Quiet Knight, invited him over to the Earl to hang. "They were so great to me in those early days," Buffett told Hoekstra.

Goodman was a Chicago native, a Cubs fan, and a former high school classmate of Hillary Clinton. He kept trying college, only to keep dropping out to write songs. He went to New York to play the Cafe Wha? He wrote "The City of New Orleans," and played it for Arlo Guthrie after securing Guthrie's attention for the cost of a beer. Guthrie, who figured to only get a beer out of the deal, got a hit in 1972, and the American songbook got another page. Two years later, a roughneck ex-con from Ohio named David Allan Coe would make another Goodman song, "You Never Even Called Me by My Name," a country classic.

Prine was ex-army, ex–United States Postal Service. Opening for Kris Kristofferson in 1971, Goodman covered one of Prine's songs. After the show, Goodman brought Kristofferson to see Prine, who, because it was after hours, was sleeping on a table at the Earl. He was staying at the club. They woke Prine and stuck a guitar in his hand. He stunned Kristofferson. "John Prine is so good we may just have to break his thumbs," he famously told *Rolling Stone*. Prine went on to prove Kristofferson right time and time again. Today he's John Prine, national treasure.

"The music business is not hard," Light said. "It moves too slow to be hard. If you're talented enough to do this, and go about it right, and do it long enough, it works. I know of no exceptions."

When Kristofferson arrived in Nashville and started pushing a broom around Columbia Recording Studios, there wasn't any reason to see the guy as anything but a scruffy janitor. When he landed a helicopter in Johnny Cash's yard? Scruffy janitor who could fly a helicopter. Then Johnny Cash made Kristofferson famous when he performed "Sunday Morning Coming Down" on *The Johnny Cash* show in 1970.

Cash was one of the few who didn't have to play by Nashville's rules. He'd won that fight the hard way, by nearly destroying everything. He could wear all black and use his band. He had his television show, taped at the Ryman Auditorium, same as the Grand Ole Opry, but the Opry didn't invite Neil Young and Joni Mitchell. The Opry wasn't singing duets with Bob Dylan or sitting next to Tony Joe White and growling "Polk Salad Annie."

After a 1954 appearance, the Opry pulled Elvis aside and told him he wasn't a good fit for the show. As late as 1968, the Opry crowd booed Gram Parsons and the Byrds, damn longhairs—all of them. The Opry audience was the Nashville Sound's target demographic, and no one's ever eager to fix a cash machine that isn't broken. But threads wear, imperceptibly at first, before they rip.

Roger Miller had covered Kristofferson's "Me and Bobby

McGee" in 1969. Gordon Lightfoot did the same in 1970. But Cash giving voice to Kristofferson's lonely hangover was a genuine moment. Things would be different after that. Attention had to be paid.

Kristofferson's songs were jagged. He wore his "cleanest dirty shirt." He was "as faded as" his jeans. His dark nights were darker and he wasn't just drunk, he was stoned. He was stoned and he wrote that he was stoned and Cash *sang* it—on national television. Right there, "wishin' Lord that I was stoned," for the world to hear. To the fainting couches, Mom and Dad.

Sharing a stage with Kristofferson once, Merle Haggard said, "Kris is going to sing a song that changed the world."

"Changed my world, anyway," Kristofferson said.

"I was there when you got an award for this song and were too drunk to accept it," Haggard said. Everyone got a good laugh at that—because history by then had proven Kristofferson right.

"Sunday Mornin' Comin' Down" won the Country Music Association's song of the year in 1970, and the establishment wasn't overly thrilled with Kristofferson's award-show performance, mumbling into the microphone while Roy Clark whispered he should say thanks and move on. "When I got to my seat, Merle Haggard was the only one who would shake my hand," Kristofferson told the *Chicago Tribune* in 1973.

Kristofferson's voice sounded like a tobacco farm drowned in a distillery and buried in a car wreck. He'd been a Golden Gloves boxer and a Rhodes scholar who'd studied at Oxford. He was sharp as his jawline, and even if he didn't beat the devil, he drank the devil's beer for free, and stole a song. Then he told the story.

"Kris came to town and created the illusion of literacy," Tom T. Hall told John Spong for a 2012 *Texas Monthly* story. "Somebody once said he and I were the only guys in Nashville who could describe Dolly Parton without using our hands."

In 1966, Bob Dylan went to Nashville to finish *Blonde on Blonde*. He returned for *John Wesley Harding* (1967) and *Nashville Skyline* (1969) and made Nashville a destination for more than just country music. Kristofferson, born in Brownsville, Texas, was Nashville in Dylan's wake.

A couple more Texans, Guy and Susanna Clark, moved to Nashville in 1971, and that meant Townes Van Zandt (Texan) and his parakeets would be by regularly. A who's-who of who-wasn't-yet—pickers like Rodney Crowell, Steve Earle—lined up to sit in Guy and Susanna's kitchen and learn to craft truth into music. Generations of writers followed, right up until Clark's death in 2016. Van Zandt gave every one of them a mission statement when he titled his 1968 debut *For the Sake of the Song*. You do it all for that.

Meanwhile, Willie Nelson's house in Nashville burned down, and by the time it was rebuilt, he'd about had *his* fill of the Nashville Sound. Looking for a move, he booked a three-day country music festival in Dripping Springs, Texas, the Dripping Springs Reunion. The festival was a financial disaster, but was a historic event. Waylon Jennings met Billy Joe Shaver, who'd write some of Waylon's biggest hits. And Willie convinced himself to leave Nashville for Texas.

Meanwhile, Jerry Jeff Walker, on his way from Florida to Los Angeles with a big-money deal from MCA Records that gave him creative control, stopped in Austin and stayed. Doug Sahm, once an East Texas country and western prodigy, returned from five years in San Francisco, where he'd tuned out and turned on. Michael Murphey returned to Texas from California, where he'd gone to UCLA, established himself in the folk scene, and had a song ("What Am I Doing Hangin' 'Round?") recorded by the Monkees.

Austin was filling with musicians, and many found their way to an old property on North Lamar. "A funky little ol' farmhouse the city had grown around," says Gary P. Nunn, who lived there with Michael Murphey. Small efficiency cabins dotted the lot. It was $50 or $75 a month for a cabin, and so it became home to a constantly changing cast of characters. "I called it Public Domain Incorporated, a Home for Runaway Fathers," Nunn says. Others called it Outlaw Cove. There was a police station across the street. Surprisingly, the police mostly left them alone.

Nunn and the rest of Murphey's band, the Cosmic Cowboy Orchestra, lived there. That same group of musicians became Jerry Jeff's Lost Gonzo Band.

There was no genre, no codified (or commodified) Texas Sound. Blues players sat in with folkies; the folkies courted the rockers. Gram Parsons and Buffalo Springfield were bigger influences than Glen Campbell and Tammy Wynette. When Willie played the Armadillo World Headquarters, the beer-bellied shirtless rednecks stood happily alongside the barefooted hippies and famously everyone got along.

"Texas has such an incredible ego," Ray Wylie Hubbard says, "but also an incredible sense of independence."

You could hear it in Dallas at Mother Blues, at the Rubiayat, at the Abbey Inn. In Houston at the Old Quarter. In Austin at the Saxon Pub, the Vulcan Gas Company, Castle Creek, and the Armadillo.

"Jerry Jeff would just kind of show up there," Hubbard says of Castle Creek. "And there were times he'd show up in a bathing suit and cowboy boots and be too drunk to play, but he could get away with it."

Today, Hubbard lives southwest of Austin in Wimberley, Texas, and he writes country blues songs in the key of long black Cadillacs, empty roads, bottleneck slides, open tunings, pistols, philosophers, and Lightnin' Hopkins. He's long sober and determined, but Hubbard began as a hard-partying folkie in Dallas who first ran into Jerry Jeff in the mid-sixties at the Rubaiyat.

"They had this little Pan statue," Hubbard says. Pan: the Greek god of the wild. Chased nymphs. Played the flute. The statue was across the room from the stage. Jerry Jeff began strumming offstage, walked on, stopped, tossed his hat across the room and onto Pan before falling back into the song in perfect time. "One of the best stage entrances I've ever seen," Hubbard says.

That night, Jerry Jeff was still a folk singer working with his birth name, Ronald Crosby, and playing Dylan and other New York standards. Hubbard remembers an old Hungarian named Andre who told Mr. Crosby he should write some songs of his own. He wrote "Gypsy Songman" and "Travelin' Way of Life." He made himself into Jerry Jeff Walker, vagabond poet.

Hubbard put together a folk group and they played some originals and a bunch of Michael Murphey's songs. "He was kind of the established guy doing all original material," Hubbard says. Murphey had cowritten a double-album Kenny Rogers & the First Edition recorded in Nashville. *The Ballad of Calico* sketched the stories of the town of Calico, California, and before the tape had barely run out on that one, Dylan's producer, Bob Johnson, got Murphey into another Nashville studio to record *Geronimo's Cadillac*, the title track inspired by a photo of the Apache chief in full white man costume sitting at the wheel of an automobile in 1905. He was a prisoner at the time. "But there's an intensity in his eyes that says, 'I may be in a denigrating position, but I survived,'" Murphey told *Texas Monthly*. "So I wrote the song."

Soon everyone was writing songs. They had to. You couldn't get away with someone else's material. "It wasn't like open mic," Hubbard says. "You had to get onstage and prove it."

If you wanted to be a Texas Songwriter, you had to earn the badge, because it meant something. As Hubbard wrote in his 2015 memoir, *A Life . . . Well, Lived*, it meant "you were a reinforced-steel-concrete-honest-to-god-walking-badass-songwriting-son-of-a-bitch who wasn't metaphor deficient, had read *Grapes of Wrath*

and knew that Townes Van Zandt believed song lyrics should stand
on their own without music and no matter how bad your twang
was, you were literate."

Austin was the Chart Room with more musicians. What emerged
was something Key West was too small to develop—a music scene
capable of sustaining those musicians. There were clubs, there was
camaraderie, and there was an eager audience. Light could keep
Buffett alive in Texas. "Once you got on that circuit," Light said,
"you could grow that."

Buffett would play Castle Creek in Austin and then crash at
Outlaw Cove. Up in Dallas he'd play Mother Blues and then play
poker in the back room with the staff and Freddie King until dawn.
One night the woman who worked the door at Mother Blues introduced Buffett to Hubbard. Hubbard remembers it mostly because
he eventually married the door girl. They're still married today. The
rest of the night's fuzzy. "I remember we were drinking," Hubbard
says. "You know, a lot."

Let's say they sang "Redneck Mother," because Hubbard figures
they probably sang that song. It is, in a sense, his "Margaritaville."
It's the reason that when songwriters ask him for advice, he tells
them to be prepared for the possibility they might write a song
they have to sing for the rest of their life.

He wrote "Redneck Mother" after a harrowing beer purchase in
the wrong Red River, New Mexico, bar. Red River wasn't Austin.
The hippies and the rednecks weren't getting along. The right bar
would have been the one farther way, the one that liked hippies.
Instead he went to the wrong one, the one full of guys waiting to
play Stomp the Hippie.

"Technically, I'm a musician rather than a hippie," Hubbard said.

That didn't help the situation. But he got out alive and wrote
the song, and when Jerry Jeff recorded it live at the Luckenbach
Dancehall in Luckenbach, Texas, in 1973, "Redneck Mother"
(also known as "Up Against the Wall Redneck Mother") became

an anthem. To everyone's surprise—and especially Hubbard's—it's still an anthem.

"This song probably should never have been written, let alone recorded, let alone recorded again," he'll say onstage. "But the way I look at it is, careers have been built on less." And twice a year, a check arrives in the mailbox. It's usually a pretty nice check.

Texas was as important to Buffett in those years as Key West, but he wasn't a Texas Songwriter. He'd fly in from Florida and then fly home, or head to Nashville for a run at the Exit/In or to take a meeting or sit in on a session. Tompall Glaser and his brothers Chuck and Jim had opened Glaser Sound Studios not far from Light's office.

"They had about the second sixteen-track recording studio in Nashville," pedal steel player Doyle Grisham says. While the scene in Austin came together, opening one front in the war against Music Row's conservatism, Tompall took the fight to the old guard in its own backyard.

Kenny Rogers & the First Edition had recorded *The Ballad of Calico* there. Waylon, Kristofferson, Billy Joe Shaver, Jessi Colter, Shel Silverstein—they all recorded at what would become known as Hillbilly Central.

Enter Grisham. Born in 1942, Grisham grew up outside Temple, Texas, picked up the guitar when he was eight or nine, and never quit. He got to Nashville in 1966 and made it to the Opry stage before moving to Maine in the fall of 1967. That wasn't a career decision. He was in the navy. Discharged from active duty in late 1968, he hit the road with David Houston, whose "Almost Persuaded" had been a number-one country hit in 1966. Houston had a top-ten hit in 1968 with "Already It's Heaven."

In 1970, Grisham went to work for the Glaser Brothers. "That's when I got into doing studio work real heavily," he says. Tompall and the Glaser Brothers had a publishing business, and so demos of songs had to be produced and shopped. Then they'd work on their own albums. That's how Grisham met Buffett.° The Glaser Brothers were recording "The Christian?" and "Tin Cup Chalice"—probably the second song Buffett wrote after getting a look at Key West.

West of Key West was Tank Island, so named because the navy had once planned a fuel depot to be marked by a dozen hulking green fuel tanks. Only two were ever built, the depot was never finished, and today it's a private island where you can buy or rent homes with enormous price tags. Fuel tanks or millionaires, the sun sets beyond it just the same, night after night, indifferent to anyone's story, troubles, or plans.

The best view is from Mallory Square, which fills with tourists and the performers and artists looking to separate the tourists from a few bucks. It's a production, organized and choreographed. When Buffett arrived in Key West, sunset was for locals. An old man sold conch salad from his bike. A tourist or two might materialize, but just as likely it'd be a few friends, a joint or two, and tin cups filled with wine.

"Tin Cup Chalice" is a memory of that one perfect evening we should all be so lucky to have. The thick salt air, the oysters and beer, the sailboats chasing the breeze as the sun slips toward the horizon—they're a daydream as Buffett concludes they should "get that Packard running" and get back to the island before the day's last light. Wherever he was when he put pen to paper, he knew exactly where he wanted to be.

When Norman Wood, captain of the fishing yacht *Petticoat III* and an early Buffett supporter, first heard the song he said, "But Jimmy, there's no honeysuckle in the Keys." Details. Details. Who cared? Someone was cutting a Buffett song. Based on Don Light's theory of separation, that was another small step from the pack. If

° Michael Ruppli and Ed Novitsky's *The MGM Labels: A Discography, Vol. 2; Volumes 1961–1982* tags the date of the recording session as December 16, 1971.

it made one of Tompall's records, Buffett might find a little money in his mailbox back home.

"He was just hanging out 'cause he wrote the song," Grisham says. "That was kind of the norm in those days. The writer would show up to watch the session."

During a break, they were sitting around and Buffett asked Grisham if he'd play on his record when the time came. "I said, 'Sure,'" Grisham says. "What the hell? I didn't know him from Adam and everyone was always telling you things, but that came true."

Eventually.

When the break Buffett was working for came, it wasn't front-page news. It was page-three news—in *Billboard*, on November 11, 1972. "ABC Buys Cartwheel Records; Hires Gant," read the headline. Followed by: "NASHVILLE—In its strong move into country music, ABC-Dunhill has purchased Cartwheel Records 'lock, stock and barrel,' hired Acuff-Rose executive Don Gant to run the operation here, and announced other activities." The story announced Gant as "one of the most talented producers in the business." Unnamed "insiders" told *Billboard* that using Nashville people was the best decision ABC-Dunhill could have made.

"Don Gant was one of the greatest music men," Buzz Cason says. "He was a heck of a singer." Like Cason, Gant was an East Nashville kid. He ran out a string of 45s in the early sixties, putting a jukebox-perfect voice (and clean-cut, parent-friendly look) to songs like Roy Orbison's "Sad Eyes" and "Daydream (Of You)." Gant went to work for Acuff-Rose Music as a writer and earned a cowriting credit on a minor Orbison hit, 1967's "Cry Softly Lonely One." By the time he left to run ABC-Dunhill's Nashville operation, he'd worked his way to Acuff-Rose's executive offices.

Nothing about that résumé suggests outsider, and Gant, as *Billboard* noted, wasn't one. He was Nashville people. But he had also formed the Neon Philharmonic. In the late sixties, Gant teamed with writer-producer Tupper Saussy to make two trippy country-pop records. But for the Oompa-Loompas, the Neon Philharmonic could have been Willy Wonka's house band.

The Moth Confesses, released in early 1969, spawned a top-twenty hit, "Morning Girl." *The Neon Philharmonic* was released later that year. Warner Brothers promoted it with an ad in *Billboard* calling "Morning Girl" a rare "hands-across-the-formats phenomena" and promising to put enough promotional push behind the new record to assure "America'll soon know Tupper Saussy is not the name of a sticky fish dish."

Also in a busy 1969, Gant produced and the Neon Philharmonic backed Orbison on "Southbound Jericho Parkway," a multi-act, seven-minute work of melodic fatalism that stands out even among Orbison's fatalism as especially fatalistic.

Gant wasn't risk-averse, in other words. "Gant called me and said, 'Tell me if I'm crazy or not,'" Cason says. "I said, 'What?'"

"I'm thinking about signing Buffett," Gant said.

"Do it," Cason said. "He's getting a following in colleges. He's the future of what's going to be happening."

Gant signed Buffett and then took the deal and Buffett's demo tape to Los Angeles for a show-and-tell session with the label's top executives. ABC-Dunhill was hoping for the next Waylon Jennings. Buffett, whatever he was, definitely wasn't that. Gant called Light and said it didn't look like he could get the label behind a Buffett record, and without their support, they wouldn't get Buffett on the radio. He offered Light a chance to get out of the contract free and clear. Light said thanks, but no. They'd stick with the deal. Worst-case scenario: they get new, better sounding demos to shop to someone else.

"If it wasn't for Don Gant, there wouldn't have been a Jimmy Buffett," Light told Peter Cooper. Jimmy Buffett had his second record contract and it was time to reintroduce the guy who'd once so glumly looked out from a pile of junk buried along a river in Tennessee.

Chapter 7

There Wasn't a Name for It

G od's Own Truck was a beat-to-hell, semi-green, holes-in-the-floor-board-and-everywhere-else 1953 Chevy 3100 pickup. It got its name from humorist Lord Richard Buckley's monologue "God's Own Drunk," a number Buffett had learned in his Bourbon Street days.

Tom Corcoran remembers how the fenders rattled and the muffler belched. You could hear Buffett coming long before you could see him. Chris Robinson recalls how those fenders were rusted so loose they'd "almost breathe" as the truck clamored down A1A, up Duval, or out to the Islander Drive-In Theater on Stock Island.

"It was a full-moon tide and half of the drive-in was underwater," Buffett said from the Exit/In's stage in 1974. *Harold and Maude* was playing. They set up nice and right: lawn chairs, blankets, fast food, and psychedelic mushrooms. "We'd wired in about eighteen speakers to the truck and were ready for the movie," he said. "And then we saw the swing set."

He was due in Houston the next day but figured if he was in by 2 a.m., he could pull six hours sleep and still make his flight. "So about 7:30, I'm looking for my toothpaste and my other pair of jeans, banging around the house, hadn't been to bed yet," he said. "And that's when the taste hits your mouth from the night before . . . It's really dragon-y, you know? Chewing gum's the only thing that can get it out for me."

From the maw of the night before came "Grapefruit-Juicy Fruit," about hangover remedies, the soul-reviving power of mortal sin, road-weary loneliness, and that pickup truck "chuggin' down the street."

On January 8, 1972, the poet and painter Kenneth Patchen died in California. An inspiration to the Beat generation, Patchen was a 1936 Guggenheim Fellow. The National Foundation on the Arts and the Humanities awarded him $10,000 in 1967 for his lifetime "contribution to American letters." In the fifties, Patchen pioneered the live reading of poetry to jazz. Whether that's good or bad depends on the listener—and the poet.

Patchen was accomplished, if not exactly appreciated. The *New York Times Book Review* wrote that many critics found Patchen naive and romantic: "Even the most generous praise was usually grudging, as if Patchen had somehow won his place through sheer wrongheaded persistence." Sure of who he was and what he was doing, he kept at the job of being Kenneth Patchen until people came around—or didn't. He didn't worry about it.

None of that was in the obituary the *New York Times* ran on January 9, 1972, but Buffett saw the news—if not the foreshadowing of his own career, which barely existed at that point, anyway. Jerry Jeff had one of Patchen's books on a shelf at his place in Coconut Grove. Buffett had gotten into it when he was first staying with Jerry Jeff.

If *Down to Earth*'s "Ain't He a Genius" voiced Buffett's ambition—to be the envy of all who'd once criticized—"Death of an Unpopular Poet" cut to a deepest fear, that the genius might not be recognized in this lifetime.

Best-selling books and poems turned into songs came too late for Buffett's poet to enjoy the rewards of his work. By the time the world turned its attention and eyes toward him, he was in Florida "with a tombstone for a crown." He never experienced his fame, and as for fortune, that was left to his dog, Spooner, to spend. "He was just a poet, who lived before his time," Buffett softly sang.

Corcoran was at the Chart Room one night when Buffett wandered in. "Whatcha you doin' for dinner tonight?" Buffett asked. Corcoran paused and realized Buffett needed a meal. Judy was making spaghetti. Buffett happily tagged along.

"He picked up my old Gibson J-45," Corcoran says, "and he said, 'I've been working on this song.'" Buffett began the story of a playboy "picking 'em up and laying 'em down" all over the Caribbean, but "when you get your kicks, Havana plays tricks," Corcoran says, reading the original lyrics to "Cuban Crime of Passion." And that's when things go south, so to speak. A tropical love triangle leads to a murder, a suicide, and sensational headlines back in the States.

"He played the song and I was flabbergasted," Corcoran says. "I thought it was *really* good." A few nights later, when Corcoran couldn't sleep, he got up and grabbed the same guitar and tried to remember Buffett's song. He zeroed in on the chords but couldn't recall the lyrics. No problem. He made up his own, lines like "half woman half child" and "in the tropics they come and they go."

"It was kind of clicking for me," Corcoran says. He called Buffett and read him what he'd come up with. "Hell, Corcoran," Buffett said. "You just got half a song." Corcoran went back to bed and forget all about it.

Buffett rewrote a line about "cheap rum," replacing it with the more specific "*añejo*," because that's what the gang was drinking. The dearly departed, quickly forgotten, Shrimper Dan–killing piano player from America was originally Billy Nine Fingers, named after the piano player at the Sands Restaurant and Cocktail Lounge whom neither Buffett nor Corcoran had met or seen perform. They liked the name—until Buffett came up with a better one.

When Corcoran first heard the finished version, "I said, 'Who the fuck is Billy Voltaire?'" But he never bothered to ask and didn't figure it out until a few years ago while he was brushing up on

Fitzgerald. Among "those who accepted Gatsby's hospitality and paid him the subtle tribute of knowing nothing whatever about him" were the Willie Voltaires, and Key West had a little more in common with West Egg.

"He Went to Paris" took inspiration from the after-hours stories the Quiet Knight's sweep-up artist in residence, Ed Balchowsky, told Buffett. Like Guy Clark's "Desperados Waiting for a Train" gave voice to an old man who lived at his mother's boarding house, Buffett weaved Balchowky's stories into a poignant life full of love and loss across the decades. Until "after eighty-six years of perpetual motion" he smiles at "Jimmy" and says, "Some of it's magic, some of it's tragic, but I had a good life all the way."

After a show at the Bistro one night in Atlanta, Buffett headed to the Marriott for a late-night bite, a little something to sponge up the booze. "A soaker," as he likes to say. Over his burger, he overheard the romantic negotiations of a man and a woman at the bar and decided to finally write a country song. "Why Don't We Get Drunk" sounded exactly like what Nashville might want—until Buffett finished his thought with, "and screw." Two little words and he was no longer singing country music. He was satirizing country music.

"I remember Tompall Glaser saying, 'I can't believe you actually did this to a country song,'" Buffett said onstage in 2015. "And I said, 'Well, Harlan Howard always said country music is three chords and the truth. So here's the truth.'"

These were the songs he'd dreamed up in the hammock and worked over in notebooks at the Boca Chica Lounge as the sun rose. He'd written them on airplanes and in hotels and crashing with friends in Texas. He made them up while nobody was looking and played them for anyone who'd listen in coffee shops, student unions, and listening rooms.

"It was moving at such a pace that we had a catalog," Don Light said. That meant they had choices to make when they traveled to Nashville, set up at Glaser Sound Studios, and made *A White Sport*

Coat and a Pink Crustacean for ABC-Dunhill. Don Gant couldn't promise label support, but he'd do all he could as producer.

True to his word, Buffett brought in Doyle Grisham on pedal steel. "They very seldom told me anything to play," Grisham says. "Just play. He had handpicked everybody. He knew what he wanted, and it was kind of a collage of different people."

That was Austin's influence. Grisham remembers being stumped by the bass player, who no one had met before, but who Buffett somehow knew. Ed "Lump" Williams played in a rock band called Jubal, one an Associated Press story from December 1972 suggested could expand the Nashville Sound into uncharted territory. Williams played bass, the story said, "with a rhythm and blues flair reminiscent of the Deep South black man's music." A year after working with Buffett, Williams worked on a jazz record, *Earth Blossom*, with drummer John Betsch. What Williams really brought to the studio was range.

Reggie Young—a guitar slinger from Memphis—took electric lead, and Goodman came down from Chicago to add some acoustic lead. Sammy Creason, the same "Sammy Creasy" Buffett had caught playing with Tony Joe White in the *Billboard* days, manned the drums. Fingers Taylor, the kid Buffett met in Hattiesburg, Mississippi, got the call on harmonica.

Then there was the piano player, the only musician in the room with a zoology degree. Michael Utley had planned on going into medicine—just like his father.

Utley was born in Blytheville, Arkansas. Stax and Sun country—Booker T., Elvis, and Cash. Early rock and roll was in the air. Utley first heard Roy Orbison's "Ooby Dooby" at the public pool. He was riding to Memphis with a friend and his family when Booker T. and the MGs' "Green Onions" hit the airwaves and pinned him to his seat. "I eventually got to play on one of Booker's albums," Utley says. "My whole musical career has been thrills."

He formed a rockabilly band in high school, and then a horn

band because the Mar-Kays had made "Last Night" and that hit Utley like "Green Onions." But he was always planning on medical school, even when, as a senior in high school, his biology teacher told him a band in Memphis was looking for a piano player. It was Bill Black's Combo. Black was Elvis's original bassist. Along with guitarist Scotty Moore, and under the direction of Sam Phillips, they cracked the code that blew open the universe.

Utley headed to Memphis to audition. It was an instrumental outfit, and so the members were interchangeable. Black wasn't even there when Utley played. But Reggie Young was in the band, and Creason was playing drums. Utley got the gig and made it a summer job for the next few years. His first summer included a tour of South Africa. "It was a great experience," Utley says. "But I'm still going to college." Still going to be a doctor.

Utley went to the University of Arkansas, and during his senior year, Bill Black's Combo went into the studio to record an album for Columbia Records. It wasn't summer, but it was spring break. At Creason's urging, Utley wrote a couple of songs, but he was still going to school, still preparing for the MCAT.

Back at school, Utley's phone rang again, this time with an offer to record with Tony Joe White. "It was during finals," Utley says. The piano-playing son of a doctor on a pre-med track had a decision to make. He could stay in Fayetteville and take the test in his quantitative chemistry lab, or he could go play with Tony Joe. The lab was only one credit. Tony Joe had made "Polk Salad Annie."

Utley skipped the final, played on *Continued*, which included "Rainy Night in Georgia," and still passed the class. "I ended up with a B-plus," he says. "I graduated."

He graduated, but he wasn't going to medical school. It wasn't the easiest thing to tell his father, that if all he ever did was play juke joints and dive bars that's what he was going to do, but his father handled it well. "Then it happened really quickly," Utley says. "I pinch myself how quickly it happened."

Jerry Wexler was one of the three most powerful executives at Atlantic Records, and he was looking for a rhythm section that would work out of Criteria Recording Studios in Miami. The Swampers, the studio crew he'd been working with in Muscle Shoals, Alabama, churning out soul hits for Atlantic, didn't want to leave Muscle Shoals. Wexler didn't want to keep commuting to northern Alabama. And he wanted some place warmer than New York in the winter.

Wexler turned to Memphis for a new group of players. Creason joined producer/piano player Jim Dickinson, guitarist Charlie Freeman, and bassist Tommy McClure in what became known as the Dixie Flyers. As they the prepared to sign the contract with Wexler, Creason and Dickinson mentioned they had an organ player who'd come in handy. "Fine," Wexler said. By the time the summer of 1970 was over, Utley was working in Miami.

"A year before I'd been listening to Aretha and all the guys in Muscle Shoals," Utley says. Now he was working with Aretha Franklin, who went to Miami to make *Spirit of the Dark*. Sam & Dave put the Flyers to work on "Knock It Out the Park," which landed a *Billboard* new and notable mention alongside "The Christian?"

Utley played with Jimmy Cliff, and Taj Mahal. He jumped in on sessions with Buddy Guy and Junior Wells, who were joined by Eric Clapton and Dr. John. But it was one of the first albums the Flyers made at Criteria that set the course of Utley's life. They backed Jerry Jeff Walker on *Bein' Free*. "That's the album Jimmy heard when he started hanging with Jerry Jeff," Utley says. That's the reason Gant called and asked if Utley would come to Nashville and play on the first record of Buffett's new ABC-Dunhill deal. By then, Utley had left Miami and joined Rita Coolidge's band. Coolidge met Kristofferson, they became an item, and Utley joined Kristofferson's band.

Utley blocked out some time and went to Nashville. In two or three days at Hillbilly Central, with an emphasis on spontaneity and feel, they completed the not-so-anxiously-awaited follow-up to *Down to Earth*.

Released in June 1973, *A White Sport Coat and a Pink Crusta-cean* came with a title twisted from Marty Robbins's 1957 country hit, "A White Sport Coat (and a Pink Carnation)," and blinked on *Billboard*'s country chart at number forty-three. True to every rejection Don Light received, Buffett didn't get much radio play. But he did get a chance to reset his career and redefine the guy who'd made *Down to Earth*.

A bare foot sticking out from bellbottomed jeans and resting on a lobster trap, the new Jimmy Buffett appeared content instead of perplexed. A brightly colored shirt flared from under the white sport coat, his new backdrop was blue skies and shrimp boats. The pursed lips of the past were replaced—or shaded anyway—by a resplendent seventies mustache. The Thompson O'Neal Shrimp Co. supplied the pink crustaceans that, according to the liner notes, "made a great cover and a fine dinner." Guy de la Valdene, a French count who'd found his way Key West in search of fish and adventure, shot the cover.

"Tin Cup Chalice," "Pencil Thin Mustache," and others would have to wait for another album. "The Great Filling Station Holdup" kicked off an eleven-song set anchored by the yin and yang of "Death of an Unpopular Poet" on one side and "Why Don't We Get Drunk" on the other. The latter, perhaps, to Don Gant's dismay.

"Let's just say my producer was a little conservative at the time and he said, 'This could destroy your career,'" Buffett said onstage in Key West in 2015. "And I said, 'Why? I don't even have one yet. How can it destroy it? This could *make* it.'"

Both sides of the album open with small-stakes larceny. Chronicling Hattiesburg-era hijinks, the sardines-and-peanut-butter heist of "Peanut Butter Conspiracy" made "The Great Filling Station Holdup" look like *Ocean's 11*.

"They Don't Dance Like Carmen No More" tipped a hat piled high with bananas and mangos in the direction of Carmen Miranda and Xavier Cugat "doin' the rhumba as no one else dared."

"I Have Found Me a Home" found one on side two, in front of "My Lovely Lady," a catch-you-later Tennessee taunt from someone promising he'll send a postcard just as soon as he's done "sailing in those warm December breezes."

McGuane, ol' Captain Berserko himself, wrote some lines for the back cover of the album, and no one ever did figure out what it meant to be "among the first of the Sucking Chest Wound Singers to sleep on the yellow line," but it sounded good. The "shadowy Club Mandible" lit the story with a little mysticism. Buffett's duties to the club "have yet to be explained," McGuane wrote. Was Jimmy as "dedicated as ever to certain indecencies and shall we say reversible brain damage"? Absolutely. "And of course he has never washed dishes or owned a puppet show." Good to know.

Buffett was a kid from Mobile, Alabama, with a college degree and a good family. He'd gotten married and divorced, recorded one album nobody bought, and moved from Tennessee to Florida. And that's fine. More interesting than most. But there's a reason Robert Zimmerman invented Bob Dylan, and then kept reinventing him. It was more fun.

McGuane helped construct the foundation of a new Jimmy Buffett with sentences like: "And as a souvenir of some not so terrible times, this throwback altar boy of Mobile, Alabama brings spacey up-country tunes strewn with forgotten crab traps, Confederate memories, chemical daydreams, Ipana vulgarity, ukelele madness and, yes, Larry, a certain sweetness."

Yes, Larry.

A White Sport Coat and a Pink Crustacean was the first Jimmy Buffett record only Jimmy Buffett could have made. It wasn't folk or country or rock. It wasn't trying to satisfy anyone. It was well traveled and sentimental. It had a sense of humor and a suntan. It came from out on the edge, but a different edge than Kristofferson and Townes and the rest were walking.

"It was like a breath of fresh air," Utley says. "In Nashville during that period, there were a lot of songs that were really dark. I was around a lot of people like that, trying to be as tragic as they could be, and it was nice to be around Jimmy. It really was."

Only a few songs had anything directly to do with Key West, but that was enough to mark the album with a touch of the exotic. Wherever you were, it was an album from elsewhere. But it wasn't alone.

At the same time Buffett gave us those two dopes at the filling station and all that fun-loving mortal sin at the drive-in, McGuane set a couple of fishing guides to war with each other in *Ninety-two in the Shade*. Thomas Skelton and Nichol Dance walked the same streets as Buffett's characters. They passed the same old bikes resting near the same bars. They spoke the same language, and they'd all recognize Buffett's winks and McGuane's nods: the sign on the garbage truck that says WE CATER WEDDINGS or the nativity scene in the plumbing store featuring "a squat chromium faucet" as Mary's head.

The heat that fueled comic antics in Buffett's world, however, stoked violent madness in McGuane's. Nashville didn't have the market cornered on darkness yearning to be tragic. Key West still had Hemingway.

In *Papa: Hemingway in Key West*, James McLendon stakes out the "Hemingway Myth, a legend, a code of *machismo*," argues it was established during his twelve years on the island, and that it "allowed Hemingway to move in an aura of self-created magnificence around the globe" for the rest of his life. McGuane, Harrison, Buffett (in his own way), and the rest were after that aura. They'd chase all the fish, drink all the booze, and romance all the women it took to get it.

To Have and Have Not was Hemingway's Key West book, and charter captain Harry Morgan his Key West archetype. "Captain," a client said to Morgan, "could you make me a highball?"

"I made him one without saying anything, and then made myself a real one," Hemingway wrote for his captain.

Dance and Skelton at war, Harrison's men in *A Good Day to*

Die drugging, drinking and screwing their way west, the Buffett of McGuane's album notes . . . they're all some version of Morgan making himself a Man's drink.

"You really got to be a little crazy to live on an island—especially this one," Buffett once said. "But in my kind of work, being a little bit crazy helps."

ABC-Dunhill had sent a film crew to Key West to make a short titled *Introducing Jimmy Buffett*. With limited time, less of a budget, and a drunk writer, Buffett quickly hatched a plan to use his pals.

"You know someone around here by the name of Buffett?" a narrator said.

"Sure, I know him," Sheriff Bobby Brown said, leaning out his squad car. "Hell of a nice guy. Shouldn't have any trouble finding him. Key West is not all that big of an island."

When the crew arrives at the Waddell apartment, they find Buffett in bed, wrapped in sheets, curtains drawn. "Oh, the film crew, right," Buffett said rolling over.

As he prepped for the day (or the midafternoon), he offered his thoughts on island life. "I guess we're all here for about the same reason," he said, turning to the camera. "Whatever that is."

"You gotta remember what was going on in Key West at the time," Buffett said on a stage a few steps from his old apartment in 2015. "Let's just say, first of all, I'm way beyond the statute of limitations."

What was going on? A lot of dope was moving into the United States, and the gentlemen of the ocean moving the supply weren't all that secretive about their work.

"I was tempted occasionally to get into it," Buffett said, "because in those days they actually unloaded in the middle of the day down at the shrimp docks. It was a whole different thing there that was going on."

More often, loads would arrive under the cover of darkness.

Sometimes people would get caught. Sometimes loads were lost. The bundles, square groupers as they were known, might wash up on the beach or get tangled in the mangroves. Someone who spent any time in the backcountry might find a stranger (or a friend) passing along a phone number in a bar. *You ever find anything out there, just give a call and tell us where it is. Don't touch it. Don't move it. We pay cash.* It's a small island. No one was very hard to find.

Buffett recalled being pulled aside and told he could make twice what he'd made for the record with a single run. "It was kind of like *Let's Make a Deal*, Key West style," he said.

Corb Donohue talked Buffett down. In the summer of 1972, ABC-Dunhill in Los Angeles assigned Donohue, who'd been its publicity director, to a newly created job as the head of the department of creative services. Seven months later, he was back atop the publicity department as well as running artist relations.

Donohue was instrumental in another Jim's career—Croce. Eventually, Donohue kicked the record business and moved to Costa Rica to surf. He later moved back to Southern California, got back in the record business, and opened his own communications company. But he was never far from waves—one reason he and Buffett remained connected over the years. When he died on October 5, 2007, two years after being diagnosed with skin cancer, Buffett dedicated that night's show in Hawaii to Donohue.

Donohue held something similar to Don Light's Philosophy of Separation. "Anything that rises above the mire is a success,"* Donohue said in R. Serge Denisoff's 1975 music business study, *Solid Gold: The Popular Record Industry*. "Anything that draws attention to itself and continues on without some sort of great preposterous hype involved is a success."

Jimmy Buffett wasn't going to be the recipient of any ABC-Dunhill–funded hype—preposterous, modest, or any adjective in

---

* More true (and more difficult) in the Internet age than it was in 1975.

between. "I don't think anybody knew what niche to put him in, and even then Nashville liked clichés," Grisham says. "They like to call you this or call you that and put you in a pocket. And he definitely couldn't be put in any normal Nashville pocket."

But Donohue liked *White Sport Coat* and told Buffett exactly that. "You really think so?" Buffett said. "I'd never heard from a record company before." All Barnaby had done is release some demos and then not release the second album. Buffett was so new to the world of record company compliments he hedged. *Thanks, but I've got this job offer, from this guy on a boat, and it's going to pay big. I think maybe I'll do that.* He had his eye on a new boat, the Boston Whaler he'd been denied when a banker in Key West told him his musician's income wasn't stable enough for a $500 loan.

That's fine, Donohue told Buffett, but go to New York anyway. Play Max's Kansas City. Max's was a big deal club and New York was nice in the summer and so sure, why not? All Buffett needed was a band. He called up Fingers Taylor, but felt he needed one more player.

"One of the first bands I had played in was a jug band here in St. Augustine," Vaughn Cochran says. "It was called the Hydraulic Banana Jug and String Band and Kazoo Ensemble."

Like Bill Black's Combo, membership was fluid. Over the years, Cochran has run into plenty of musicians who, when they first meet and talk turns to music, say, *"I* was in the Hydraulic Banana Jug and String Band and Kazoo Ensemble, too." Most he's never met.

Vaughn and Cydall Cochran owned one of the couches Buffett first crashed on when he got to Key West. Their Stock Island home with the two-car-garage-turned-pottery-studio was right behind the Boca Chica Lounge. "We were all in the same boat at that time, struggling and playing music at night," Vaughn says.

Buffett asked him if he wanted to go to New York and play some shows. Cochran's was an easier decision than Buffett's. Cochran didn't have anything else to do and had never been to New York.

They flew north and opened for Andy Pratt, who'd released a self-titled record on Columbia. ABC-Dunhill put them up in a Park Avenue hotel and picked up the tab.

The shows went well. A tight review ("Andy Pratt Is Heard At Max's Kansas City") landed in the *New York Times* on June 18, 1973. "The unknown-genius-of-the-week spot is always a rough one," Ian Dove wrote, referring to Pratt, not Buffett, who hadn't even ascended to flavor of the week. Pratt, Dove decided, was "self-indulgent" and "disjointed," and his falsetto "reedy." His sizable band: "flabby."

"By contrast, the imagery of the country singer (and writer) Jimmy Buffett was clean, rooted firmly in Buffett's own existence," Dove wrote. Fingers was "good," Cochran a "low-phosphate washboard scrubber." In conclusion, while Pratt focused inward, "Buffett looks outside and takes notes."

"We had great sets, great fun," Cochran says. He remembers women would come over to the hotel and ask what kind of music they played. "I'm not sure what you call this," he'd say. "Tropical rock? There just wasn't a name for it."

There was a fourth member of their traveling party, a woman from South Carolina, a student at the University of South Carolina who'd come to Key West on spring break. Buffett saw her from a distance one day—blonde, beautiful, and put together. He didn't meet her that night, but he kept looking until he ran into her in the phone booth outside the Chart Room.

Buffett and Jane Slagsvol quickly became an item, and she brought a touch of professionalism and practicality to a touring operation that otherwise wouldn't have been interested in much of either. Cochran remembers the final morning in New York. They were set to fly back to Florida, but Jane needed an iron. There wasn't one in the room, and so she went across the street and bought one. "We were at breakfast and when we went to sign the check, they said, 'Your room's closed out,'" Cochran says.

They went around the table and pockets were empty. "Why none of us had any money, I'm not really sure," Cochran says. Probably because they were all still broke. They were only playing rock star for the length of the stay.

Jane walked back across the street, returned the iron, took the cash, and paid for breakfast. Problem solved. They returned to Key West wrinkled, but victorious. Maybe Jimmy Buffett wouldn't make that dope run after all.

Chapter 8

He Meets the Bear, Finally

Don Light's phone rang one morning. It was Margie Buffett. "Where is that son of a bitch?" she said.

Margie had gotten the Mercedes in the divorce. Buffett had taken it for one last drive. As Light recalled the story to Peter Cooper, Buffett pulled up in front of Light's office just as Light was arriving. Jimmy waved, opened the door . . . and a passing truck folded that door to the fender. Jimmy and a friend drove the car to a nearby golf course and assessed the damage. Seeing no easy fix, they removed the door and put it in the backseat. The next assessment was of Buffett's options. They figured that best done at a bar.

The next morning, when Margie left for work, she found the car where it was supposed to be, safe and sound. Backed into the driveway. Just like new. Until she walked around to the driver's side and discovered her four-door was down to three.

"I later learned when I talked to Buffett that they'd pushed the car into the drive," Light said. The plan they came up with over drinks had been to make as little noise as possible, face the damage away from the house, and get away without facing Margie. Buffett went straight to the airport and got the hell out of town.

"And Buffett could do that," Light said.

Light had a receptionist and she had all the duties receptionists have, plus one. When Buffett walked through the door, she was to get his car keys. "Otherwise we'd be turning the building upside down looking for them," Light said. Every time.

Buffett once borrowed Light's car to get to a gig at Vanderbilt. Light went to the show separately, and later, as someone from the club read off the license plates of cars being towed, he knew. "I didn't know my license number," he said, "but I was sure it was being towed." Buffett was dispatched the next morning to retrieve the car. Even God's Own Truck eventually ended up impounded and crushed in Key West.

Then there was the night outside Roger Miller's King of the Road Motor Inn in Nashville when Buffett couldn't find his rental car but found plenty of trouble while he was looking around.

Four months after working Max's Kansas City, Buffett was back recording in Nashville, this time at Woodland Sound Studios. "The deals back then were two albums a year and Jimmy kind of lived up to it," Michael Utley says.

The basic tracks for *White Sport Coat* were cut in about a day and half, Buffett laying down scratch vocals and fine-tuning those when the band was done. The new record was tackled at a more leisurely pace. "We were doing two sessions a day for four days and then on Friday we'd all get together and have a listening session at the studio," Doyle Grisham says.

The cast of musicians was largely unchanged from *White Sport Coat*. The songs, if they skewed any direction at all, skewed west. To Texas, Montana, and California as settings for songs about distance—between Buffett and Key West, between men and women, now and then.

Max's Kansas City hadn't been the sum of the *White Sport Coat* tour, not even close. The summer of 1973 kept Buffett on the run, sometimes with Fingers Taylor, sometimes with Vaughn Cochran and Taylor. A lot of the time it was Buffett and his guitar, a one-man band lighting out into the territory, as his old pal Huck Finn liked to say. The songs he took into Nashville for the new record reflected the disjointed sense of time and place that develops when you bounce from one end of this very large country to the other.

"Pencil Thin Mustache" threw back to the fifties and "the way that it used to be." On a road trip from San Francisco, Buffett and writer Richard Brautigan stumbled upon Ringling, a "dying little town" about forty-five miles north of Livingston, Montana, that appears out of nowhere and disappears just as fast.

Ringling didn't have much, but it had a bar, and across from that bar, Buffett spied beer cans piled like stories. "Imagine all the heartache and tears in twenty-seven years of beer," he wrote in "Ringling, Ringling."

He rescued "Livingston's Gone to Texas" from the unreleased *High Cumberland Jubilee* and then, in "West Nashville Grand Ballroom Gown," rescued a hitchhiker whose well-planned future in Nashville's high society had been "cancelled with a swing of her dear father's hand."

"I'd like to ride the rodeo, but I've got Brahma fear," he sang in "Brahma Fear," a concession, perhaps, that while he was spending a lot of time in Texas, he wasn't going to be mistaken for a Texan. He was more comfortable in that Whaler he'd managed to finally get, "somewhere below the sunlight, somewhere upon the sea."

"Brand New Country Star" was another success story, one about a crossover singer—"he can either go country or pop"—who'd shed his sequined suits and dropped his custom "pearl-inlayed" guitar in favor of Japanese-made electric and a shot at the kind of money that lets you put your name on a chain of bowling alleys.

One of Buffett's Austin acquaintances, Willis Alan Ramsey,* wrote "Ballad of Spider John." Like "He Went to Paris" (and Guy Clark's "Desperados Waiting for a Train"), its voice was an old man's

---

* "Ballad of Spider John" appeared on Ramsay's acclaimed, self-titled 1972 debut. He's yet to release its follow-up.

looking back on adventure, misadventure, and misbegotten love: "She thought I was a saint not a sinner gone astray."

Buffett's pen pushed memories of colorful and wild old New Orleans into "The Wino and I Know," where dark bars full of "tattered and torn" old men willing to give a kid his first scar lurk just around the corner from the sweet delights of the Café du Monde. "It's a strange situation," he sang, "a wild occupation. Just living my life like a song."

He'd prove himself against that final lyric time and again, but never more than after they'd knocked out one last New Orleans number, that old Lord Richard Buckley gem, "God's Own Drunk."

The band settled in, in front of a live studio audience in Nashville. Buffett picked at tipsy seventh-chords, adding little slides that slurred and hiccupped; Utley sprinkled tongue-in-cheek honky-tonk piano fills; Sammy Creason kept casual time on drums.

"Well, like I explained to y'all before, I ain't no drinking man," Buffett began. Laughter filled the studio, and for the next six minutes he played the part of a decent enough guy, one who'd promised his brother-in-law he'd watch his still for a few hours.

Like he said, he wasn't a drinker, but who among us has not known temptation? So he took a drink, and then a few more, and then another until he was not just drunk, "but God's own drunk and a fearless man."

Then came the bear, "a Kodiak lookin' fella about *nineteen*-feet tall." He and the bear looked each other over carefully and came to a delicate détente. He offered the bear a drink. It was the polite thing to do. Not one to be rude, the bear accepted. Soon the new best friends were drunk and dancing in the moonlight until, exhausted, our man lays down for a restless sleep. When he wakes up, the bear's gone and, along with him, the still.

"That's a take!" Buffett shouted. The new album, *Living and*

Dying in ¾ Time, was finished. Champagne corks popped. Toasts were made. Buffett and Creason crawled into a bottle of tequila.

"And got *real* drunk," Buffett said four months later at the Record Plant, in Sausalito, California. It was February 19, 1974. Buffett was taping a session for San Mateo's KSAN.* *Living and Dying in ¾ Time* was freshly released and Buffett was in good-but-ragged spirits after a big night in Los Angeles delayed his Bay Area arrival.

"I ran into some nice things in L.A.," he said.

"Nice things in L.A.?" someone in the studio audience said.

"Yes," Buffett said. "Can't mention names, though. I was out *stargazing*. I wanted to buy a map to the stars. They have those maps, Homes of the Stars. I was in the Polo Lounge at the Beverly Hills Hotel. That's the last of Hollywood, it really is." He was wistful, as he always was when talking about the way things used to be.

Near the end of the taping, Buffett turned back east, to Nashville, to what happened after he and Creason opened that bottle of tequila, the mere mention of which drew an "Ooooooooh," from his audience.

"Yeah, but it makes you real crazy," Buffett said. "It's like, you know, peyote and tequila come from the same plant and there has to be a little crossover there somewhere. The only thing worse than that is mescal, with the worm in it."

Real drunk, Buffett and Creason headed to the King of the Road Motor Inn, worked their way to the club on the top floor of the hotel, took over the stage, and banged on a guitar and drums until they'd dismantled music. Then they got hungry and left. In the parking lot, they couldn't find Buffett's rented Gremlin because, of course, they couldn't. He never could. He was lucky he had his keys.

---

* Two weeks earlier, the Symbionese Liberation Army kidnapped Patty Hearst. They'd use cassette tapes sent to KSAN to communicate their demands.

Buffett was wearing a pair of shoes he'd picked up in a thrift store in Miami. They were golf shoes, and even though he'd pulled out the cleats, they clicked when he walked and sounded like tap shoes on the Cadillac he climbed atop. He was on the hood when a voice said, "You're under arrest."

"You can kiss my ass."

("I guess it was his car I was standing on," Buffett said.)

Creason found the Gremlin and waved Buffett over, one ornery stranger in pursuit and threatening more than just arrest now. Creason apologized and said ABC-Dunhill would pay for any damage Buffett had done. "Which was awful generous of Sammy, because he didn't have the authority to say so," Buffett said. "Being a good company man, I took up for my company and said, 'No they won't and I'm still going to beat your ass if you don't leave us alone.'"

At that, the gentleman reached into the car and yanked a handful of blond hair from Buffett's head and punched Creason in the face. Creason slashed back with a BIC pen that was in no way mightier than a sword. Buffett tried to focus on his seatbelt, because he couldn't start the car unless the seatbelt was fastened, and he was too drunk to perform the task. "So we sat there while this man pounded the hell out of both of us," Buffett said, telling the tale again, this time to a Nashville crowd at the Exit/In. It'd been a month since Sausalito. He was coming off a week of one-nighters at colleges across the Midwest and the story had improved. "I looked over at Creason and I said, 'Sammy, I don't want to die in a Gremlin.'"

Buffett got his seatbelt fastened and they got away, got some barbecue, and on the way back to the hotel, hit a bridge. "But luckily there was nobody around, so we just backed up and headed for the hotel," Buffett said. The lobby of the King of the Road was still buzzing from the parking lot confrontation. They hadn't just aggravated any old guest. They'd aggravated Buford Pusser.

"Oh," Buffett said.

The sound of Pusser's name shook him sober. Pusser, the former sheriff of McNairy County, Tennessee, was the man who'd taken on the State Line Mob. His wife had been murdered, and he had survived numerous shootings and stabbings. Hollywood made a movie about Pusser, *Walking Tall*.

Buford Pusser was big and tough and mean. "He killed, like, twenty guys with a stick or something," Buffett said. The stick even had a name: the Buford Stick. The Drive-By Truckers wrote a song by that name, framed through the eyes of the gangsters. "Ask him for a warrant, he'll say, 'I keep it in my shoe,'" Truckers cofounder Patterson Hood sings.

For his first fight since junior high school, Buffett had chosen to take on *that guy*. Buffett tangled with a tall tale come to life. Armed with this new information, he retreated to the safety of his room and locked the door tight and didn't emerge until he had to leave for the airport and return the dented Gremlin.

After performing "God's Own Drunk" for years, he'd finally met the bear and lived to tell the story—at length. Again and again. Light wasn't kidding. The guy could talk, and people loved him for it. He was quick, and he was topical. "He was good about getting to town and finding a local newspaper," Light said. Whatever Buffett might find in the *Mattoon Journal Gazette*, or the *Dunkirk Evening Observer* or any other little paper in any other little town where he was playing, was fair game.

Had he seen the February 26, 1974, edition of the Mattoon paper, where his upcoming show at Eastern Illinois University was announced (admission: twenty-five cents), he might still be talking onstage at the Martin Luther King Jr. Student Union. Above the page from "Buffett Sets EIU Concert" was this bit of breaking news: "Doctor claims puritanical views rob elderly of sex."

He could have done twenty minutes on that and then segued directly to "Why Don't We Get Drunk." Putting that one on *White Sport Coat* hadn't ruined him, as Don Gant had worried, or made him the star, as Buffett had hoped. Released as the B-side of "Great

Filling Station Holdup," the more liberal-minded FM stations dug it (a little), and the song became a jukebox hit, selling more than 50,000 copies by mid-1973, according to *Billboard*.

"I thought, *My God, this is it*," Buffett said in Key West in 2015. *"I'm going to get to buy a Boston Whaler or something . . .* The thing about it was the mafia controlled the jukeboxes in those days and they didn't pay royalties on jukebox plays. That's true.

"I never made a dime off of the jukebox plays because they wouldn't pay you and I wasn't going to ask. *Hey, Carlo, where's my fucking money?*" He flashed a finger gun. "Nope."

For better or worse, "Why Don't We Get Drunk" became the first song Buffett couldn't escape. Back in Sausalito, recording for KSAN for a second time in 1974, Buffett remarked how nice it was not to have a club full of drunks shouting "Why Don't We Get Drunk and Screw." Near Philadelphia early that summer, amid a flurry of requests, someone shouted out "Why Don't We Get Drunk."

"Nah," Buffett said. "We don't do that anymore. Tasteless song."

Not that Buffett was onstage discussing the finer points of French Impressionism or adapting Bach for one man and a guitar. The artist drank. The artist was prone to tasteless asides.

"It lets my feelings show," he said, referencing another *Living and Dying* track, "Brahma Fear." "Boy they were showing all over last night. That's not called showing your feelings, that's called showing your ass."

Or: "Last night? You can write that off. I did. Last thing I remember is being in Maloney's and buttering my plate instead of my biscuits."

Or, again referencing his prized Boston Whaler* back in Key West: "I gotta scrape my bottom when I go home. I scraped it last night when I left here." (Pause.) "Cut that out, Buffett."

---

* Buffett's style of onstage embellishment makes it difficult to figure out when, exactly, he got that damn boat. But he did get it.

At the Exit/In, he poked another bear. Richard Nixon was headed to town to sing "God Bless America" and christen the new Grand Ole Opry House alongside Roy Acuff, who would give Nixon a yo-yo lesson on what had to be one of Nixon's better nights of 1974. Dedicating it to the president, Buffett did stoop to play "Why Don't We Get Drunk."

Onstage, Buffett had become part Ramblin' Jack Elliott, part barstool philosopher, and everybody's stoned best friend. He was a run-on sentence, punctuated by an occasional song. And he was busy.

He found himself far away from Key West for longer periods of time. And so he was far away from Jane for longer periods of time. He'd turned the distance he'd felt the summer of 1973 into one more song for *Living and Dying in ¾ Time*.

At summer's end, he'd found himself heading north toward San Francisco to play a show with Country Joe McDonald at the Lion's Share in San Anselmo, California. "It's one of those places where you feel real comfortable," Buffett said at the Record Plant in early 1974. "You know you can fall down. The floor's real dirty and they don't care."

Before catching up with Country Joe, he'd again been in Los Angeles, killing time at the Continental Hyatt House rather than the Polo Lounge. Originally the Gene Autry Hotel, the Hyatt House became known as the Riot House and earned its place in seventies Sunset Strip lore.

John Bonham drove his motorcycle up and down its hallways. Jim Morrison dangled from a balcony. Robert Plant stood on another, looking out on the city and a Led Zeppelin billboard, and declared himself a golden god. Various Rolling Stones would wreck the place for fun. In the middle of "freak city," as he described it, sat Jimmy Buffett in a pair of comfortable Hush Puppies, feeling out of place. Buffett wrote "Come Monday" about "four lonely days in a brown L.A. haze," and about being oh so close to heading back to see Jane.

"By the time we did 'Come Monday,' I thought that was an unbelievable song," Utley says. He was sitting next to Doyle Grisham during playback at the studio. Utley remembers Grisham turning to him and saying, "This is going to be a hit."

"People weren't saying things like he was saying," Grisham says of Buffett. "They weren't writing the chord progressions. That song's pretty intricate for the time it was written. And he was unique in that way. Some of his ideas were really fresh."

He points to the song's bridge, suspended by major seventh chords. "Those were almost jazz chords, what we'd call 'em at the time," Grisham says. "Now they're more commonplace." On the other side of that bridge, Grisham played a sweeping pedal steel solo adrift with the loneliness and longing Buffett carried back on the road. There'd be no slowing down.

"Folksinger in Concert" read a nearly hidden headline on page nineteen of the third section of *Dolton Pointer* on February 28, 1974. Jimmy Buffett in concert at noon on a Monday in the Student Faculty Center on the campus of Purdue University Calumet in Hammond, Indiana, read the story. Admission: free. That's not a gig you play for fame. You play Hammond, Indiana, at noon on a Monday in early March because it's your job.

In Commerce, Texas, in April, the ad read Jimmy Buffett, with the African Music Machine. Admission: $2, but that got you free pool and Ping-Pong. Any gig, anywhere that would have him. For every Lion's Share or Quiet Knight, there was a college or coffeehouse that never earned a reputation.

It's hard, even for those who were there, to remember when Buffett was in Key West in 1974. In May, he headed back to Montana where director Frank Perry was shooting a screenplay McGuane wrote. Buffett had agreed to do the soundtrack. Starring Jeff Bridges, Sam Waterston, and Elizabeth Ashley, *Rancho Deluxe* was a misfit cowboy picture set in and around Livingston, a railroad town sprung to life in the late 1800s.

In 1968, McGuane's debut novel, *The Sporting Club*, made him enough money to buy fourteen acres in Paradise Valley, south of Livingston. Tom Corcoran remembers sitting in McGuane's living room listening to Bridges, fresh from his costarring role with Clint Eastwood in *Thunderbolt and Lightfoot*, singing and playing guitar. "I thought, *That's cute*," Corcoran says, "*maybe singing isn't in your future*."

Rancho Deluxe was one film project. Sometime that summer, Buffett and Jane went to Europe to work on another. Guy de la Valdene and his brother had been shooting a documentary about tarpon fishing in Key West, and Buffett was going to do the music for *that* while Jim Harrison handled narration. There wasn't a lot of money, but there was a free trip to France. They'd stay in Guy's family's castle and work in Paris. The castle had a moat, and they had a key to the wine cellar, and as Buffett told *Men's Journal* after Harrison's death in 2016, they scored a bag of pot from Spain. So they were good.

While the filmmakers cut *Tarpon* down, the next studio over was editing the soft-core porn flick *Emmanuelle*. Harrison and Buffett were more excited about that than they were their own documentary.

New songs, meanwhile, kept pace with Buffett. A funny little tune about the benefits of "skinny tires and wires" called "Peddler Not a Pusher" was introduced in Sausalito as his meditation on the energy crisis, and dedicated to Walter Cronkite. It was funny, he said, because he couldn't write serious or sad. Another nearly finished (and possibly never finished) song was called "I Bet Mel Blanc Has Money in the Bank."

In Nashville, he played "You Never Used to Need a Reservation at the Preservation Hall," an ode to Sweet Emma Barrett pounding the piano when Buffett would slip into the hall after playing the Bayou Room. He'd gone back and things had changed; there were paintings all over the walls and it had become an art studio.

"And that depressed me a whole bunch," Buffett said. "Not in the fact that it was like that, but the fact that people let the past slip away, and the future looks so dull and crapped up we should go back to the past."

Ben Jaffe, whose parents founded the Preservation Hall, says he and Buffett talked about that song in 2015 when Buffett played a late-night set alongside the Preservation Hall Jazz Band. They even ran through the song backstage, but didn't play it. He told Buffett the hall had never been turned into an art gallery, and had always been as it remains. But Sweet Emma played out, there were other piano players who were regularly mistaken for Sweet Emma. Buffett figured he must have been somewhere else entirely. Those were blurry nights in New Orleans.

Another song new to the set was "Migration," an ode to his favorite Texas songwriters (Michael Murphey, Jerry Jeff, and Willis Alan Ramsey), a punch at the trailer parks filling up the Keys (aluminum eyesores better off as beer cans), a recommendation against marrying too early, and a fantasy of one day sailing away to live out his years on Martinique as a make-believe Bogart with a parrot on his shoulder.

But by the chorus he'd cast his thoughts toward the people he passed on the road. The ones who weren't going anywhere but to another day exactly like the last. Buffett wasn't exactly sympathetic to their cause. With so much wonder in the world, he wondered, how was it so many had "never even seen a clue." Well, not him. No way. No how. He could "travel and rhyme." He had his "Caribbean soul," with a little Texas tucked away in his heart.

Speaking of which, in May, before Montana and Paris, Buffett found himself back in Austin, at Castle Creek, working a three- or four-night run. No one quite remembers. Castle Creek was a good room for a solo set. It fit Buffett's style. "It wasn't a honky-tonk," Ray Wylie Hubbard says. "You were there for the music."

Roger Bartlett was there to open the show. He had been

playing mandolin, bass, and guitar with Bill Callery, whose "Hands on the Wheel" would be recorded by both Willie Nelson (on *Red Headed Stranger*) and Jerry Jeff Walker.

Bartlett had hooked up with Callery (and his brother Will) in Nashville, and they'd headed to California and worked their way back to Texas. They got to Dallas, where Bartlett's parents were living and then headed south to Austin. "It was like magic land down there," he says, likening it to Paris in the twenties, the way everyone in Key West at the time likens *it* to Paris in the twenties.

By the time Bartlett got to Austin, he was in the throes of a Django Reinhardt crush and in possession of all the necessary sideman tools. When he first got into bands, he played trumpet. He picked up drums whenever the drummer was too drunk to play. He could write a song when inspiration struck. He could sing, but he was nobody's front man. "I'm not a terrifically social guy," he says. He wasn't listening to pop or very much country. He was into "arcane shit nobody likes."

But Bartlett knew the popular influences and could apply them on demand. He had grown up with the source material in Shreveport, Louisiana, home of KWKH and its tentpole program, *Louisiana Hayride*. Roger's father, Ray, worked prominent positions for both the station and the show.

Powered by 50,000 watts, KWKH, "1130 on Your Dial," celebrated twenty-five years of service in 1950 with a publication highlighting its staff and shows. Ray Bartlett, looking not unlike a young George McFly in *Back to the Future*, his smile bright and hair tight, hosted *Groovie's Boogie* and was a *Louisiana Hayride* announcer.

"My dad was on the radio all the time," Bartlett says. "And he played stuff like Muddy Waters and Johnny Otis and Cab Calloway and Duke Ellington."

The *Hayride* was "the premier jamboree of folk music in the Southwest," according to that KWKH anniversary publication. It was a barn dance, in semi-competition with the Opry, and hosted Hank Williams, a young Elvis, Johnny Horton, Tex Ritter, Moon Mullican, and hundreds of others over the years.

Groovie's Boogie, starred Ray Bartlett as Groovie Boy, his jive-talking alter ego, who spun black music and pitched sponsor Stan's Record Shop's mail-order deals. The station was powerful enough to reach Minnesota, where a young Robert Zimmerman listened intently.

KWKH had reach, but it was a product of its immediate geography. It was close enough to New Orleans to catch all the sounds Buffett had picked up in Pascagoula and Mobile, but it was well above the salt line and just as influenced by the hard-dirt country and juke-joint blues buzzing about north Texas, Mississippi, and Arkansas.

When the Bartletts moved to North Little Rock, Arkansas, Bartlett picked up the same Memphis R&B that had shaped Michael Utley's world. Bartlett was eleven when his uncle taught him a few chords on the guitar. He was fourteen when the Beatles arrived. "When I was twelve, I went with my dad to the Opry," Bartlett says, "and we went out and had dinner with Roy Orbison and Stonewall Jackson." Hank Williams used to visit his house, though Bartlett was too young to remember.

By April 1974, Bartlett had left Callery's band, but he was still living with Callery and another guitar player, Jeff Ragsdale. When Bartlett moved to Austin, he put the word out that he was giving guitar lessons. Ragsdale, looking for some flatpicking help, gave Bartlett a call. When Callery needed a new guitar player, he asked Ragsdale. When Callery was called on to open for Buffett, Bartlett asked if he could sit in. They were all still friends, so why not?

"And one night, might have been the second night, might have been the third, Bill and I had just finished playing and we went back into the green room," Ragsdale says, "which was more a broom closet with a couch in it."

Buffett came back and joined them in the break between his two sets. "And Roger all of a sudden pipes up," Ragsdale says. With no shortage of confidence, Bartlett approached Buffett and said, "You need a lead guitar player—me."

Buffett said no he didn't. He was a solo act. All he needed was his guitar. It was working out. "Roger was very insistent," Ragsdale says. "I was kind of taken aback. 'I think it'd really help you out if I was playing guitar, and backing you up. Give me a try.' And Buffett kind of relented and said, 'Okay. Come up with me on the next set and it'll be kind of an audition. We'll see how you do.'"

Buffett returned to the stage and introduced Bartlett, who knew everyone in the club. He'd been playing there for two years. He kept an eye on Buffett's hands so he could chase him through the songs. "Sang some harmony too without really knowing the words," Bartlett says. "I just made sounds that matched the sound of the words he was singing."

At the end of the night, Buffett hired him. It wasn't an easy decision. Playing solo allowed Buffett his onstage wanderings and extended monologues. People liked those. They paid to hear him talk as much as sing.

Until then, Buffett's band, which he'd nicknamed the Coral Reefer Band, was a collection of imaginary friends with tongue-in-cheek names like Kay Pasa, Al Vacado, Kitty Litter, and Marvin Gardens. Would a little magic be lost sacrificing Marvin for Roger?

Depends. Marvin was a good gag, but he wasn't much of a foil, or musician, because he didn't exist. Bartlett was funny. He could play a wry straight man to Buffett's rambling stoner. He could sing harmony—even better once he learned the words. His guitar playing was instinctive: rhythmic when Buffett needed rhythm and melodic when a melody was called for. "It was the right place at the right time with the right thing," Bartlett says.

Buffett wrapped up the Castle Creek run and hit the town at least once in the process. Boz Scaggs was in town as well, playing the Armadillo World Headquarters. Ragsdale remembers a big house with a grand piano, and the who's who of Austin was there. Jerry Jeff brought a cooler full of sangria. Scaggs's piano player took a seat at the grand. Ragsdale grabbed a guitar. Scaggs was playing harmonica and standing next to Buffett and they played old rock-and-roll songs for hours.

Bartlett told Ragsdale and Callery he'd continue to pay his rent, and then jumped on the road with Buffett. Their first gigs were in Los Angeles, at the Troubadour, opening Hoyt Axton's five-night stand. Axton had written the Kingston Trio's 1962 hit "Greenback Dollar" and Three Dog Night's 1971 hit, "Joy to the World." His mother cowrote "Heartbreak Hotel." Then they headed across the country to open for Three Dog Night in the northeast. They flew on the band's Douglas DC-3. In Boston, the local promoter with his local accent, kept telling Buffett and Bartlett, "the Dauugh has to be on by 10." They taped a television show called *Your Hit Parade* with host Chuck Woolery.

Aside from the optimism of a full calendar, there was another reason Buffett felt he could afford a guitar player. Radio was loosening up. On May 19, "Come Monday" entered *Billboard*'s singles chart at number ninety-six. A week later, it inched up to number ninety-one. Then an eleven-spot jump, and it took off.

In Montana, Corcoran and his son, Sebastian, drove from Livingston to Bozeman to scoop Buffett from the airport. Buffett's plane arrived on time, but he'd missed his flight. As the Corcorans were driving away, Tom somewhat annoyed, "Come Monday" came on the radio and Sebastian shouted that they needed to turn back, that Buffett was there. Tom couldn't help but smile. Buffett arrived on a later flight.

Grisham was right about "Come Monday." By the beginning of July, the song had cracked the top forty. By July 13, it was number thirty and a problem on the other side of the Atlantic for the BBC: "the BBC advised Dunhill executives in England they could not play the song, 'Come Monday,' because 'Hush Puppies' constitute a brand name," *Billboard* reported. "Thus it was a commercial." Buffett and Gant returned to Woodland for a twenty-minute recording session to change "Hush Puppies" to "hiking shoes."

The song peaked at thirty, but spent fourteen weeks on the chart before being snagged in the northeast United States, which preferred Dave Loggins's "Please Come to Boston," another song about distant love that reached number five in August.

Living and Dying hadn't exactly kicked down the door to *Billboard's* album chart, but reaching number 176 had to at least qualify as a neighborly invitation in for a beer.

In Montana, Buffett filmed his big-screen debut in *Rancho*, sweating and hollering a song about bar fights, underage girls, and the "whorehouse on the edge of town where anybody's able to screw." Backing Buffett as they filmed the performance of "Livingston Saturday Night" in Livingston's hippie bar, the Wrangler, was a band that included Tom McGuane pretending to play mandolin and Warren Oates faking Fingers Taylor's harmonica runs. Across the bar, Harry Dean Stanton busied himself by beating Jeff Bridges at Pong and telling him he knew he was the one rustling the cattle owned by an ex–beauty parlor magnate from Schenectady, New York.

To record the film score, Buffett and his studio band, plus Bartlett, returned to Woodland in Nashville, this time surrounded by televisions for playback of the film. Bartlett took lead vocals on "Left Me with a Nail to Drive," a low-down story of a man caught cheating and the woman who stole his truck. Working on a budget, they knocked the score out in one twenty-four-hour session.

"That's a lot of coffee," Buffett said during a show in Nashville in 2016.

"It wasn't coffee," Utley said. "Please."

In the middle of the summer, just as "Come Monday" was hitting

its stride, Buffett, Bartlett, and Fingers Taylor went back to Texas
for more than a coffeehouse or college gig. This one was bigger
than Castle Creek and it was bigger than the Armadillo.

Willie Nelson was having another festival. Willie Nelson's 4th of
July Picnic was set to go down over three days at the Texas World
Speedway in College Station. Aside from Willie, Waylon was atop
a guest list that included Leon Russell, Jerry Jeff, Michael Murphey, Doug Sahm, Tompall Glaser, Billy Joe Shaver, Ray Wylie,
and Buffett.

The lineup and set times were adjusted on the fly. No one had
a contract. Cars caught fire° as shirtless stoners helped firefighters
attack the blaze. Gary P. Nunn remembers a woman coming up in
the middle of Jerry Jeff's set and drunkenly slurring, "Thrbeenadth!
Thrbeenadth!" *What?* "THRBEENADTH!" Finally someone figured out she was saying there'd been a death. Nunn never figured
out if she was right or not. He'd gotten to sing his hit, "London
Homesick Blues," early in Jerry Jeff's set. Most of Jerry Jeff's songs
were lost to the commotion.

When Ray Wylie Hubbard went to the hotel to pick up his cre-
dential, a Waylon Jennings record was playing and the promoter
was on the phone doing a radio interview, pretending to be on-site
and suggesting there was a chance some Beatles maybe might stop
by, but who's to say for sure? You'll just have to come down to the
speedway and find out for yourselves, kids. Tickets still available!

It was anything goes—especially where there was a buck or
two involved. Outlaws before the outlaws had a name. And Willie
Nelson knew who Jimmy Buffett was. Light stood on the side of
the stage and saw a little more progress. "The audience, as deep as
I could see, were singing the words to every song," he said. "They
didn't hear those songs on the radio."

° Including one belonging to a Texas A&M student named Robert Earl Keen who'd
one day write the classic, "The Road Goes on Forever."

They knew those songs because they'd bought a record, or a friend had bought a record and played it for them. They knew those songs because they'd caught a show. Then caught Buffett again the next time he was in town, and brought those friends. The music business ran on rules because those rules worked. Almost always. But . . .

"There's an old axiom," Light said, "that you can always find exceptions."

Chapter 9

Tire Swings, Hurricanes, and the Coral Reefer Band

B uffett's crash pad on Waddell Avenue, above Chris and Sonia Robinson and next door to Louie's Backyard, had an owner—the Spottswood family. Unless you're spending sunken treasure, Spottswood money is as old as money gets in Key West.

Colonel Walter C. Maloney, of the "July 4, 1876, speech so boring the town was happy to watch a bar burn down" Maloneys, is the Spottswood patriarch. His great granddaughter married Colonel Robert F. Spottswood, a descendant of Alexander Spottswood, the first colonial governor of Virginia, in the early 1900s. In 1940, Maloney's great-great grandson, John Maloney Spottswood founded Key West's first radio station, WKWF. In the sixties, Spottswood bought the Casa Marina and La Concha hotels. In 1962, Spottswood coaxed the Warner Bros. production of the film *PT 109* to his private retreat, Little Munson Island. Like nearly everywhere else, there's resort there now, and the Spottswoods still have a law firm and a lot of real estate.

WKWF didn't have 50,000 watts, but it could get a signal to Cuba and, in favorable conditions, as far north as Tallahassee. What it needed in the seventies was a jolt, an identity. For that, the Spottswoods turned to a former taco cart operator turned bartender.

"I was there to change the format," Tom Corcoran says. "There was a well-established country DJ who I didn't mess with that would play from seven until noon, and so to ease into it I had to pay homage to the country guy, Old Duke, who wasn't old and he was not a Duke."

Corcoran would play Flying Burrito Brothers, Eagles, Linda Ronstadt, Dan Fogelberg, and Paul Simon. "Mid-seventies," Corcoran says. "James Taylor and some unknown folks like J. D. Souther. It was a pretty good radio station."

He played plenty of Buffett, too, who'd show his appreciation by stopping by the studio and saying whatever came to mind in whatever shape he was in. "I interviewed Jimmy one time when he'd been out in the boat all day long," Corcoran says. "I said, 'Obviously you've got a great career in front of you with all this creativity and music. What if it all goes to hell?'"

"I'm going to open up some sidelines," Buffett said. "I'm already thinking about one. I'm going to open up a plant on Stock Island and make guitar picks out of pressed plankton."

Corcoran ushered Buffett off the air, saying they had to get him to dinner with friends. "I wish I'd taped that one," he says.

By the sixties, World War II—and the depression that preceded it—was still in America's side-view, closer than it appeared to the boomer kids, but not their parents. "Those beach blanket movies, those were fiction," Corcoran says. Nobody was spending all that money it took to go play in the sand. Remembering the icy winters of a childhood in Michigan, Jim Harrison's *A Good Day to Die* narrator described the few who could afford a trip to Florida "vaguely decadent."

Even as the middle class rapidly expanded, there were worries within as to whether or not it would hold. Better be safe and save a little than be sorry, right? Anyone who'd experienced before was cautious after. The Beach Boys, Jan and Dean, Annette and Frankie—they were for the kids. Then the kids grew up and paradise seemed within reach. The little towns along the Gulf Coast and the Atlantic Ocean began to grow: Pensacola, in the Florida panhandle (the Redneck Riviera), Daytona Beach, Tampa, and St. Pete, Fort Lauderdale, Hollywood, Miami. Orlando had Mickey Mouse. South Florida had Travis McGee, John D. MacDonald's tanned and capable "salvage consultant."

But Key West was still a haul, and then came the gas shortage. If you're going to drive more than a hundred miles to the end of a string of islands, best to know you'll be able to fuel up and get home. All the billboards in the world near Disney weren't going to solve that riddle. "The joke in seventy-three and seventy-four was the chamber of commerce had someone stationed on the Seven Mile Bridge to call ahead when a car was coming," Corcoran says. "Then everyone would race down Duval Street and open their stores."

On March 29, 1974, Admiral John Maurer lowered the American flag at the Key West naval station and 151 years of military operations in Key West came to a close. The economic impact trickled down and the streets soon were emptier still. To illustrate the point, historian Tom Hambright flipped through a stack of photos in his office in the back of the Monroe County Public Library on Fleming Street. He settled on one snapped at the corner of Fleming and Duval on December 8, 1974. There are two people in the shot, a mother pushing a child in a stroller across Duval. What's now a Banana Republic was an empty storefront. All the storefronts in the photo are empty, save for a single bar, the Boat Bar, which Hambright recalled as a risky proposition. It grew up to be a T-shirt shop.

Steve Thompson drove from Seattle to South Florida in 1971 and got a bartending job, where he met Chris Robinson. He'd always planned on returning to the West Coast, but figured he should get a look at Key West before he left. He arrived late in 1973 with $500 in his pocket.

"It was so quiet," he says. Lost among the stories of smugglers and boozy nights, the heat-fueled, drug-fueled, youth-fueled craziness of that time is the fact that Key West was peaceful. "Deserted might not be the right word," Thompson says, but it's close. He pulled his car onto Duval Street and parked anywhere. On a half-deserted misfit island in 1973, $500 went a long way. It got him settled. "It wouldn't last a day now," Thompson says.

It might not even last a night in the wine bar where he'd grabbed a table as powerboats paraded down Duval toward the marina, the annual ceremonial kickoff of another race week. At the other end of the table, Thompson's wife, Cindy, told the story of her Key West arrival. She'd come to the island a little more than a year after Steve, setting south from Wisconsin.

She'd already seen the world, been to India and back and was living in Denver when she began to miss the water. After a trip to the library, she settled on two options: Savannah, Georgia, or Astoria, Oregon. Key West only entered the mix when a friend mentioned the island. "I didn't even know there were islands in the United States," she says.

She tossed a backpack into the backseat of her Volkswagen and drove home to Wisconsin to see her parents. The windchill was forty-five-below when she turned south from Milwaukee, and she didn't stop until somewhere in Kentucky, out of fear her car wouldn't start back up in the cold.

She still has the backpack she arrived with, and she and Steve go to the Chart Room every Thursday night, as they have for decades. And they recall their arrivals in fairy-tale terms. "Couldn't believe it when I got here," Cindy says. "Could not believe it. It was magical."

"It changed real fast," Steve says. "Overnight, almost."

"Right when Jimmy started to get famous," Cindy says.

Before Cindy arrived, and well before the two met, Steve had settled in on the island and opened a business, Key West Taco Company and got ahead of the T-shirt curve on Duval.

He hadn't been around town long when he walked into a party at Vic Latham's house. Buffett was there and everyone wanted Thompson to meet the musician. Elizabeth Ashley, who'd been in *Rancho Deluxe* and would star in the Tom McGuane–directed adaptation of his novel *Ninety-Two in the Shade*, was also at the party. Steve wanted to meet her.

"I was more impressed with that," he says. "They were just people to me, short people, and I had no idea who they were."

Buffett got Thompson's attention when he picked up a guitar and played a song about a bartender they all knew. "I'm not sure if Phil was there or not," Steve says, "but he was one of the few people I knew."

"Did you know it was about him when you heard it?" Cindy says.

"I did," Steve says, "because my first thought was, *Nobody's going to know who you're talking about*. I thought this was a local thing for the local bars. Nobody was going to buy it. Thirty years later, I go back to Seattle and everyone knows it."

Buffett wrote "A Pirate Looks at Forty" for Phil Clark, who was indeed a smuggler. Or at least he had smuggled. He had made money and lost money. He had married and divorced. Married and divorced. Married and divorced. Maybe married and divorced again? No one's quite sure of the number. He was smart and savvy, well traveled, and he told a good enough story that even his friends weren't sure where fact separated into fiction.

"Had a big toothy smile and a big voice and I want to say one time he captained the sailboat the *Ticonderoga*," says Chris Robinson, who'd fallen into his Chart Room job because Clark was leaving town. "These are just stories I heard. When I got here, he'd already gotten caught for smuggling. He was working on a shrimp boat.

"He had cowboy boots on with the silver toes and he could stand at the bar and almost pass out and then he would get up and stomp that heel down."

In Clark, Buffett saw an anachronism, and he loved those. Two hundred years earlier, and Phil Clark would have been an honest-to-god pirate. Instead he was a guy who couldn't quite fit his times—or wouldn't.

When Buffett returned to Woodland in Nashville in August 1974, "A Pirate Looks at Forty" went to wax, sequenced to introduce the second side of *A1A*—his second album of 1974. "A1A is the beach access road that runs occasionally on and off U.S. 1," Buffett wrote, taking over liner notes for the first time in his career, which, after "Come Monday," looked a little more like an actual career.

A1A, he noted, could take you to some of Florida's best beaches and "right through the middle of 'Wrinkle City,' better known as Miami Beach and ending suddenly 90 miles north of Havana and four blocks from my house."

ABC-Dunhill sent photographer Peter Whorf to Florida to work out concepts for what wouldn't be Whorf's most famous photograph. He shot the cover of *Whipped Cream & Other Delights,** the 1965 Herb Alpert and the Tijuana Brass album that featured an alluring Dolores Erickson wearing nothing but whipped cream and a come-hither stare. That she wasn't really naked under the whipped cream, and that the whipped cream was really shaving cream, did not matter. The illusion, as is often the case, was the appeal.

"After several hard skull sessions at Louie's Backyard," Buffett wrote, "we started up A1A to Miami. So the cover was the trip and the trip was a cover."

Jimmy Buffett as not just another entertaining singer and songwriter, but as a laid-back *ideal* began on the cover of *A1A*. He's

---

* The album's title track, "Whipped Cream," was written by Allen Toussaint (though credited to Naomi Neville, his mother's maiden name) and first recorded in 1964 while he was still in the military. He went into the studio with his army band under the name the Stokes. "Whipped Cream" played an integral role in *The Dating Game* when it debuted in late-1965. Alpert's record also included a cover of the Leiber and Stoller hit "Love Potion No. 9," which Buffett would throw into his solo sets.

slouched in a white rocking chair in the shade of his backyard. Dressed in his own cleanest dirty clothes—a yellow T-shirt and cutoff shorts—he's got a bottle of Michelob on his right and beyond his beer there's nothing but blue sky and blue water.

"We had the whole Pacific Ocean in front of us, with nothing to do but do nothing and be comfortable," Mark Twain wrote in *Following the Equator*, and there was Buffett, living Twain's words in lazy defiance of Watergate, the energy crisis, the recession, work obligations, family frustrations, rush hours, long lines, bills, and to-do lists.

The gatefold was built from a nautical chart of the Keys—the kind tacked to the Chart Room's ceiling. More than a dozen photos of a beach bum in inaction highlighted the path back to the mainland: Buffett lounging in a hammock; Buffett gnawing on a chicken wing; Buffett at a picnic table with a Budweiser outside a crab shack; Buffett sitting in the back of God's Own Truck set against a backdrop of palm trees and blue skies he'd replicate for decades onstage. He could just as easily have titled the album *Wish You Were Here*.

Side A of *A1A* was another collection of road-dog songs, the exception being "Door Number Three," a cowrite with Steve Goodman and the kind of song you stumble on when you're road weary enough to be inspired by Monty Hall and the costumed contestants of *Let's Make a Deal*. "The man was dressed like a cucumber," Buffett said, back at the Record Plant with Roger Bartlett in October 1974. "The lady was an oil and vinegar setting." And they traded down, lost their television and refrigerator. It was all so tragic.

"Makin' Music for Money," was an Alex Harvey song about *not* doing that. "I'm gonna make my music for me" was the promise. Bartlett wrote "Dallas" as a warning: stay away lest you end up mentally imbalanced and talking to chairs. He'd written it in Dallas when he was in the band Baccus. Influenced by the Band and Crosby, Stills & Nash, Baccus was named for Bacchus, the Roman god of wine and drunkenness. "We spelled it wrong," Bartlett says.

"I was living with a girl there who was sort of my high school sweetheart," he says. When that fell apart, he got a song, and that song turned out to be his second big credit of 1974. In October, when the low-budget slasher classic *The Texas Chainsaw Massacre* was released it featured Bartlett working out his Django jones on "Fool for a Blonde."

John Sebastian wrote "Stories We Could Tell," but Buffett got his hands on the song through an Everly Brothers record he borrowed from Corcoran. "Never saw that record again," Corcoran says.

"Presents to Send You" was written by a busy mind. Buffett packed it with thoughts of Jane (a "fast moving angel who dresses like the city girls do"), distant love, the ever-present danger of tequila (including an allusion to the Buford Pusser Incident), and the thought of sailing away to Barbados, a plan that fell through when he "smoked the whole lid" and went exactly nowhere. He'd no doubt earned a stoned day in the hammock.

Another rental car had to die to make "Life Is Like a Tire Swing," but so it went. "It's a really weird story," Buffett said at the Exit/In in 1974. "I guess that's how you write 'em."

He'd been working on a song about childhood trips to see his aunt and uncle and cousin Baxter in Gautier, Mississippi. They lived in a big antebellum house with a tire swing. "I'd written about two verses of the song and I was in Illinois doing a bunch of one-nighters . . . college dates," he said. He flew into Peoria, picked up a car, and drove to Macomb, cruising at sixty-five miles per hour and listening to Hall & Oates's "When the Morning Comes," when he looked over and saw a house with a tire swing out front. What a coincidence.

The next morning, he was racing back to Peoria for a 6 a.m. flight when he fell asleep at the wheel and hit a telephone pole in front of that same house. "I had the ending of my song," he said. "It was a hard way to do it."

The flip to Side B finally brought Buffett's music fully in line with the image he'd been fashioning and featured some of his best writing. "A Pirate Looks at Forty" was about Phil Clark, yes, but Steve Thompson's friends in Seattle would eventually memorize it because it was just as much about feeling out of sorts. "My occupational hazard being, my occupation's just not around," Buffett sang. You needn't have dreamed of being Blackbeard to feel like you missed your shot, in one way or another.

"Migration" was next, followed by "Trying to Reason with Hurricane Season," Grisham's pedal steel dancing sweetly through the palm fronds, a storm building over the Gulf Stream, and Buffett passed out again in that hammock before coming to sometime after noon and heading over to Louie's for a drink. "I must confess, I could use some rest," he sang. "I can't run at this pace very long."

In "Nautical Wheelers," Buffett finally told the story of the great Tequila Regatta, pairing it with the imagery of a square dancing group who'd play "fiddle tunes under the stars" at the old city hall in Key West on Friday nights. "Square dancing's fun," Buffett said during a show near Philadelphia in 1974. "You can do-si-do your ass off." He dropped in one night, found his kind of people, old island folks who were "more than contented to be living and dying in three-quarters time."

"I was real stupid," Buffett said. "I named the second album after a line in a song I did on the new one." Stupid? Possibly. Or he was on island time. As he added, "The pace of life slows the farther south you go in the Caribbean. It really does.

"Oh, I've been here five years," Buffett said, mimicking conversation.

"What do you do?"

"Nothing."

Sit and watch the sunset like everyone else, maybe with a cup of wine. "Tin Cup Chalice" finally found its home at the end of A1A.

In a little more than a year and a half, Jimmy Buffett had recorded *A White Sport Coat and a Pink Crustacean, Living*

and Dying in ¾ Time, A1A, and the *Rancho Deluxe* soundtrack
and scored *Tarpon*. He'd played every coffeehouse, beer joint,
and student assembly room from Boston to the Keys to San
Francisco and back. He continued to work Nashville, whether
Nashville liked it or not. He could make a living in Texas. He had
a beat-up truck, a nice little boat, and a minor hit. He'd grown
his one-man band to two. He had his wit and his charm and went
right back to work.

In October 1974, Buffett and Bartlett played a Don Light–
sponsored showcase in Nashville. They hit another booking
conference in Commerce, Texas, arriving to the news that the
Commodores were coming.

"Now, the Commodores in that time were moving in style,"
Buffett said in 2012, telling the story onstage in Seattle. They re-
leased their debut album in 1974. They played *Soul Train*. "They
had a bus that looked like the Starship *Enterprise*," Buffett said.
"They had outfits that would put Parliament-Funkadelic to shame.
And they could *play*."

The last thing anyone wanted was to have to follow the Commodores. Straws were drawn, and Buffett and Bartlett had to follow
the Commodores, who walked in from their space ship and threw
down for fifteen minutes exactly as everyone knew they would.

"What are we going to do?" Bartlett said.

"First, we're going to start drinking heavily," Buffett said, "and
I'll figure this out."

Here's what they did: They took the stage, Buffett took a swig
of tequila, and for twelve minutes he talked about the brilliant
performance they'd all been lucky enough to witness. For the last
three minutes, they played "Why Don't We Get Drunk."

"And got just as many goddamn bookings as they did," Buffett
said.

By the end of October they'd worked back to the Record Plant
to record another KSAN session. This time the audience was Jerry

Jeff and the Lost Gonzo Band and the microphones captured bags of beer rustling, bags of beer falling off stools, and shorter bursts of entertaining but random thoughts:

"We're doing a national phlebitis campaign here. For anyone's leg that puffs up!

"We're going to do a rope trick later on . . .

"But the main purpose of our business is music . . ."

He paused for a beat, then broke up laughing.

"What a thing to say," Bartlett said.

An hour later, they were on their way to the next town. "We sort of did a circuit for about a year," Bartlett says. Up to Boston, down to New York. "I think we opened for Bo Diddley at Max's Kansas City," he says. Down to Atlanta. Over to Nashville. Up to Chicago. Out to Los Angeles. Up to San Francisco and back again.

The rooms got bigger, two-night stands turned into four-night stands. Buffett handled every challenge the way he handled having to follow the Commodores, with ease. When things got too wild or went awry entirely, he invented a scapegoat, an alter ego named Freddy Buffett.

It was only in the quiet moments, in the car between gigs when Bartlett would try to talk to Buffett about his past that Buffett seemed almost shy. For whatever reason, Bartlett doesn't recall him ever opening up much. But put him on a stage and he could own a room.

"I had more of a musician kind of background, and he had more of a performer kind of background," Bartlett says. "That whole folk thing where they're kind of stand-up comics." Buffett liked the spotlight. So much so that Steve Vaughn, who'd later join the touring cast as a roadie, says the running joke was that if Buffett opened a refrigerator, he'd stand there for ten minutes just because the light was on.

Not that he shut down when the light went off. He couldn't. "Jimmy did everything," Light said. Buffett didn't necessarily think the art department could present his music better than he could. Buffett didn't think someone else should write the liner notes. He had a case file full of evidence the record company didn't get him, or couldn't figure him out.

"At that point, there's nobody out there but you," Buffett said in Key West in 2015, defending himself against charges of narcissism. "Yes I'm a confirmed narcissist because there was nobody back there who gave a shit at the time. You were on your own, and you better be good."

Said Light: "He was the most take-control artist I've ever been around."

The magic was making the world believe Buffett was barely in control, that he wasn't anything more than the semisober performer they saw onstage. And he could do that as easily as he could wreck a rental car. What he couldn't do, as "Trying to Reason with Hurricane Season" so plainly admitted, was continue to run at the pace he was keeping. There was physical toll, but the creative cost was the tricky one.

Light described a natural attrition to the songbook that occurs when an artist has a hint of success. You've got a stack of songs, Light said, throwing out fifty as a working number. You make your first album and cut maybe fifteen of those. "It's going to surprise you how quickly they're going to ask for another record," Light said. But you're busy promoting the first record and you haven't refilled the tank. Then the label wants a third record. You're touring. You're doing press. You're taking meetings. You're managing business. Life has changed. The songs don't come as fast or as easy. The stack gets smaller and smaller again.

"A Pirate Looks at Forty" stalled out a spot below cracking the top one hundred. "Door Number Three" pushed its way to number eighty-eight on the country singles chart. Neither came close to replicating the success of "Come Monday."

The album, however, did well. *A1A* worked its way to number twenty-five on *Billboard*'s albums chart, and did so without radio. For ABC-Dunhill, Jimmy Buffett had become a small profit center. "We were in the third album before we ever spent $25,000 on a record," Light said.

There was opportunity there. In Los Angeles, a label rep named Dennis Lavinthal was pushing for an expansion of the Coral Reefer Band. The risk when Bartlett joined the band hadn't changed. Light remembered how fans took a while to warm up to Bartlett after having seen Buffett play solo. Fans seemed to like Buffett best however they'd first experienced him, and there'd be pushback to a full band. "Because he had to have a smaller percentage of talking," Light said. "They missed those stories and the funny things. He lost some comedic content. Quite a bit of it. They resented it—until he got it to be a pretty rocking band."

There's a natural resistance to change. "We should go back to the past." Buffett said it himself when he thought the Preservation Hall had been lost for good. But he had to make a change. "At a certain point, we decided the venues were getting too big," Bartlett says. "We did one festival as a duo in Oklahoma and it was 135,000 people. So I'm really glad I drank. You talk about stage fright."

When the *next* album, *Havana Daydreamin'*, was released early in 1976, Buffett would write of a night in Raleigh, North Carolina, when he and Bartlett were trapped in a dressing room by a horde of fans looking to party: "I turned to Roger (the mono-Reefer then), and calmly screamed, 'I can't do this shit much longer. If I don't get a band I'll go crazy.'"

In March 1975, the Coral Reefer Band convened for rehearsals in Key West. To Corcoran's many professions, he'd added proprietor of a leather shop, F. T. Sebastian's Leather Co. He made hats and bags.

Located at 531 Fleming Street, near Fausto's market and down the street from the Monroe County Public Library, Corcoran set up shop in what had once been a gas station. He told Buffett his new band could rehearse in one of the old repair bays.

"When we got down there, we didn't really know each other," Bartlett says. He knew Fingers Taylor a little, because they'd played some shows as a trio. Gove Scrivenor, an autoharp player who'd spent time in Key West (jamming with Vaughn Cochran, among others) and who was also managed by Don Light, recommended bassist Harry Dailey. Bartlett had a passing acquaintance and the phone number for the drummer from Texas. "I'd been playing an acoustic duo," Bartlett says. "He was one of the three drummers I knew."

Phillip Fajardo was hooked into the blues scene. Growing up in Amarillo, he'd started on the drums early and then set them aside in favor of Texas's national pastime: football. As a senior halfback at Amarillo Palo Duro in 1966, his announcement he'd play his college ball at the University of Houston made the newspapers.

After college, Fajardo arrived in Austin in 1970 and found a suitable replacement for football: drugs. "Dropped in and dropped out," he says. "I was kind of in search of the truth." He played a little with Waylon Jennings and in a pickup band full of other starving musicians who liked to play the blues. He found some work in the studios around town. He set out for Key West as soon as Bartlett called.

"It was a week before we even picked up any instruments," Fajardo says. "We just partied. It was just a big party. Rolling thunder." Bartlett says they got right to work, but he also remembers they got down there at different times. Both remember the sound of a band-in-progress ricocheting off the repair bay's concrete floors and colliding with acoustically unfriendly walls.

"But the truth was, we could rehearse all afternoon and into the early evening and then we'd go out and get totally plotzed," Bartlett says. "The sound problem was irksome, but it didn't really bother us."

Why would it? Bartlett and Fingers knew the scene. Bartlett had once even been in possession of keys to an apartment in Key West. It took him a month to realize the keys weren't worth the rent he was paying on an apartment he'd never occupy. But they'd met the people. They knew the dance around Duval. For Fajardo, it was nothing like anyplace he'd been.

He and Buffett took the Whaler out snorkeling and spearfishing. "I went down into a shallow coral reef canal and as I turned the bend in the canal, I ran headlong into a small sharpnose shark," Fajardo says. "We both did immediate 180s. That was my first and last encounter with a shark."

Fajardo decided to get his ear pierced—left ear, as was the pirate's fashion—and since earrings came in pairs, Buffett joined him. They chose a fourteen-karat-gold option. They hung out in the apartment on Waddell, at the Chart Room, Captain Tony's, and anywhere else they could get a drink. "It was really loose," Fajardo says. "Getting to meet the locals and hanging out, and, boy, that was quite a time. Unbelievable."

Rehearsals wrapped, they played a debut show at Logan's Lobster House, and nobody recalls a thing about it other than it happened. Vic Latham was managing the restaurant. There was an open bar for the band. Things went sideways, probably. Then they hit the road. "After we finally did get down to business," Fajardo says, "our lives were like a hurricane."

In their rearview, Key West continued on quiet and peaceful and weird. But just as Jimmy's fame was growing, the island and island life were changing in ways that wouldn't surface for a few months.

In 1973, Florida Governor Reubin Askew asked his law enforcement officials to look into Key West's open secret: all those drugs. Askew didn't think much of local law enforcement, and so he asked Broward County, not Monroe, to take lead on Operation Conch. "Marijuana in their mindset is no different than shrimping," Ken Jenne, a former assistant Broward County prosecutor told local historian Stuart McIver in a 1996 *South Florida Sun-Sentinel* piece. "Theirs is simply a different moral and legal system."

If it had just been marijuana, Key West might have continued to fly under Tallahassee's radar, though coming in by boat was still the most common approach.

"They're going sixty miles per hour and they're only drawing a few inches and they'd have a flashlight at a certain time at a certain place," Steve Thompson says.

"They have no running lights," Cindy Thompson adds.

The runners knew those waters better than anyone trying to catch them. Everyone else knew the score. So no one could have been *that* surprised when, on September 9, 1975, the agents of Operation Conch swept into town and arrested nineteen suspected drug dealers. Included in the indictments was one Joseph "Bum" Farto, Key West's fire chief, aka El Jefe.

Bum Farto's father had owned a restaurant on the corner of Greene and Duval. He sold the building to Sloppy Joe Russell in 1937. Bum picked up his nickname hanging around firehouses as a kid. As an adult, he drove a lime-green Cadillac, preferred fire-engine-red clothing, and saw the world through literal rose-colored glasses. A baseball fan and a voodoo practitioner, he'd drive his car up to the field when Key West's high school team was playing and light a candle for good luck.

He also liked to move drugs from fire stations: marijuana first, and then cocaine. Ask around, and the same people who knew who was running what are in agreement about when things changed.

"Nobody shot anybody over marijuana," Chris Robinson says. Cocaine piled bodies. Bodies brought attention. In 1971, Richard Nixon declared war on drugs. In 1973, he backed that up with the creation of the Drug Enforcement Agency. Mandatory minimum sentences came into vogue. Gerald Ford was slightly more pragmatic about addiction than Nixon, and Jimmy Carter would eventually run for office with decriminalization of small amounts of marijuana as part of his platform, but there was no sympathy for smugglers and dealers. The game got way more dangerous. Between 1975 and 1977, the Monroe County sheriff's department seized more than 207,000 pounds of narcotics worth more than $82 million.

Bum was run up on charges of moving both marijuana and coke and found guilty by a Key West jury after thirty minutes of deliberation. He disappeared before he could be sentenced. Farto had rented a car from a gas station in Key West, told his wife he was going to Miami, and was never seen again. Was he killed? Obviously that was one theory. Did he run off with a pile of money he'd stashed away? That was the romantic's hope, that Bum skipped south and was spending freely on a beach, fishing all day and lighting candles for Key West High's starting pitcher at night.

Whatever happened to Bum Farto, his story became part of what Key West was before the dopers unloading at the shrimp docks gave way to civic improvements aimed directly at the wallets and purses of tourists. The Downtown '76 revitalization project was designed, the *Citizen* wrote, to "capture the precious essence of what it once was, tempered with the taste and dignity of modern life." And it was underway as Farto went on trial, and he was a ghost by January 1977 when the *Citizen* declared the project a success: "The proof is found in a casual stroll down Duval Street as it is in the faces of thousands of tourists flocking to the island in ever increasing numbers. It's in the new charm of Old Key West which lured them here; it's in the new face of Old Key West which intrigues them."

Finally, people were going there, doing that and buying the T-shirt—sometimes the same T-shirt being worn onstage by Key West's most visible ambassador. "Where's Bum Farto?" it said.

❋ Chapter 10 ❋

Euphoria

Inner southeast Portland, Oregon, isn't much to look at, just blocks of squat warehouses packed alongside each other. The streets are narrow and cracked. Freight trains rumble through and back up traffic. Noisy and claustrophobic, the tropics it ain't. But there used to be a pretty good rock club there called the Euphoria Tavern.

The Euphoria fell nicely into a West Coast tour, either on the way to or from San Francisco, Los Angeles, and San Diego. It was a good room. High ceilings and wood beams gave it a warm sound. There was a big dance floor and an L-shaped stage. George Stevenson was a regular. He was in law school the summer of 1975 and had just wrapped up a summer job with the Yamhill County District Attorney's Office when he figured he'd head to the Euphoria to celebrate.

When he got there, he found a tour bus parked alongside the club and a pack of musicians outside the back door. Their leader—compact, with a flop of blond hair and a droopy mustache—was pounding on the door.

"I walked up and suggested I could lead him to the front door," Stevenson says. Before Jimmy Buffett had a chance to respond, the back swung open and the Coral Reefer Band was in the building to set up and get to work. It could have been any other night on the road—it *was* just another night on the road—until time made it something slightly more.

The contract for that show, August 23, 1975, resides in Gainesville, Florida, filed away in a quiet room in a library named after former United States Senator George A. Smathers, the same Smathers Key West named a beach after.

The money wasn't bad. The deal for the Euphoria was a flat guarantee, $1,250 (half up front, half before the show, "cash or cashier's check only") for two shows ("T/B/A"), "artist to receive 100% headline billing." The club's responsibility was a professional sound system at no cost to the artist. Signed, Jimmy Buffett, local number 257, care of Don Light. Buffett's name was spelled correctly; the club's wasn't. "Europhia," it read.

David Leiken signed the deal for his Double Tee Promotions, and he still has Double Tee Promotions. He operates it out of a corner office behind another venue in another part of town.

"That was a crossroads show," Leiken says. He remembers the tickets went on sale on a Saturday, and when he arrived at his office on Monday and casually asked how the show was selling, he was shocked to hear both shows had sold out. They added another night.

The new Coral Reefer Band was finding its sound. Earlier in August, they'd been in North Carolina to open for the Eagles, "the best American band of my generation and many to follow," Buffett wrote online in 2016 after Eagles cofounder Glenn Frey died. "No band worth their salt didn't start out as an opener for somebody. Opening for the right band at the right time could be your stairway to heaven."

One of the Eagles road managers invited Buffett and the Reefers to sound check. Wandering back to their dressing room after, Buffett turned "and I said to my band, 'That is the kind of band we want to become,'" he wrote. Later, Frey popped into the dressing room, wished them luck, thanked them for being there, and told Buffett he liked "A Pirate Looks at Forty."

"It wasn't your ordinary gig by any stretch of the imagination," Buffett wrote. By that standard, the Euphoria was an ordinary gig, but a good one. Good *ones*, actually. Four shows in two nights and another market outside Buffett's Southern stronghold conquered, a new front opened. One more reason to celebrate—beyond all the usual reasons to celebrate, which, to be honest, were any reasons at all.

There was ongoing competition for the D&O Award—Drunk and Outrageous. "If you threw up, it was an automatic win," Roger Bartlett says. He was still drinking like he was trying to drown stage fright, and the scene around Buffett had only grown wilder.

"I'd bring a girl backstage and go out to get us drinks," he says. By the time he got back, she'd be with somebody else. "And I had two drinks to get rid of," he says. "That's how I ended up with a drinking problem."

At least there was plenty of cocaine to pick them up and kick them on down the road to the next city. Bartlett half remembers someone gifting a garbage bag full of blow in the Northwest, maybe Seattle, but possibly at the Euphoria Tavern. The party (and the party people) gravitated toward Buffett.

"Nobody thought about anyone having a drug problem, because everyone thought you could do this with impunity," Bartlett says. "Everybody had a problem."

On the tour bus, driven for a while by a guy named Hack, valuables were kept under bunks, visitors were kept in the main lounge, and Buffett had the stateroom in back. They used the buddy system in truck stops, lest some amped up redneck on the long haul from Knoxville or Cincinnati decide he was bored enough to pick a fight with a longhair. Bob Seger wasn't making anything up when he wrote "Turn the Page."

"One of the trips we made, we were in Portland and had to drive to Houston, and we drove it straight," drummer Phillip Fajardo says. "I had to learn how to drive the bus. There was a lot of speed."

Buffett soon upgraded from the first bus to a Silver Eagle, dispatching Fajardo and his freshly acquired skills behind the wheel, and another driver, Curly Jones (who also drove the Oak Ridge Boys), to Brownsville, Texas, to pick the bus up. "It was just an empty shell," Fajardo says. "It was a big aluminum box." They got a mattress, threw it down in the back, drove straight to Nashville in shifts, and delivered the bus to Hemphill Brothers Coach Company, where it was built out with a nautical theme. "Driftwood and barn lumber," Buffett told *High Times* in December 1976. "It's just a cruiser. You get in there and it's like being on the moon."

"We had every episode of *Star Trek* ever," Steve Vaughn, one of the roadies, says. They played those videos constantly, Captain Kirk, Mr. Spock, and the rest of the crew booming from a top-of-the-line sound system.

Given the option of custom destination markers, Buffett opted for Key West, Havana, Teens for Christ, Governor's Staff, Loretta Lynn, and Enterprise. "Loretta Lynn" would get them more latitude at a truck stop than the buddy system; "Teens for Christ" drew the occasional missionary to the door hoping to discuss the good book with partners in service of the Lord.

The D&O Award changed hands with regularity, and Buffett was riding in style, or at least *a* style, one befitting the screwballs and misfits in his band, in his crew, and in songs they'd bring to life each night like never before.

"Okay. If we can get the lights out in the kitchen, we'll get going with a little bit of Florida right here in San Diego," came the introduction in September 1975. "Jimmy Buffett and the Coral Reefer Band!"

The miles between Logan's Lobster House and the Backdoor, on the campus of San Diego State University, had built that first Coral Reefer Band into a stoned wrecking crew. Midnight juke-joint hot-shit blues? They could play it. They could make "God's Own Drunk" sound like Hendrix burning down "Red House," Fingers

Taylor and Bartlett trading harmonica and guitar licks like dirty jokes. But when they needed a lighter touch, say on "Trying to Reason with Hurricane Season," they could take you and put you right on the beach behind Buffett's apartment.

"Jimmy sort of had to feel his way into the thing, because he wasn't used to playing with a band," Bartlett says. "There was no such a thing as a musical director. I was the de facto musical director at the time."

Bartlett's leanings became the band's arrangements, and his leanings (with apologies to his Django crush) were blues and rock, perfect for Fajardo, who could throw in a country beat when necessary. Harry Dailey brought a folkie's touch to the low end. Fingers could do it all, do it better than anyone else, and then step offstage and keep going until sunrise. One of Steve Vaughn's jobs each morning was to check on Taylor. "He had, like, a makeup kit, and that was full of his feel goods," Vaughn says. "He knew people everywhere."

They all made friends easily. "We were living our lives like the song we recorded, 'Kick It in Second Wind,'" Fajardo says. At San Diego State, they parked that one near the end of the set, closest to the 1 a.m. barroom scene the song opens on, where the crowd is screaming, the booze is flowing, Buffett's "belly hummin'," and some poor soul is locked in what had to be an unpleasant bathroom. "I pity that man but from where I stand, it's looking like the prisoner is me," Buffett figured. His mind wanders from his perch to the ocean and a boat where it's just him and Jane (who cowrote the song). That fantasy is broken by shouts of last call and the bass player tipping over. Improbably, they're out of coke, and as 3 a.m. rolls around, they're left with adrenaline and one certainty: "tomorrow's a day and we've got to do it over again."

"Here for a good time not a long time," Buffett liked to say onstage. "Every night's a Friday night, every day's Saturday. Been wrong so long we gotta try it one more time."

Night after night, cities and stages blurred together like landscapes out the tour bus window until Buffett and band could get back into the studio to work out the last album on his ABC-Dunhill contract. With the chart success of *A1A*, and three albums under his belt, he felt his footing solid enough to push back against one of Don Gant's more traditional Nashville beliefs: Thou shall use studio musicians. Buffett had a road-tested band and he wanted to use it. He had a title for the new record, *Kick It in Second Wind*, and a collection of songs for every hour of his endless days.

"My Head Hurts, My Feet Stink, and I Don't Love Jesus" remains an all-time hangover song, the story of an escalating night at the Snake Pit, the next morning's checklist of cures (Darvon, orange juice, chocolate milk from Fausto's), and the inevitable broken promises that follow: "Trying to convince myself my condition is improving, and if I don't die by Thursday, I'll be roaring Friday night."

Buffett talked the Oak Ridge Boys, who also worked with Don Light, into singing background vocals, their gospel background making a funny song funnier when William Lee Golden dropped his down-so-low baritone on the line, "Oh my Lordy it's bad."

"Woman Goin' Crazy on Caroline Street" was set in another bar about a block up Duval, its troubled and lonely star desperately trying to convince a crowd that she'd once been a dancer. "But I don't think she's cut a rug in years," Buffett sang, looking on as she drinks cheap beer, sways to the jukebox among "lurking eyes," and promises a trip to her place for the first guy who shows some small kindness. But it isn't that kind of bar, or at least that kind of night, and "in a flash" a fight breaks out. "Be careful when you go to swing your partner," Buffett warned, because "someone just might take a swing at you." On the test pressing, the song was credited to Buffett, Steve Goodman, and Shel Silverstein, another famous pen who'd found Key West.

Goodman wrote "This Hotel," an accounting of every item in a hotel room by a guy who'd been gone so long that when he finally glanced in the mirror he couldn't believe what he saw: "That couldn't be me in that gorilla disguise."

"Big Rig," written by Fingers, was all amphetamines and fifth-gear grooves, Buffett singing about how "drinking and snortin'" wasn't really who he was, and that if he had his way, he'd be headed home to Alabama and then . . . hello. Who's that? "It's a good lookin' blonde with a bottle of scotch and she wants to go home with me." Been wrong so long . . .

"Please Take Your Girlfriend Home" was about a fifteen-year-old, not *exactly* new territory for Buffett, who'd noted in "Livingston Saturday Night" that "fifteen may get you twenty." Not wishing to risk it, his new request was straightforward: "Please take your drunken fifteen-year-old girlfriend home." Backstage at a rock show was no place for anyone that young. The punch line lands when she tells him she likes the harmonica player more, and Jethro Tull puts on a better show.

Buffett cut Keith Sykes's "Train to Dixie" and powered it with horns and fiddles chasing lightning-quick guitar fills that couldn't outrace time any more than the railroad lady: "The years are passing faster than that train could ever run."

For emotional depth, Buffett lifted "The Captain and the Kid" from the obscurity of *Down to Earth*, and another ballad, "Wonder Why You Ever Go Home," from *Rancho Deluxe*, reorienting a song written for McGuane's characters into a universal lament set in the conflicted headspace between youth and maturity. Not that anyone who saw the movie would have known. The lyrics were left out of the final cut.

Kick It in Second Wind was finished with a combination of Coral Reefers and studio pros (including Utley and Grisham), and then never released. Summer turned to fall, fall turned to the holidays, and even without a new release, the Coral Reefer Band returned to Key West to play Mallory Square.

For the many who'd missed the Logan's Lobster House debut,

it was their first chance to see Buffett with a full band. Just in time for the show, the weather turned, the temperature plummeted, and the wind whipped up out of the northwest, blowing onshore. Situated as Mallory Square is, on the northwest corner of the island, the show took a beating.

"That was the Christmas I moved here," Cindy Thompson says. "It was soooo cold, and my boyfriend at the time, out at Stock Island, he said, 'You gotta hear this guy; he's pretty good.' So we went in to hear him and, 'Yeah, this is amazing.' But it was so unbelievably cold. There were puddles everywhere. It was so dark and it was so windy and it was so cold. I couldn't believe he played, really."

"I got a cold that night that hung for three weeks," Tom Corcoran says.

"I do remember that one," Bartlett says.

Buffett bundled up in an Irish sweater, threw on the old white sport coat, and according to Corcoran, drank a bottle of Chivas Regal during the set and was still so cold he walked off stage sober.

"You know, it doesn't work that way," Bartlett says, chuckling.

When the calendar flipped to 1976, the follow-up to *A1A* was finally released not as *Kick It in Second Wind*, but *Havana Day- dreamin'*. The cover illustration found Buffett squinting into the sun, smiling wide with blue skies blending into the blue of the ocean behind him. Things were good.

"Train to Dixie," "Wonder Why You Ever Go Home," and "Please Take Your Girlfriend Home" had disappeared. As, with his consent, had Shel Silverstein's name from the writing credits for "Woman Goin' Crazy on Caroline Street."

Taking one of those spots was "Cliches," the third-person story of his relationship with the one person who was always on his mind— Jane. She'd been the far-off inspiration for "Come Monday," and made appearances in "Presents to Send You" and "Saxophones," but "Cliches" was the first song where she was present.

"She's got a ballpark figure, he's got a ball point pen," Buffett sang. She played a little guitar, but just for fun. He wondered where he could get a cheap cigar. He watched *Star Trek* while she watched him. "Hiding his cookies when he gets the munchies, trying hard just to keep the boy slim."

In *A Pirate Looks at Fifty*, Buffett called Jane a "compassionate Vulcan," which is something like a practical dreamer. "Jane," he wrote, "is an amazingly adaptable woman." Over the years, he'd seen her as comfortable in rooms full of the rich and the famous—say Milan, for fashion shows, or every year in Hollywood at the *Vanity Fair* Oscar party—as she was in the galley of a sailboat whipping up a meal. "She's a great road manager and operates with a lot more patience and common sense than I ever could," Buffett wrote. On the trip that framed that book, for example, he wanted to go to the Amazon, and *she* found the luxury hotel that made it work for the whole family. And she'd been like that from the start of their relationship.

"Jane grew up well off," Corcoran says. "And it probably didn't take her too many months in Key West to realize she didn't want to live the hippie life."

Her father, Thomas Slagsvol, founded an insurance company, Greater South, in the 1940s. As its website proudly declares, it's now the country's "#1 insurance brokerage for poultry processors." They do the everyday insurance work as well: home, life, auto, etc.

She'd arrived in Key West on spring break from the University of South Carolina and never went back. The guys at Outlaw Cove in Austin remember her accompanying Buffett on one trip. Corcoran remembers them returning from Nashville once with a Mercedes she'd talked Buffett into leasing. "So suddenly he's driving a Mercedes," Corcoran says. "He could barely make the payment, and he was making money."

When Jane got the idea to spend some time in Provincetown, Massachussetts, because that's where the influential spent time, Corcoran and Gordon Larry "Groovy" Gray, another South Carolina expat doing this and that on Key West, were enlisted to drive that Mercedes north from Key West. "I don't even want to talk about that," Corcoran says.*

Jane saw the big picture, and was making a few of her own. *Havana Daydreamin'*'s gatefold featured a few of her photos—shots beyond the barely-in-focus Poloroids Buffett mentions in "Cliches."

Havana Daydreamin' also included "Something So Feminine About a Mandolin," a tune Jane and Jimmy cowrote about a sweet night in a "pasture somewhere near Austin" where a woman picks gently on a mandolin. It carried with it a wish, that Buffett might one day have a daughter who could learn to play with the same subtle charm.

"Defying Gravity" filled another spot on the finished record. Written by Jesse Winchester, a Southern gentleman working in Montreal because he'd chosen Canada over Vietnam, the song was a sweet, simple ode to life on a big spinning ball.

The new title track set Buffett's imagination loose on mythical Havana, where his father had taken his first steps and where so many of his grandfather's stories were set. For added inspiration, Buffett turned to Peter Matthiessen's *Far Tortuga* "and fell in love with the description of the men on that turtle boat," he wrote in *The Parrot Head Handbook*.

Buffett's protagonist, Jesus, was working product more profitable (and dangerous) than turtles as he moved from Ecuador to Mexico in a sharp suit and carrying big plans. Waiting for a "mystery man" to arrive with hard-earned cash, his mind drifts to his father, who'd

---

* "All I know is, we made it all the way from Key West," Corcoran says. "We got a letter from the sheriff saying these two guys really do belong in this car. We made it all the way to Richmond drinking beer. I don't know how. And I finally, we were in a gas station, I said, 'We haven't eaten.' Richmond, Virginia. Groovy said, 'Oh yeah.' So he went in and he was gone, like, ten minutes. I went, 'all right, good. He's getting some sandwiches made.' No. He walked out with a Smithfield ham, a smoked ham. He put it on the console, got a knife out of his pocket, sliced it open, and we used the knife to feed ourselves dried Smithfield ham."

dropped dead chopping sugar cane, and then to a hotel room where the ceiling fan swirled cigar smoke and the pillow held the fragrance of a beautiful woman and the memories of an evening of spilled wine and laughter that would last long after he'd moved on—and he'd be moving on soon enough.

There's some Phil Clark in Jesus, and in them both a little of McGuane's rustlers from *Rancho Deluxe* and countless other dreamers. Two hundred years ago or tomorrow, someone's always going to wish themselves away from wherever, and what kept Clark and company restless wasn't a yearning for lawless seas. It was plain old fear—of becoming just like everyone else. "Same occupations and same obligations," as Buffett wrote in "Wonder Why You Ever Go Home." And there he was, sneaking up on thirty, feeling all the clichés that come with the end of one's twenties.

Havana Daydreamin' peaked at number sixty-five, forty spots below *A1A*. But by then the label had come to understand that chart performance and radio plays alone didn't define Buffett's success. Costs remained manageable. Buffett didn't have to sell *that* many records to make money for ABC-Dunhill, because ABC-Dunhill wasn't spending any money on him.

"We'd had some action with him," Jerry Rubinstein says. Rubinstein moved into the president's office at ABC Records early in 1975, and had begun to negotiate Buffett's next deal. That action was "Come Monday," two albums earlier, but promising enough. "We'd already had that. I liked it and it did enough business that we thought he was an artist. We wanted him. We felt he was both good and a good investment."

And Buffett had been a semi-loyal employee. He hadn't always been pleased with the promotion of his records, but when Sammy Creason told Buford Pusser the label would pay for any damage to his car, Buffett said, "No they won't." When Corb Donohue suggested Buffett hit the road and work, Buffett got out on the road and worked. He'd pretty much stayed on the road, jamming more hours and miles into each day than the laws of time and space would seem to allow. He'd proven himself capable of writing and recording, putting together a band, keeping that band on the road and getting it onstage each night no matter what.

"There's a lot of shit that goes on in life," says Michael Utley, who was touring with Kris Kristofferson by then. "A lot of curve-balls. The road's not an easy place. You're cramped up with a lot of people. And no matter how much you respect them as musicians, we're different.

"As easy, as luxurious as we have it now, it's still travel. And it still has its moments when it's testing you. As far as Jimmy, I've never known him not to have a positive attitude toward life."

Which doesn't mean there weren't times when he was ornery or demanding. That came with the job of being in charge and being detail oriented. "He is the benevolent dictator when he needs to be," Utley says. "When it needs to happen, that's what he calls himself. The benevolent dictator. I think I can say that."

Steve Vaughn was eighteen when he signed onto the road crew. The ground rules, as explained by Buffett were simple: "I don't give a shit what happens 22½ hours of the day," Vaughn remembers. "The only thing that matters is the ninety minutes we're onstage. If you had a shitty load-in day or shitty load-out and you're just dragging ass, don't want to hear about it. Don't complain. What matters is the ninety minutes onstage.

"That's what made Buffett tick. That's what made him good."

As luxurious as they have it now, as Utley says, they didn't back then. The bus had its charms, but the road, the pace, the lifestyle they were living, it wasn't for everyone—at least not for very long. "I really wanted to change," Fajardo says. There was too much booze and too much dope. "I had to reexamine the whole thing," he says. "Why am I doing this?" he wondered. When he couldn't come up with a decent answer, he was out of the band.

He took eighteen months off, got married, found God, and then went on the road with his old teammate from the University of Houston, Larry Gatlin. Fajardo had been with Buffett about a year. Looking back, he says, he's reminded of something Hemingway wrote in *A Farewell to Arms*: "The world breaks everyone, and afterward, some are strong in the broken places."

Michael Gardner replaced Fajardo and in May 1976, Buffett and the Coral Reefer Band returned to the West Coast for a tour that began at the Backroom then moved north to Los Angeles for two nights at the Roxy.

Don Light flew from Nashville to Los Angeles to continue negotiations with ABC. Light landed, went straight to the Roxy, and ran right into Buffett. "Coming down the hall in shorts, no shoes, T-shirt, guitar, and lyrics," Light told Peter Cooper. "Yellow notebook."

In the notebook was a song Buffett began in Austin after drinking away an afternoon in a Mexican restaurant in a strip mall near a freeway. With hours to kill before a flight, he'd wounded a few of them with a friend and some margaritas. "She drove me to the plane and I thought, *Those tasted good*," Buffett said at the American Library in Paris in 2015. "I started it, and I'd get off the plane in Miami and I'd drive the Overseas Highway to Key West and on the Seven Mile Bridge there was a traffic accident and I sat there for an hour and a half and I finished the song."

In three minutes, he told the audience in Paris. Added to the three minutes* he spent on it in Austin, he'd made quick work of "Margaritaville." And then the song sat in the notebook for a while, which was typical. "Tin Cup Chalice" hadn't arrived on record until 1974. "Pencil Thin Mustache" got bumped from the first record to the second. Another ballad about the push-and-pull between home and the road—home in this case being Alabama, where he just wanted to "feel that southern sun upon my arms"—has, dis-

---

* Six minutes is the low end of Buffett's estimates of how long it took to write "Margaritaville." Usually it's in the neighborhood of fifteen, never more than twenty.

appointingly, never made any record. Tom Corcoran has a demo on his computer.

That night at the Roxy, with Rubinstein in attendance, Buffett played "Margaritaville." By Light's recollection, it was the song's debut. "It wasn't then," Utley says. "It was at San Diego State." Utley was living in Laguna Beach, and since he was home from touring, he sat in with the Coral Reefers at all those Southern Californian shows.

Light remembered Buffett playing the song solo. By the second night at the Roxy, the band had worked it out. "None of the songs were that complex," Bartlett says, though to the specifics of that particular song, he was at a loss. He didn't recall ever playing it and didn't think he was in the band when Buffett added "Margaritaville" to the arsenal. But Bartlett was drinking a lot. There were plenty of drugs. It's foggy. He was wrong.

"Harry Dailey always said I came up with the melody at the top," Bartlett says. Dailey, who died in 2003 at the age of 51, might have been right. A bootleg of the second Roxy show captures Buffett introducing the band right before "Margaritaville," and the first Reefer he turns to is "Mr. Humble, Roger Bartlett." Bartlett was as surprised as anyone to hear that.

The song was fully formed that night, the lyrical differences between stage and studio small. After cutting his foot on the pop-top in the final verse, Buffett was "bleeding so bad" he had to limp on back home. Instead of blenders and frozen concoctions in the final verse, it's pain and cocaine that's been gone since early in the morning (huge applause at the mention of cocaine, too).

In the years to come, Buffett would reprise that version of the final verse, playing it like drug-addled, outlaw stagecraft set in contrast of the recorded version. But cocaine was probably the original lyric. At the Roxy, he introduced the song as "Wastin' Away Again in Margaritaville," an insignificant difference that would prove to be of some future consequence.

"I liked it," Utley says.

"Yeah, we knew it was hit," Light said.

If that's true, that they knew they had a hit song, what happened next was neatly timed and expertly executed. "I went backstage to do my mandatory thing," Jerry Rubinstein says. "Security stopped me and told me I wasn't allowed in."

The rest of the ABC Records staff passed through to the party. The president of the label turned and left. He wasn't happy about it, either. "I knew exactly what he was doing," Rubinstein says. "It was a negotiation. It was very interesting. No one ever did anything like that—to me anyway. Sometime after that, I got a call from Don that Jimmy said it was okay for the attorneys to continue work on the agreements."

Three weeks later, outside Missoula, Montana, Buffett and the band caught up with Jerry Jeff and the Lost Gonzo Band to play a festival with Heart at the K-O Rodeo Grounds.

William "Daddy" Aber, a professor of Greek at the University of Montana from 1895–1919, had long ago begun a day of on-campus service. Students and faculty would plant trees and clean the place up and chip in for the common good. They called it Aber Day. In the 1970s, someone had the bright idea to raise money for the library by hiring some bands and ordering some kegs of beer. In 1974, the Aber Day Kegger was born.

"The Guinness Book of World Records Beer Drinking Contest" Bartlett says. For a small amount of money, everyone in attendance was given what was essentially a plastic beer pitcher. Not a mug, a pitcher. "And so you went around to the kegs and filled up your pitcher and people were totally blitzed and we'd been on the road for six or eight weeks straight without a break," Bartlett says. Then the wind kicked up. "A quarter inch of dust on everything we owned," Steve Vaughn says. Then it rained. Tempers flared.

Buffett and the Coral Reefers stepped onstage and Bartlett, in his role as quasi-musical director, counted off the opening number and Gardner,* the still relatively new drummer, said, "Wait a minute." He was having trouble with his bass drum pedal. Bartlett counted off the song a second time. "Wait a minute," Gardner said.

From Gardner's perspective, he needed the pedal. From Bartlett's, there were thousands of extremely drunk people in front of them so, you know, *play*. There is no "wait a minute" in that or any other situation. "We almost got into a fistfight onstage then later back at the hotel," Bartlett says.

When the tour turned toward Canada, Buffett and Bartlett flew to Portland to appear with Georgia Governor Jimmy Carter as he campaigned for president. News of the Euphoria Tavern sellouts had made its way to Carter's people. "He invited me to go out on the campaign plane, which I did for a day," Buffett said in a December 1976 *High Times* interview. "I thought *I* worked hard."

Bartlett remembers walking offstage with Buffett and straight into a conversation with CBS News's Ed Bradley, who'd soon become the first African American to cover the White House for a television network. When Buffett and Bartlett returned to the tour in Vancouver, British Columbia, Bartlett had an apology to make. He'd left a hash pipe under his mattress. It'd been discovered at the border.

Like Fajardo before him, Bartlett took a look around, took a look in the mirror, and then compared notes. They'd been working a circuit, and so they'd see the same people every few months. Those faces, he'd noticed, were getting "crispier and crispier," he says. An honest self-evaluation revealed he was getting "crispier and crispier," too.

Soon he'd find himself in New York, in a club, watching a guitar player burn the place down. After the set, after lifting his jaw from the floor, Bartlett introduced himself.

---

* Gardner died in 1991 at the age of 44 from what his obituary in the *Memphis Commercial Appeal* called "complications resulting from dental problems."

"I'm working for this guy named Jimmy Buffett and you're amazing," Bartlett said. "I could recommend you for the job. It's like $250-a-week."

"I'm sorry," the guitarist said, "I'm working for a guy named Herbie Mann and making $1,000 a week."

So Bartlett had to pick his jaw off the floor again. The mystery guitarist introduced himself as Elliott Randall, who'd played on a bunch of Steely Dan records; was indeed working with Mann, a jazz flautist; and would, somewhat incongruously, become a touring member of Sha Na Na for a while.

"Big, big studio guy," Bartlett says.

Whether he found his own replacement or not, Bartlett wasn't long from making his move. He wanted them to say, "Roger went to New York to be a jazz guy." There was style in that, sophistication and cool. *Jazz Guy*. Perfect for a guy who liked all the arcane stuff he liked. There was one last adventure with Buffett before that, however, and it was back down in Tampa, Florida.

Joe Nuzzo was surfing Florida's Gulf Coast before anyone knew that was a thing that could be done. In 1954, his mother scooped up four kids, left her husband on Long Island, and headed to Florida. Nuzzo went into the military, got out and went to California to surf. In '62 or '63, he returned to Florida for a visit.

"And I went for a paddle one day from our house and went out to the Gulf and there were waist-high waves and I was surfing," he says. Until that moment he'd never considered it a possibility. He moved back to Florida and got a job fixing airplanes. He was asked to cut his hair, so he quit that job and went to work for a surf shop. *They* asked him to cut his hair, and that was just life in the early sixties. "The city wanted to get rid of us because we were surfers and we drank wine and smoked pot and they banned surfing here for a while," Nuzzo says. Police would stand on the beach with rifles and megaphones and order surfers out of the water.

Organizing against such injustice, he and some friends formed the Suncoast Surfing Syndicate and sold T-shirts ("I PROMISE TO BE A GOOD SURFER GUY") to raise the money to hire a lawyer to challenge the surfing ban. Nuzzo figured the city didn't own the waves, and he was right. They won. In 1966, he opened Suncoast Surf Shop in Treasure Island, Florida. "Surfing flourished from there," he says. "I never made a lot of money. You know, you make enough for the next surf trip."

In the early seventies, at the beginning of the surf industry, when everyone knew everyone, he'd run up to New Jersey to see a surfboard maker named Tinker West, a literal rocket scientist who worked out of a warehouse that was home to his board-making business and a rock band he was managing. At day's end, West would shout at Bruce Springsteen to come help clean up the shop. That was part of the deal.

Down in Florida, time on and around the water meant an almost unavoidable familiarity with the Trade, as Buffett termed it on Radio Margaritaville before a 2015 show near Tampa.

"Can you explain what the Trade is?" Utley said, knowing full well what Buffett meant.

"They were dope dealers," Buffett said. "These guys liked to party, and they paid in cash."

"There was a lot of marijuana dealings going on here," Nuzzo says. "This was the headquarters, I think, in the state of Florida. I went to jail for a couple years."

He says it the way you might say it rained last Tuesday. Wasn't the nicest day, but it happened and now the sun's out. Suncoast celebrated its fiftieth anniversary in 2016. Nuzzo threw a party and John Prine came and played a few songs.

The shop's original location burned down in 1995, but Nuzzo reopened and the new shop is stacked with surf gear. No space is wasted. Florida still isn't anyone's first thought as a surf destination, but the recent popularity of stand-up paddleboards has been good for business. A book about the rich local history of dope smuggling was displayed on the counter. The wall alongside the stairs was packed with framed photos, a few with Nuzzo and Buffett on different boats at different times. "I've got photos of Jane and Buffett on the boat," he says, adding somewhat apologetically, "but he's in a Speedo."

What you won't find advertised, but you will find hidden among the racks of T-shirts, is a piece of Buffett history, shirts marking the July 9, 1976, Wine & Dine Under the Stars cruise aboard the *Tom Sawyer*. Departing from St. Petersburg with Jimmy Buffett and the Coral Reefer Band headlining. Cost: $75 per person or $125 per couple.

The T-shirt design is nearly identical to the original poster, but the T-shirts spell Buffett correctly. The original misspelled poster is framed on a wall in the little house next to the shop. "We're not going to dinner!" Buffett shouted at Nuzzo when he saw the poster.

They were kind of going to dinner. Wine *and* dine, it said. It's been a while since Nuzzo saw Buffett. He stopped by the shop not long ago, but Nuzzo wasn't there. He eventually lost backstage privileges (he blames tour managers, not Buffett), but Buffett will still dedicate a song to him when he's in Tampa. Buffett and Nuzzo go back. The details of how they met, when they met, and who introduced them? Less than clear. Nuzzo starts those stories and then ends them, saying, "Let someone else tell you that story."

A few work through the filter. There was the time Nuzzo picked up a new twenty-three-foot SeaCraft and Buffett was in town. He was supposed to fly back to Key West. Nuzzo talked him into taking the boat instead. Midway, they stopped on Cabbage Key for margaritas and cheeseburgers.

Referring to "Cheeseburger in Paradise," the *Naples Herald* asked in a 2016 headline, "Was Cabbage Key Truly Jimmy Buffett's Inspiration?" It wasn't, but Buffett's photo and a dollar bill are framed on the wall. "We wound up spending the whole afternoon there," Nuzzo says, "because we went up to the top of the fire tower and did our things, whatever, and looked out at the world, got our minds a little bit better for the rest of the trip."

Which would have been a nice, fine, and good—certainly in keeping with the times if not coast guard regulations—but they forgot to fuel up and ran out of gas before they made Key West.

They were close enough for the radio to pick up WKWF's limited signal. Corcoran was on the air. He played "Nautical Wheelers" for an audience that had no idea the song's author was stranded at sea. They got a kick out of that on the boat.

The hell of it was, Nuzzo *had* extra cans of gas. He'd left them home. There was no way they'd need those. The bag filled with fifty outdated flares on the other hand, *that* he'd brought along. "We shot off every flare in the bag," he says. "We lit up the sky."

When the coast guard arrived, there were questions. Such as, "Why isn't this boat registered?" Buffett got a lift into Key West, went to Captain Tony's, hopped onstage, and played damn near until dawn. The authorities looked at Nuzzo and said, "You're in a world of shit, boy."

It was a good line, delivered with the menace of authority, but being with Buffett in Key West meant, at worst, a neighborhood of shit.

Keith Sykes had his guitars stolen from a van on Key West once. Nice guitars, a 1968 Fender Telecaster and a 1966 Martin D-28. "Somehow Jimmy found out about it and made some calls for me," Sykes says. Buffett found them. Sykes had to buy them back, but he got them. "The thing is, the Telecaster at that time was worth two hundred dollars soaking wet with rocks in its pockets," Sykes says. "The Martin was more expensive, but I paid fifty dollars for it and sixty dollars for the Tele—because it was electric."

Nuzzo was put through the motions once or twice and then sent on his way. "So I showed up late," Nuzzo says, "and Jimmy was singing and playing on the stage. It was crazy . . . but the Wine & Dine cruise . . ."

Yes. The Wine & Dine.

Nuzzo had some friends (in the Trade) and they had this idea to hold a cruise, with Buffett and the Coral Reefers on the *Tom Sawyer*, an old paddle wheeler. "Tampa Bay can be a treacherous body of water," Buffett reminded Utley, who wasn't a part of that show. "This was a riverboat, packed."

The idea was solid, if not the funding. When Nuzzo's pals encountered a capital shortage, Nuzzo became an investor and tickets were sold through Suncoast. He also knew Buffett, which didn't hurt in securing Buffett. For his effort, Nuzzo got three front row center seats, which he used to bring two female friends. In fact most of his stories involve two female friends. "Just to have fun," he says, shrugging.

Playing in Florida in 2016, Bartlett had a chance to catch up with Nuzzo and try to relive that night. "We were all so artificially inspired we had to piece little memories from this one and that one into a whole memory," Bartlett says. "And whether that memory is the truth is up for debate."

With certainty, Nuzzo remembers a pig and cow—may they rest in peace. Both were butchered on a pier the night before the cruise. The pig had spent the previous night in a bathroom, and might have gotten loose. The police might have been involved in the roundup.

Buffett was right about the conditions on the bay the night of the cruise. A squall blew in and tossed the *Tom Sawyer* like it was the S.S. *Minnow*. Depending on the level of inebriation, the crowd aboard either had no idea they were in a storm, or were convinced they were going to die. Someone pitched down the stairs with a full case of Cutty Sark. No one remembers the show. "There was," Buffett told Utley, "a moment we thought the *Tom Sawyer* might go down."

Jimmy Buffett and the Coral Reefer Band continued to be as dedicated as ever to those "certain indecencies" McGuane alluded

to in the liner notes to *A White Sport Coat and a Pink Crustacean*.
Buffett was still sleeping on that yellow line. When he slept, anyway. Then he'd wake up, dust himself off, and carry on. The boat
didn't sink, because Buffett's boat never sank. Things had a way
of working out for Jimmy Buffett.

Don Light and Jerry Rubinstein hammered out a new contract,
and Rubinstein delivered two checks. The first, for $100,000, was
to start work on the next record. The other, for $132,000, was to
renew. Light met Buffett for breakfast, thinking about the banker
in Key West who'd told Buffett he needed to stabilize his work
schedule before he could get a $500 loan for the Boston Whaler.
"You want to take this check and say, 'Is this stable enough for your
ass?'" Light told Peter Cooper. "He didn't want to do it, which
surprised me."

Rubinstein knows the one thing Buffett did want. After refusing
backstage access to the man who was, technically, his boss, Buffett
asked Rubinstein to come sign the paperwork aboard Buffett's new
boat. It wasn't a Whaler.

"I flew into Miami with the contracts, with the signature copies,"
Rubinstein says. "And we went for a great Cuban dinner and on a
beautiful moonlit night we were sailing on his boat and we signed
the agreement. We've always gotten along since then."

On October 18, 1976, Buffett and Corcoran met at the Flagler
Marina in Palm Beach, where a broker handed Buffett the keys
to his new sailboat, a thirty-three-foot Cheoy Lee ketch. Buffett
was wearing the lime-green shirt he'd taken as a souvenir from
the Euphoria Tavern. Corcoran, who'd added photography to his
résumé, snapped the shot. "There was a look of contentment like
no one had ever seen before," Buffett wrote at the beginning of
his first book, *Tales from Margaritaville*. That look, and the T-shirt,
named the boat.

On the first page of the *Euphoria*'s logbook, Buffett kept it
simple. He and Corcoran departed the marina at 4:30 p.m. with

forty-five gallons of fuel. Corcoran says the plan was to cruise the Intracoastal Waterway south to the Boynton Inlet and then head out into the Atlantic Ocean for the rest of the trip to Coconut Grove—where Buffett's Floridian adventure had begun almost exactly five years earlier.

There he'd found his gig at the Flick delayed long enough to go to Key West. Key West had inspired the songs that put him back on the road. The road had given him a chaotic, exhausting, and yes, euphoric living. Against the backdrop of bus tires on asphalt and rock band histrionics, the *Euphoria* was thirty-three feet of serenity.

He and Corcoran were headed to Coconut Grove instead of Key West because Buffett was due in the studio in November and he wasn't going back to Nashville. They'd record at Criteria. They had a budget three times what they'd spent on the last record and nearly fifty times what he'd spent to make *Down to Earth*.

The Atlantic was angry, and so they sailed past Boynton Inlet and kept to the Intracoastal. They sailed all night, stuck waiting for drawbridges to open, left screaming at the top of their lungs to get the attention of other operators. To their west, U.S. 1 pointed toward the Keys. To the east, A1A pulled drivers to the beach. They watched the sun set off toward the Gulf of Mexico and saw it rise over the Atlantic.

"I live on audience response and intuition, and I react to it," Buffett told *High Times*. "Have all my life . . . You gotta be calculating, you gotta bust your ass if you want to do anything. For me, it's like I can't just be a sensitive artist and still be out here surviving. Certain things have got to be done in order to get where you want to go."

He was talking about why he was supporting Jimmy Carter, about how he saw those things he valued in the candidate. Usually when the *High Times* interview is written about, the attention is on Buffett threatening to kick the writer's ass if he's misquoted.

It's the least interesting moment of the conversation, tough-guy posturing for no good reason. Comfortable in the pages of a magazine celebrating a subculture, his words surrounded by ads for bongs and pipes and "POTenizers"—"For the Blast that Lasts"—Buffett was more introspective than he'd been to date.

On his past conflicts with ABC Records, he said all he wanted was his fair share of attention. "I think some people at ABC are coming around to that now," he said. Did he want to be a number one artist? "Shit, no," he said.

"What do you think about artists who pretty well shun their followers?" *High Times* asked.

"I don't think they'll be long-lived," Buffett said.

He knew what his fans wanted. On page nineteen, below an ad for another bong, one that asks "What goes Chugga Chugga?" there's an ad for Jimmy Buffett T-shirts. Out on the ocean, there's a darkened boat—no running lights. On shore, a topless woman holds a signal light.

"Our fans are listening to the songs," he said. "And that's the satisfaction I get out of it. As long as I can do this, and as long as I know that I'm doing it, I'm going to be content to stay at a certain level.

"I'm not going out there to try and sell my lifestyle to America. Because they ain't going to buy it. They never have."

* *Chapter 11* *

Changes in . . . Everything

W. C. Handy, the father of the blues, was born in Florence, Alabama. There's a statue of him playing trumpet there in Wilson Park. Sam Phillips, the founder of Sun Records, was born in Florence and grew up picking cotton before moving to Memphis and setting Elvis, Johnny Cash, Roy Orbison, and rock and roll loose on the world.

"When I was a kid I went to school here in the city because we had a house out in the north flats area," Norbert Putnam says. "And my father had been a musician. My father's family, he was one of eight children, and the youngest one always had to play the bass."

Putnam's father's bass became his bass, and that instrument took him around the world and brought him back to Florence, where he lives in a dignified two-story home built in the 1830s and set on four acres, a short walk from Handy's statue. The walls, which stretch to especially high ceilings, are fitted with fine art and memories. There's a poster from the time he played a show with the Beatles in 1964 at the Washington Sports Arena. There are photos, of late-night recording and bullshit sessions with Elvis, of a black-tie night Kris Kristofferson decided was black tie optional. A platinum record for Joan Baez's *Blessed Are . . .* hangs by the front door. A gold record for Buffett's *Changes in Latitudes, Changes*

163

in Attitudes is in the kitchen. Another gold, also for *Changes*, sat on the floor of his office next to a drill.

In that office, the shelves are full of books about art, and about music, including a copy of *A Pirate Looks at Fifty*. In one corner, near the bathroom, a bouquet of cables and cords loop over a coat-rack. Next to a computer, a black bass rested on a stand next to a Fender amp and a stack of recording gear. Putnam is semiretired, but someone had sent him a new singer, and he punched up her record, excited, and hit PLAY. No one ever really quits music.

Norbert Putnam and an award for a record he produced.
Florence, Alabama, 2015.

Author's photo

In 1976, with a new ABC Records deal on the way and a bigger budget, Buffett won his creative-control. He could unleash the Coral Reefer Band—and only the Coral Reefer Band—in the studio. Gant agreed to step out of the producer's role, and Don Light called Putnam.

"Jimmy wants to talk to you," he said.

Putnam's pretty sure he'd met Buffett once before, when Buffett was a *Billboard* writer poking around studios. Their paths had to have crossed. Putnam's equally certain he saw Buffett play the Exit/ In a time or two. He was charming, but background music. "I was there on other business," Putnam says. He noticed *A1A* and *Living and Dying in ¾ Time*, but hadn't paid them much attention. Like most people in town, he'd heard "Come Monday," liked the song, but wasn't sure what to make of the singer.

At Light's request, Buffett and Putnam met at Julian's, an upscale French restaurant with a basement fireplace. It was August in Nashville, but Putnam says they sat by the fire as Buffett talked up the Reefers. "He says, 'My band, we're more Rolling Stones than Nashville,'" Putnam says. "I'm pretty sure that's exactly what he said. He may deny it now, but why would he?"

They had a gig in Nashville in a week. So Putnam didn't have to take Buffett's word for it. He could hear for himself. "Sure," Putnam said reflexively, but his mind had drifted. He was trying to imagine the Rolling Stones playing "Come Monday."

"It's not computing," he says. "And so the next weekend, I had a couple of cocktails and went out there."

A few years earlier, Putnam had produced New Riders of the Purple Sage in San Francisco. They were . . . unruly. As he tells it, they did all the drugs, drank all the Jack Daniel's, and chased that with all the beer—and then they tried to make a record. "And when Buffett's band came out I thought, *My God, these guys are like the New Riders*," Putnam says. "They're all half-stoned and they're jumping around and their amps are too loud. I thought Jimmy Buffett was this folk singer, and here he is with this band and the people are jumping up and down."

Putnam was an interesting choice to produce a road band. He was a studio pro. In high school, he'd picked up his father's bass with a partial blessing from his old man, who taught him how to tune it and left the rest to his son to figure out. From there, Putnam set out to learn Bill Black's bass lines on Elvis's Sun recordings for a high school band that began to tour colleges in the South. Years later, Putnam would tell Elvis that story and Elvis would say, "That was only three chords. If it had been Sinatra you'd never have figured your way out the first verse."

Rick Hall began producing soul singers in Muscle Shoals, and Putnam began playing on the sessions that gave the small river town in north Alabama an international reputation. He played on hits by Arthur Alexander, and the Tams—the songs Johnny Youngblood was playing on the guitar when he taught Buffett those first three chords.

In the studio in Muscle Shoals, Putnam was making $5 an hour. In Nashville, there was a musician's union and the union dictated $57 every three hours, and you could work four sessions a day if you were in demand. He moved to Nashville with his friend David Briggs, a piano player, and within a year they were making $100,000 and working with J. J. Cale, Tony Joe White, Kristofferson, and, a little farther down the road, Elvis. He did *Hee Haw* with Ray Charles. Post-Dylan, everyone was coming to Nashville to record. The Nashville Cats, as Putnam and the other studio aces became known, profited.

Putnam and Briggs took some of their money and opened Quad-raphonic Sound Studios and started a publishing company. Putnam began producing, and when he helped Baez go platinum in 1971, his phone lit up with managers hoping he'd work with their clients.

Putnam left Buffett's gig thinking about the songs, and the band he'd seen onstage. Then Putnam thought about Dan Fogelberg. He'd worked a lot with Fogelberg. They shared a love of classical music. So much so that when they were working on Fogelberg's 1972 album, *Home Free*, they swiped a chord from Aaron Copland and used it on the opening track, "To the Morning."

"It became obvious to me that I could probably succeed with Dan Fogelberg with symphonic rock," Putnam says. But he'd noticed something else about Fogelberg's work—it was better when he was at home in the mountains of Colorado as opposed to the concrete sprawl of Los Angeles.

"I'm now going to apply that to Jimmy Buffett—only we're going to use Trinidad steel drums, and wooden flutes and anything else I could think of that was nautical," Putnam says. And they were going to get away from Nashville. They'd go to Miami and Criteria Recording Studios. It'd be November. The weather would be lousy in Tennessee anyway. "He didn't immediately jump at this," Putnam says. "I could tell he was hedging. I said, 'We *need* to.'"

A few days later, Buffett called back. He said he got it. He got it, and he'd written a new song inspired by it, "Changes in Latitudes, Changes in Attitudes."

"Then I said, 'Jimmy, I'm not one of those guys who works fourteen-, fifteen-hour days anymore,'" Putnam says. Experience told him people got sloppy after six or seven hours. They'd work from 11 a.m. to 5 p.m., and they'd try to get two tracks done each day. At 5 p.m., the workday would end and they'd take the tapes to the marina, climb aboard the *Euphoria*, and check the day's work.

Putnam booked two weeks at Criteria, and Buffett's people booked a mansion where everyone would stay. Finally afforded the opportunity to take his band into the studio, Buffett was taking the whole team. The road crew was going as well. It took one phone call to find a mansion for a rock band in Miami.

Cindy Johnson and Jeri Jenkins had been best friends since they were eight years old. They were going to school together at Miami-Dade Junior College in the mid-seventies and living in a funky, cool little frame house surrounded by twenty other funky, cool little houses originally built to house circus performers in the offseason.

The college didn't have a cafeteria. It had a vending machine. To make a little money on the side, Johnson and Jenkins would make sandwiches and sell them next to the vending machine, undercutting

on cost and greatly improving the quality. One of their classmates
was Atlantic Records executive Jerry Wexler's nephew.

Atlantic had Stephen Stills in town recording, and they needed
a couple of people to do some cooking and cleaning. "We went in
and we interviewed with twenty guys in the kitchen in this old house
on N. Bay Road," Cindy O'Dare (formerly Johnson) says. "An old
1926 house with a beautiful courtyard, and we literally walked in
on twenty men: Nils Lofgren, the Memphis Horns, Stephen Stills,
Dr. John, Boz Scaggs."

They held their own and got the job. For $1.25 an hour, they'd
get to the house at 3 p.m., make breakfast, wake everyone up, and
get them to the studio by 6 p.m. Later, they'd go to the studio and
bring dinner. Sometimes they cooked. Sometimes they bought
takeout, repackaged it, and passed it off as homemade.

"I drove this little beat-up Volkswagen and lived in a little
wooden house and then I'd drive over to this sparkling Biscayne
Bay mansion," O'Dare says. She was a junior college student hanging out with rock stars. It was surreal.

When the record was done, the band packed up and left. Jeri
and Cindy returned to making sandwiches to sell at school and
working at a health food store in their spare time. That's where
the phone rang one day—because they didn't have a phone at the
circus house. Eric Clapton's manager was on the line. Clapton had
heard good things from Stephen Stills. Were they available, and
could they help find a house? They were, and they could, and to
pull it off they borrowed money from their parents and leased a
mansion. They moved Clapton into 461 Ocean Blvd.

Next came the Bee Gees. "After the Bee Gees, I don't even
remember," O'Dare says. Home At Last, as their new company
was called, grew to nine houses and eighteen employees. They
housed the Eagles while they made *Hotel California*. They took
care of David Sanborn, Crosby, Stills & Nash, Joe Cocker, and,
naturally, Andy Gibb.

For Buffett, they set aside 5242 N. Bay Road. O'Dare remembers she and Jenkins standing behind the house, waiting for Buffett when he arrived aboard the *Euphoria*. "Jimmy taught us all how to make shrimp creole that first night," she says.

"So we've got everybody living in this big ol' mansion, and we've got a chef and a maid," Putnam says. "And the roadies have set up a bar at the studio—a complete bar at the house and the studio. And when I say complete, I'm not talking about six bottles of gin, vodka, whiskey. There are forty bottles up there. Fully stocked."

"Studio B," Utley says. "The small room."

He knew it well. Criteria had been home base in the Dixie Flyer days. Putnam says Utley was like a second producer when they got to work, and they kept to schedule. They'd hit the studio at 11 a.m. At 5 p.m., Buffett and Putnam would grab the day's tapes, head to Coconut Grove, and board the *Euphoria*. They'd open a couple of beers and check the work.

"You know, this stuff is sounding really good on a sailboat," Buffett said to Putnam after one of the earliest sessions.

"I said, 'It is, isn't it?'" Putnam says. "And Jimmy says, 'You know, if we could make a record that was good to put on boats, how many records could we sell?'" Putnam leaned back, took a sip of his beer, surveyed the harbor, and saw dollar signs flying like signal flags above each and every boat between them and the horizon.

On about the second or third morning, before heading to the studio, Buffett dropped "Margaritaville" on Putnam. "It's sort of a day and night in Key West," Putnam recalls Buffett saying. "It's semiautobiographical. I'm going to call it 'Margaritaville.' I cut my foot one night leaving the bar, and there's some other stuff in it."

"Margaritaville?" Putnam said.

"Yeah, 'Margaritaville,'" Buffett replied.

"I wasn't that excited about the title," Putnam says. "A part of me sort of hoped he'd come up with a better song idea."

They tackled other songs first, songs about people and places that were fraying. In "Changes in Latitudes, Changes in Attitudes," Buffett wished he "could jump on a plane," and dreamed again of the ocean, and of Paris and other faraway places. "If we weren't all crazy we would go insane."

"Wonder Why We Ever Go Home," its feeling for moving growing even stronger since *Rancho Deluxe*, found a new home (and a pronoun shift from "you" to "we"). In 1976, after Buffett had earned a little name recognition, those "lost" *High Cumberland Jubilee* tapes were found and released by Janus Records. Buffett reclaimed "In the Shelter" and rerecorded it in Miami, giving the new album another song about another untethered soul.

Steve Goodman always seemed to know when Buffet was going into the studio and, coincidentally, would be ready with something to pitch. "He was a voracious song plugger," Buffett told Dave Hoekstra on WGN Radio in 2015. "And the thing of it was, every time he did it, they were great songs."

Then again, Buffett was always rushing back into the studio, and Goodman was a great songwriter. Alignment was inevitable. "Banana Republics" was an ex-pat's lament from somewhere south of the border where try all you want to fake it, but "none of the natives are buying any second-hand American dreams."

"Tampico Trauma" was about wearing out your welcome in the same Mexican town where a down-on-his-luck Humphrey Bogart kicked around for a little spare change in the beginning of *The Treasure of the Sierra Madre*. Even "Lovely Cruise," about exactly that, is really about the end of that ride. "We'll bid our farewell much too soon," Buffett sang.

"Biloxi" was the second Jesse Winchester song in as many records. Buffett's Biloxi was lit by neon and illicit possibility. Winchester's was warm, gentle, and sweet, a place where the stars look down and "see their faces in the sea," where children dig in the sand, and a couple sneaks a naked swim in the ocean. And where the sun sets and the storms build in the direction of New Orleans.

Winchester's "Biloxi" was touched by melancholy, like it was written on a cold, exiled Canadian morning, and by a guy longing for home. It might have been.

"Landfall," on the other hand, was hot—a rocker asking an open-ended question: "What would they do if I just sailed away?"

The *Euphoria* gave Buffett the option. She was insurance against an industry that hadn't ever fully figured him out and didn't offer any long-term assurances. He set the sound of the tour bus's "big diesel boom" against "the smell of fresh snapper fried light," and that doesn't seem like much competition, though, for Buffett, they weren't in competition. The road made him appreciate his time off; his time off readied him for the road. "It just makes my whole life come alive," Buffett sang.

Straightforward as it was, there was a mystery hidden in "Landfall," and it involved old Bum Farto. Bum, according to the handwritten lyrics that accompanied the album, was down in "Queros," having a ball. Buffett's handwriting was difficult enough to decipher that *Euphoria* was turned into Eudaurm in the liner notes, and so it's possible he put Bum in Quepos, Costa Rica. Corcoran, running around Criteria snapping photos, remembers a version of the song that found Bum down in Caicos. Buffett told Corcoran someone—and Buffett wouldn't say whom—pulled him aside and said he needed to keep ol' Bum out of it altogether. Wherever he was, Buffett definitely wondered what *he'd* do on another landfall.

Buffett and Fingers Taylor wrote "Miss You So Badly" about that time "it all blew up in Missoula," and the other time the Holiday Inn was filled with stripper-loving surgeons, and all those times aggressive hotel maids knocked on doors, and the rolls and rolls of Rolaids consumed while "losing track of the long days since I've been home."

"We're two or three days from finishing when he walks in one day to Criteria with his legal pad," Putnam says, *he* being Buffett. "And he puts it on the music stand and he says 'I've got that song.'"

"What song?"

"Margaritaville."

Buffett sat down with his guitar and began playing eighth notes, not his usual finger picking, more like an approach the Eagles might take. Putnam's ears perked. "And when he started the story, wow," Putnam says. "It'd be a wonderful short film. A night and the morning after with Jimmy Buffett. I remember when I was in high school. A literature test. I missed the question: What is the most important aspect of every great story? I don't know what I wrote, but the answer was conflict."

He dug where Buffett was going, a lazy afternoon on the front porch swing, shrimp boiling, tourists baking in the sunshine. But where was the conflict? It's great that you're drunk. It's too bad that you can't find your saltshaker. Where's the conflict?

"Some people claim that there's a woman to blame . . ."

There it was.

"And then he admits his guilt and we have to let him off the hook for great humility," Putnam says. "This is textbook stuff, you know what I'm saying? Now I'm saying, 'This is a hit song.'"

But it wasn't a happy song, not exactly. It came with a dispirited note; it was disillusioned, its narrator unsure why he'd stayed around town as long as he had. What was there to show for the time—besides the tattoo? Had he accomplished anything at all? Well, had you, Jimmy Buffett?

And then there was the verse about "old men in tank tops" ogling younger women and wishing they had more control over their lives. Buffett had tossed that one in when he'd played the song for friends in Key West.

"That was about the transition period of Key West," Buffett told *Rolling Stone* in 1977. "I could see it changing from the funky little town I loved into something touristy. I was thinkin', 'Was I a part of that?' So I was tryin' to justify it to myself."

Putnam was on board and all they had to do was get the song

they'd been working on the road for months down on tape. They cut the verse with the old men, "because it didn't make sense musically," Utley says. It took the verse-chorus-verse-chorus structure and doubled up verses at the end of the song. Also, they wanted to shorten it for radio.

Utley, having played the song a few times live had an idea how he'd work into the song. "I played the Wurlitzer, because that was kind of a happening thing at the time," he says.

There was one snag. "I remember the rhythm tracks not working," Steve Vaughn says. As a roadie in the studio, he didn't have a lot to do once things were set up. They kept the bar stocked, mixed a few drinks, lent a hand with an instrument when needed, but more or less they watched everyone else work. "And I remember Norbert," Vaughn continues, "Norbert had his shit together."

Putnam had been wise enough to bring an insurance policy disguised as a percussion player. Kenneth Buttrey was one of the best session drummers in Nashville. He played on Simon & Garfunkel's "The Boxer." He played on Neil Young's *Harvest*. Buffett wondered right away why Putnam wanted to bring a famous drummer along when they'd already agreed this record belonged to the Coral Reefer Band. Putnam told Buffett it was because Buttrey was multitalented. "I didn't want to tell him that there's one guy in the band, if he can't perform, you're dead," Putnam says. "And that's the drummer."

Sure enough, they get into "Margaritaville," and Michael Gardner couldn't find the song. For whatever reason, maybe inexperience in the studio, maybe just a bad day, but it wasn't working. Putnam turned to Buffett and convinced him to let the seasoned pro give it a try. "We stick Buttrey in, and I think the second take is the one you've heard all these years," Putnam says.

They had a record. Utley helped Putnam arrange some strings and flutes, and when that was finished, Putnam told Buffett they needed to go to Los Angeles and present it to the promotions department at ABC, because if they didn't, everyone else with a record coming out would, and *Changes* would get lost in the pile. They flew west and played the album for Charlie Minor. "Charlie Minor?" Putnam says, pausing. "Put a question mark next to that."

"Charlie was one of the great promotion people of all time," says Steve Resnik, who worked side by side with Minor in ABC's promotions department. In the free-spending golden age of the record industry, Minor was also a fantastic character, living larger than even his professional reputation. "Every Saturday night for years, rock 'n' roll blared from the outdoor speakers of Charlie Minor's rented Malibu beach house," the *Los Angeles Times* wrote in 1995.*

If Putnam and Buffett flew to Los Angeles for a meeting, it would have been with Minor, and Resnik would have been there—unless he was on the road. He doesn't recall being at that meeting, and so he probably was out of town. "There were meetings every twenty minutes," Resnik says.

The previous three years had been frustrating for everyone. Resnik thought *A White Sport Coat and a Pink Crustacean* was great. "If he'd have been a James Taylor name at that time, he'd have had three or four hits off that record," Resnik says. "Second album was also terrific. We just couldn't get him arrested. It was tough going."

That summer, Buffett had come across a news story where Resnik had been interviewed about ABC's plans to promote *Whistling Down the Wire*, the second record from David Crosby and Graham Nash. Resnik hadn't talked about the promotional budget (he says he wouldn't have known it), but the dollar amount found its way into print anyway and caught Buffett's attention. He wrote Resnik a quick note, on personalized stationery, suggesting the Crosby-Nash

* On March 19, 1995, Minor was shot and killed by a Suzette McClure, a twenty-seven-year-old stripper with whom he'd had an affair. There's an *E! True Hollywood Story* about the case.

backing was the kind of backing he deserved. Buffett believed in his songs and his work.

That was in August 1976—before Buffett re-signed with ABC. The risk, as he and Putnam flew to Los Angeles, was that it was too late. Program directors aren't much different from record executives. They're risk-averse. However tentatively, they'd tried Buffett, and no matter how much they might like him, or the songs, there hadn't been a hit. And each miss lessened the likelihood of a breakthrough. "Usually radio stations won't touch it because they're scared," Resnik says.

Usually, but not always. The meeting in Los Angeles went well. There was reason to be encouraged. Putnam went home to Nashville, and Buffett flew back to Key West reflecting on five years of perpetual motion.

His instincts, that ability to read a crowd or a situation, had always worked. He'd been proven right more often than wrong. However dire any day might have seemed, he always came out smiling by the end of the week. He'd been flat-ass busted more than once. He'd played to nearly empty rooms and done multiple sold-out nights. He'd built a loyal little following around the country. He was a cult act and he was perfectly happy about it. Should it change, well, what would they do if he just sailed away?

Sitting aboard the *Euphoria* in Coconut Grove in December 1976, days away from his thirtieth birthday and scribbling the liner notes to a new album, there wasn't much to say. When was the last time Jimmy Buffett didn't have much to say?

Thanks, then, to the fans who enjoy the music and the people who helped make the records. "This album is dedicated to the Coral Reefer Band. Boys, it's been a long time comin' —Popps."

* *Chapter 12* *

To Bimini and Beyond

The guidebooks said don't sail into Bimini at night. The entrance was narrow, the sandbars shifty, and the coral destructive. You didn't go into Bimini at night—unless you absolutely had to.

Anchored thirty yards from the western shore of North Bimini, the *Euphoria*'s crew felt the pull of necessity at the end of a long, exhausting day. The trip had been Captain Buffett's idea. The newest Captain Buffett—Jimmy. He'd called Corcoran and suggested a run through the Bahamas. Thanks to the United States Navy, Corcoran could read a chart and plot a course. Thanks to the Chart Room, he could ready a drink. He picked up two new job titles: navigator and beer-stowage consultant. If the boss wanted to go to the Bahamas, to the Bahamas he'd go.

On January 13, the *Euphoria* set out from Coconut Grove for a quick sail to No Name Harbor on the southern tip of Key Biscayne. They dropped anchor that evening and, according to the logbook,* "commenced cocktail routine." They noticed the anchor was dragging, repositioned the boat and dropped anchor again. "No further dragging noticed," Buffett wrote. "Crew and captain, however, were dragging noticeably."

About that crew. There was of course Captain Buffett, and first

---

* The logbook, in this case, reproduced in *The Parrot Head Handbook*.

mate Jane. *National Lampoon*–managing editor P. J. O'Rourke, identified as "itinerant journalist, jester and Big Apple raconteur" was aboard. He and Corcoran had become good friends at Miami University in Oxford, Ohio. O'Rourke visited Corcoran often in the early seventies and even put his name on *National Lampoon's* masthead for a time. He and Buffett hit it off, and Jimmy and Jane would visit when they were in New York.

There was Corcoran, of course, and a deck aid named Juan. The logbook gave no last name, but the last name was Thompson. Juan was the twelve-year-old son of Hunter S. Thompson. Jane and Jimmy had been spending time in Aspen, Colorado, and met Thompson through mutual friends.

But Hunter wasn't aboard. He and his wife were fast fighting their way toward divorce and thought it would be better for Juan to go sailing with Jimmy Buffett. He knew how to sail and loved boats. What could go wrong?

Captain Buffett was awake at 7:15 a.m. the next morning. Breakfast was scrambled eggs, bacon, "and green and yellow motion pills." By 11 a.m., they were cruising comfortably on Biscayne Bay, listening to James Taylor and preparing to tan. "Domestic beer served, imported cigarettes consumed."

Soon the *Euphoria* would make south for Key Largo and anchor in Jewfish Creek. The plan from there was to set off across the Gulf Stream for Bimini, which they did despite dense fog. Fog so thick they were nearly run down twice—by the same tanker. "It was a Gulf supertanker, but it came so close all we could see was the *U*," O'Rourke wrote in his 1988 book *Holidays in Hell*.

"I have to assume they had a radar and knew where we were, or they would have been all over their foghorn before they struck us, but who knows?" Corcoran says. "We'd have never been heard from again."

Once their heart rates returned to normal, they picked up an AM station in the Bahamas, dialed in the onboard radio direction finder, and Navigator Corcoran charted them across the Stream in rough seas. Every hour or so he'd check the signal, see how the Gulf Stream was moving them, and adjust. Buffett, wrapped in yellow foul-weather gear, stretched out with a copy of Hemingway's *A Moveable Feast*.

They found Bimini—after dark—as conditions continued to deteriorate. They could hear waves breaking on the beach, and however calming that sound might be to a vacationing couple from Cleveland lounging onshore, it's unnerving aboard a boat. Options were considered. Decisions were made. Corcoran, wrapped in *his* foul-weather gear, took the dinghy ashore to look for someone who could guide them into the harbor.

He tried a church first and the minister recommended a guy named Boaty the Loadie. Boaty could get them in, even loaded, and the working assumption remains he was, or else why the nickname?

Corcoran tracked down Boaty and got him back to the *Euphoria*. Boaty took control and cleanly navigated the cut between North and South Bimini. The *Euphoria* tied up at Brown's Marina in Alice Town, a few steps from the Compleat Angler Hotel* where Hemingway stayed as he worked to finish *To Have and Have Not*. Or at least that's how it was advertised. They got to charge more for one room that way. Buffett had paid the extra few bucks when he first made the trip to Bimini in 1971 aboard a Chalk's Ocean Airways seaplane from Miami.

The next day, Corcoran, Jane, and O'Rourke caught a seaplane back to Florida. Buffett waved good-bye from shore, bundled in a long-sleeve shirt, his Euphoria T-shirt peeking out from underneath. O'Rourke headed back to New York. Jane was going to Fort Lauderdale for a few days. Corcoran needed to check on his wife and an ex-girlfriend who'd come to stay with them. Buffett and Juan watched a storm roll in.

* The Compleat Angler burned down in 2006.

The skies over Bimini darkened, temperatures dropped, and the wind twisted palm trees sideways. Buffett later swore to Corcoran he saw snowflakes. Two hundred miles west-northwest of Key West, a 410-foot Panamanian tanker capsized in eight- to twelve-foot seas and thirty-five knot winds. In the Bahamas, twenty miles northwest of Nassau, a four-masted schooner, with 127 on board, was stranded on a sandbar and battered by fifteen-foot waves.

On Wednesday, January 19, the *Key West Citizen* reported three endangered shrimp boats near Shoal Channel. A twenty-eight-foot cabin cruiser run aground near Boca Grande. One sailboat was in trouble in Boca Chica Channel and another ran aground near Safe Harbor Channel, which had to be frustrating, to be so close to *Safe* Harbor Channel.

In an attempt to save crops from the freeze, helicopters hovered over vegetable farms on the edge of the Everglades. Citrus growers set tire fires near Fort Lauderdale. Temperatures dropped to twenty-seven degrees in West Palm Beach and twenty degrees in Orlando. Snow was reported in West Palm and Orlando, in St. Petersburg and Fort Myers, in Christmas, and even in the town of Frostproof—though city officials said they had no plans to change its name.

Farther north, in the nation's capital, jackhammers chipped ice from Jimmy Carter's inaugural parade route. In a generous act of bipartisanship, Republican senator Ted Stevens, of Alaska, invited Carter to move the festivities to Anchorage, where the high was forecast in the forties, compared to the twenty-degree outlook in Washington, D.C.

The weather sucked all over, and there was Jimmy Buffett, freezing his ass off in Bimini. With the *Euphoria*'s high-end radio up and running, he gave an assist to the coast guard as it attempted to find another stranded vessel.

When the weather finally improved, the group (minus O'Rourke) reconvened and set south for Nassau and then farther south still toward the Exumas, an archipelago of hundreds of small islands like Little Hall's Pond Cay,* which appeared deserted when the *Euphoria* arrived.

After casual exploration, the landing party prepared to claim the island in the name of cocktail hour when a woman emerged from a building wondering 1) where they'd come from and 2) if they'd like to stay for dinner. It'd be served at 5 o'clock. A couple more boats were expected from Staniel Cay. Cost was $12 per person. Grouper was on the menu.

The crossing to Bimini was a memory by then, another funny story, another near miss they could laugh about. They had perfect water, perfect weather, and perfect music for the cruise. They'd packed along Joni Mitchell, Jackson Browne, and Little Feat. Corcoran had left his job at the radio station in Key West, which was fine by him, but it upset Vic Latham, who had opened the Full Moon Saloon.

The Full Moon would quickly become known as the Full *Spoon* Saloon, a nickname it earned for rare was the occasion you'd find fewer than two sets of feet in any bathroom stall. Latham had intended to use Corcoran's radio show as barroom entertainment. In its place, he asked Corcoran if he could make some mix tapes to play. Corcoran did, and packed a few aboard the *Euphoria*.

Especially popular was *Greatest Hits of the Lesser Antilles*, where Tom Waits's "Shiver Me Timbers" captured clouds "like heaven on a new front-page sky," and where James Taylor hoisted "Captain Jim's Drunken Dream." Leon Russell urged himself "Back to the Island," and Jimmy Cliff was just "Sitting in Limbo."

Corcoran even snuck "Havana Daydreamin'" into the mix. Buffett would pick up a guitar and play along with Waits or sing a few of his own. If he was drunk—*really* drunk, like so drunk he

---

* While shooting *Pirates of the Caribbean*, Johnny Depp came across Little Hall's Pond Cay and bought it in 2004 for $3.6 million. It's forty-five acres and includes six beaches, one of which is named Gonzo in honor of Hunter S. Thompson.

could barely sit up (yeah, God's own drunk)—he might even inhabit another alter ego, Blind Lemon Pledge.

And they hadn't left Florida without the new one from the Eagles, *Hotel California*. Buffett had struck up a friendship with Glenn Frey and the rest of the band since that first nervous gig opening for them in South Carolina. The Eagles had recorded at Criteria not long before Buffett made *Changes in Latitudes, Changes in Attitudes*, and it had continued to rocket them to a level of stardom few bands have attained—an altitude Buffett dreamed of.

They'd closed their new album, however, with an especially earthy, seven-and-a-half-minute lament about how we ruin every good thing we get our hands on. Don Henley wrote "The Last Resort," wondering why we'd ever call anything paradise, because all it ever does is invite the bulldozers. "You call some place paradise," Henley sang, "kiss it good-bye."

Had Buffett been home in Key West, he might have pulled up at Louie's, on the Afterdeck, ordered a beer, paged through the *Citizen*, and learned 1976 was a banner year for Air Sunshine. The carrier moved 112,274 passengers in and out of the Keys—more than double the business it had done in 1975 and 14,000 more passengers than the entire airline industry carried a year earlier.

During the recent Christmas holiday, Key West sold out of hotel rooms, forcing the chamber of commerce to turn to its list of residents willing to rent rooms to tourists. A spokesman for one hotel told the newspaper the heaviest traffic seemed to be folks from Ohio, Indiana, and Illinois—with a noticeable increase in travelers from Europe and South America. The manager of another estimated a 35-percent increase in business in 1976.

Not that Buffett needed to read that in the newspaper. He'd written all those tourists, baking under a tropical sun, into the first verse of "Margaritaville," and then added the portly caricatures into the verse he cut in the studio. They were real, and they hadn't been there five years earlier when he arrived with Jerry Jeff and

Murphy. They'd called it paradise back then, and now the beaches were filling and strangers would knock on his door offering a six-pack because everyone wanted to get drunk with Jimmy Buffett. Key West wasn't the same as it was, but what ever is? Don't like it? Keep moving forward in search of whatever's next.

The *Euphoria* made south for Staniel Cay, home of the Staniel Cay Yacht Club. "An oasis of tropical charm," according to its brochure. There was a new 3,000-foot airstrip, and for those arriving by private plane, Staniel Cay Yacht Club monitored Unicorn 122.8. They even took American Express. "A get-away haven on a happy island."

There, in a squat yellow building behind a white door lined by windows, there was a phone. The sign outside said Bahamas Telecommunications Company. Buffett and Corcoran were strolling past when Buffett, half-joking, said "Maybe I better call L.A. and see if I still have a job."

© 2017 Tom Corcoran

Corcoran waited outside while Buffett dialed back to the world, to his *job*. Corcoran recalls the half of the conversation he was privy to:

"*That* wasn't supposed to be the single," Buffett said.

He thought "Changes in Latitudes, Changes in Attitudes" would be the new album's lead single.

"It's *what?!*" Buffett said.

Radio was showing interest in "Margaritaville." It was looking like a hit.

Change of plans. *Get your ass back to the bus, Buffett, and fire up those diesels.* Unexpectedly, they had someplace to be. Oh, they celebrated the news that night, sure. But they set out fast for Great Exuma. A few days—and a few more celebrations—later, a chartered Beechcraft King Air turboprop landed in Georgetown. Larry "Groovy" Gray, Corcoran's road-trip partner to Provincetown and Jane's old college friend, was there already and he'd take care of the *Euphoria*. Vacation was over.

Buffett had to reassemble the Coral Reefer Band. It was time to tour, and he couldn't possibly have imagined as he lifted off from the Bahamas that the tour would never really end.

* *Chapter 13* *

Fool Buttons

Maybe four people actually wore flowers in their hair
before Scott McKenzie sang "San Francisco." Afterwards,
the place looked like a botanical exhibit. Now people are
drinking margaritas like it's been a tradition.
                              —Tom Corcoran, *Crawdaddy*,
                                  December 1977

The tour kicked off in Savannah, Georgia, in the middle of February. Shortly thereafter, "Margaritaville" cracked *Billboard*'s Hot 100 and began a slow climb into a long hot summer—the summer of *Star Wars*, of rolling blackouts, of the Son of Sam.

"Margaritaville" crept into the top fifty by the end of April, and on May 21, while Stevie Wonder's "Sir Duke" held the top spot, "Margaritaville," broke into the top thirty. That made it bigger than "Come Monday."

"Hotel California" was a monster for the Eagles that year. Glen Campbell made a hit of Allen Toussaint's "Southern Nights" despite turning the original, so otherworldly, into something Kermit the Frog and Fozzie Bear might sing on a road trip. On June 11, "Margaritaville" moved into the top twenty while KC and the Sunshine Band hit number one with, "I'm Your Boogie Man." On July 2,

"Margaritaville" moved to number ten, followed by two weeks at number nine and two more at number eight.

In the top spot those weeks: Shaun Cassidy's saccharine cover of the Crystals' "Da Doo Ron Ron," Barry Manilow's saccharine "Looks Like We Made It," and Andy Gibb's saccharine "I Just Want to Be Your Everything." Interesting summer.

The tour put Buffett back in front of the Eagles' audience in some of the biggest venues in the country. Buffett visited the White House for a little face time with another Southern boy done good, President Carter, and few of the roadies got high in a bathroom next to the Oval Office.

One day Buffett walked on the bus with a wad of cash. "I couldn't have done it without you," roadie Steve Vaughn remembers Buffett saying, as bonuses were distributed.

At an after-party somewhere in the South, maybe Memphis, they got off the bus, walked through an alley, into a backyard, "and there's this huge swimming pool," lighting director Clint Gilbert says. "Pristine. Right out of picture books." There was a bar along one side of the pool and it was waiting for them, lined with margaritas. "I don't know who it was; it might have been Fingers," Gilbert says, "who just walked in ahead of everybody, walked in with his arm stuck out knocking them all into the pool. And nobody said a word."

Corcoran was called to duty to take photos, and then put behind the wheel of an auxiliary vehicle, an RV nicknamed the Green Weenie.

"How's that smell?" Buffett asked him one day.

"How do you think it smells?" Corcoran said.

Buffett pulled fifty bucks in petty cash and gave it to tour manager Mike Wheeler with instructions to buy Odor-Eaters for everyone. First two pairs on the house, but required from then on. Like J. D. checking boxes for Alabama Dry Dock and Shipbuilding, Jimmy was down in the details. While he took care of the smell, Jane took care of the look.

"When it hit," Corcoran says, "when we realized things were going to change overnight and there was going to be a stream of income, Jane dictated no more Levi's with holes in the knees, and no more shirts without collars. Jane said, 'You gotta look a bit like you're important.'"

Corcoran shares that not to suggest micromanagement, but to assure credit where it's due. "She kept him clean," he says. As sure as she hid his cookies when he had the munchies.

Older systems, meanwhile, had been fine-tuned. Vaughn, who had T-shirt duty on top of his other jobs, says they had a distributor in Hawaii who'd stack the merchandise on top of bags of Hawaiian weed and ship them to wherever they needed to go to catch the band, which had a few new faces.

After stepping in for Gardner on "Margaritaville," Buttrey took over road duties as well. "And we went through guitar players like shit through a goose," Vaughn says. Michael Jeffry had been hired to replace Bartlett, and fired while they were recording *Changes in Latitudes, Changes in Attitudes*. Bartlett flew down to Miami to chip in on a couple of tracks and help finish the album. Tim Krekel* took over the touring gig.

In North Carolina, the Holiday Inn marquee read WELCOME TO MARGARITAVILLE. In South Carolina, like she'd stepped out of "Big Rig," a good-looking blonde walked into the party not with a bottle of Scotch, but with a Buck knife and a bag of white powder, and only after everyone had taken a hit off the blade did they realize it was PCP.

"We've been through a horrendous tour," Buffett said comically, introducing the Coral Reefer Band in Central Park on August 2 before launching them into a song about "a little crazy town called Margaritaville" that was in its last days as a top-ten single, but would spend twenty-two weeks in the Hot 100. *Changes* hit number twelve

---

* Krekel died in 2010 after a short battle with cancer. He was 55.

on the albums chart, number two on the country chart, sold more than a million copies, and made Buffett a star.

In the middle of Manhattan, a day later than scheduled thanks to rain, and at the height of his success, Buffett sounded . . . grateful, and energized. Even at the end of a long tour. "I'm going to have a good time in the Apple tonight," he said introducing "Wonder Why We Ever Go Home."

Kiki Dee opened the show, and was joined by Elton John on "Don't Go Breaking My Heart." Reviewing the set for the *New York Times*, John Rockwell noted that Buffett, despite a big hit, didn't pack the place, but the Coral Reefers played with "jumpy, infectious spirit." And of Buffett: "He has a lively sense of humor. And he has a sensitivity usually reserved for that awkward hybrid, the singer-songwriter."

Buffett had returned the cocaine reference to his hit's final verse—to loud applause—and reinserted the "lost verse" about the sad old men and their three-day vacations. Into "Why Don't We Get Drunk" he added "a little good Columbian gold" and "after all of that shit," if anyone could move, well, you know.

But when Buffett stepped out front alone with just his guitar and "He Went to Paris," he found the weight of all eighty-six of his character's years. "Thank you very much for being so nice," Buffett said.

The tour (briefly) over, he pointed himself not south, but west to Aspen and another gig with the Eagles—who were going to play his wedding. For the occasion, he and Jane had booked Redstone Castle, a 42-room, 24,000-square-foot home built in 1897. The invitations said simply there'd be a party, and, at some point during that party, Jimmy and Jane would get married. Then the party would go "until it is over."

Why Colorado? They'd bought property in Snowmass, a quiet cabin near Glenn Frey's. They had to walk across a covered bridge to get home. There was room to breathe in the mountains, in part because the area was filling with celebrities.

Members of the Byrds had moved to the area. Jack Nicholson was hanging out when he wasn't in Los Angeles or on a movie set. Steve Martin would swing by. Hunter Thompson had Owl Farm nearby, and the rich and the famous and the curious would arrive hoping for an audience in the kitchen. Business executives were snapping up lots. With 1972's "Rocky Mountain High," John Denver had done for Colorado what Jimmy Buffett would do for Florida. But on Key West, Buffett was a big celebrity on a little island. He was just another recognizable face around Aspen, one of many, and less famous than most.

He'd been clear about fame as far back as *A White Sport Coat and a Pink Crustacean*, when he sang about how he didn't want that confusing kind where you're recognized on a plane. So Aspen had become the next great place to be. More comfortable than Key West in the summer, too.

The night before the wedding, Thompson strutted through the bachelor party in a three-piece suit offering acid on a silver tray and cocaine with a silver straw. Joe Nuzzo swears it snowed (real snow) that night and that he and his date (just one, because it was out of town) made snowmen at 3 a.m. Those snowmen were the only evidence left when the crowd awoke in the middle of the next day.

Chris Robinson, Buffett's neighbor, was mistaken for a rock star—not uncommon with hair down to his waist. "I love your music," a waiter said. When Robinson protested, the waiter, feeling like Robinson was just being modest, said, "Well, I mean, I like the rest of the band, too, but you're my favorite."

Juan Thompson dressed in a white tuxedo with a blue cummerbund his mother had bought him in New York. "I even had a walking stick," he wrote in 2016's *Stories I Tell Myself: Growing Up with Hunter S. Thompson.* "I'm sure I was the only child at that wedding reception, which I learned later was an evening of high debauchery."

True to the invitation, the party went until it ended, and then Jimmy and Jane headed to the islands.

"The University of Florida did this thing called the Halloween Ball; it was the most insane thing you've ever seen," Bob Liberman says. "It was a free concert by the library, and people would come dressed in costumes. There must have been 20,000 or 30,000 people there."

Buffett played. Liberman, a student, worked it and the two met there. They ran into each other again when Liberman was working at the Great Southern Music Hall in Gainesville. Liberman was still in school when he got an offer to work on Bob Dylan's Rolling Thunder Revue tour in 1975. When pieces of that tour (including T Bone Burnett) reassembled to form the Alpha Band, Liberman hit the road with them. He was driving a cab in Fort Lauderdale in 1977 when dispatch flagged him.

"Driver Liberman, your mother just called."

"I call home," he says. "God bless her heart, Jewish mother. 'Ma, what's so important? I'm at work. Everybody heard you call me.'"

"I thought it was important," she said. "Jimmy Buffett just called and he wants you to call him back."

"That *is* important, Ma. Thank you!"

Liberman called Buffett right back.

"What are you doing?" Buffett said.

"Driving a cab."

"Would you like to come work for me?"

"Yeah," Liberman said. "When do you need me?"

"Tomorrow."

"Where do you need me?"

"Atlanta."

Liberman got on a plane without asking what job he'd accepted. "You'll learn," Buffett told his new assistant tour manager. If you were right for the job, Buffett's confidence was enough to make it work.

Deborah McColl was back in Atlanta—the nearby suburb of Buckhead—playing a show when Buffett came by to catch her set. Things had changed since he'd hitchhiked up in 1972 and sat in with McColl's old band at the Bistro. She was working a solo act, and Buffett was building out his sound. "I think that night when we were talking at the table he asked me if I wanted to be on the *Son of a Son of a Sailor* album with him," she says.

Success had presented opportunities—some he'd hoped for, and some Buffett hadn't planned on. Around the time Don Light closed the new deal with ABC, he and Buffett renewed their partnership and extended their management contract. Light had believed in Buffett when no one else had, and advocated for him when no one else would. Buffett had done his job and they'd all, finally, profited. Still, Light was in Nashville, and Nashville was where they made country stars. Buffett wasn't one of those.

In Aspen, he was hanging out with Hollywood. Frey and the Eagles did their business out of Los Angeles. Buffett began to collect business contacts and lawyers on the West Coast. He didn't get rid of his apartment in Key West, but Colorado became home.

To fit his new terrain, Buffett had gotten rid of a Mercedes and bought a Chevy Cheyenne pickup in Nashville. He was complaining one day about how much it was going to cost to have it shipped to Aspen, when Steve Vaughn said he'd drive it there.

Outside Leadville, Colorado, a couple of good ol' boys with a fully stocked gun rack pulled up alongside and started flipping middle fingers and shouting at the long hair—but otherwise Vaughn's trip to Aspen in Buffett's new truck was uneventful. When he got there, the newlyweds were at the movies. They'd gone to see *The Bad News Bears*. When they got back, Buffett took Vaughn to Hunter Thompson's farm for an afternoon of firearms and chemicals.

Hunter was never far from Buffett in Aspen. Footage remains

on YouTube of the night Buffett dropped in to play a fund-raiser Thompson was hosting. With Glenn Frey on guitar and Steve Weisberg, of John Denver's band, playing dobro, Buffett (in a pressed and collared shirt) dutifully sang his hit.

He believed you give the people what they want, but there was one move he had to make for himself. Buffett told Light he wanted out of their recently signed extension. He was going to put his career in Irving Azoff's hands.

Azoff is a five-foot-three industry giant. He's ambition in compact, combustible form. As Cameron Crowe wrote in his June 15, 1978, *Rolling Stone* profile of Azoff: "He is the enfant terrible of the music business. To get his clients top dollar, he'll rip up a contract, yell, scream, terrorize, stomp, pound and destroy inanimate objects . . . gleefully. He is the American Dream taken by the balls. Many of his clients will spend their off-hours watching him 'kill' on the phone."

"What wedding present do you get for the guy who's already *taken* everything he wanted?" Frey asked Crowe. A paragraph later, Don Henley called Azoff, "Napoleon with a heart." But he could comfortably dispense with that heart if you weren't on his side.

Jerry Rubinstein, then the head of ABC Records, had occasion to work with both Light and Azoff. "You can't even talk about 'em in the same breath," Rubinstein says—if only because Azoff sucks up the oxygen in any sentence. That wasn't a knock on Light, precisely. Azoff, Rubinstein says, is one of the best ever, period. New paragraph.

"It's a tough business and you need to be aggressive to represent any artist," Rubinstein says. "Certainly Irving is one of the more aggressive managers around."

Azoff pulled Joe Walsh's career from the gutter, pushed the Eagles to the top, and as documented by Crowe, even talked them out of a dope jam at customs in the Bahamas. Norbert Putnam once watched Azoff grab a map and a pencil and reroute an entire

Buffett tour—while he was on the phone yelling at someone for something else.

Azoff and Light negotiated the deal. When Light felt he wasn't getting what he deserved, he reminded them he didn't have to do anything. He had recently signed that management contract with Buffett. That tended to get the conversation back on track.

Among the concessions, Light got 25 percent of "Margaritaville," which he'd later sell back to Buffett for $100,000 when "Margaritaville" wasn't making him but $10,000 a year. That was the late seventies, maybe early eighties and proved to be a mistake. Everyone told him you never sell publishing. "One hundred percent of the blame rests squarely on me for that," Light told Peter Cooper. "If we're going to be fair about it, and we try to be. That was my call."

Now Buffett had high-powered representation and, a year after telling *High Times* he wasn't selling his lifestyle because nobody was buying, well . . .

"When Jimmy Buffett sings 'A Pirate Looks at 40' . . . every pot dealer with dreams for bigger things in America thinks Buffett wrote the song just for him," Corcoran wrote in the December 1976 edition of *Crawdaddy*. "They're not too far off. Poetry always gets stretched to please the musical audience, of course, and play with listeners' fantasies, but the end result seems more and more to have the audience stretching their lifestyles to match the songs."

That "rather affable freak who sold tacos from a pushcart," as Jim Harrison had described Corcoran, *could* write—just as Harrison figured the night the two met outside Captain Tony's. From the driver's seat of the Green Weenie and the angles presented by his all-access photo pass and friendship with the boss, Corcoran had sniffed out an absurdity central to Buffett's appeal.

Corcoran called it the "Everyman's dream of escape from civilization," and the farther Buffett sailed from the Everyman—and the Everyday—the more he appealed to people who fit the definition of both. People weren't enamored with Jimmy Buffett because he was one of them; people were enamored with Jimmy Buffett because he could have been, but wasn't. He was some imagined version of a better, freer self.

Those cars rolling down from Ohio, Indiana, and Illinois—and every other state full of white picket fences and American Dreams—they didn't want to get caught up in a deal gone wrong (or gone right), but it was fun to think they could.

They even didn't have to hit the road. They could hit their turntable or their tape deck and listen to the same thing the smugglers were listening to and it didn't matter if Jimmy Buffett ever smuggled an ounce of anything. Smugglers liked Jimmy Buffett. It was in *Rolling Stone*. It was in "A Pirate Looks at Forty." That the real pirate, Phil Clark, had gotten caught up in a bust at Immokalee airport and was on probation in Tarpon Springs* didn't matter any more than Buffett's own pirate credentials. For four minutes, everyone was a pirate when Jimmy Buffett sang about pirates.

"He can pit a hangover against a sunrise and make his audience want the experience every day," Corcoran wrote. "Buffett can paint a picture of decadence and make it elegant. And he wonders why all these funky people, the perennial fuck-ups and two-bit adventurers, are drawn to the ocean, to a place of such beauty."

He'd seen the ocean, and the islands rising green and inviting from it. He'd found time that spring to sneak away to Tortola and St. Thomas (Juan Thompson back aboard). He'd run to the Caicos Islands (where Bum Farto was or wasn't) with Glenn Frey. They boarded the *Euphoria* and made for the Dominican Republic, where they found peace and quiet and, Corcoran wrote, good cheer and free beer aboard a neighboring boat packing only Buffett and the Eagles tapes.

The *Euphoria* had been everything Buffett had dreamed she'd be—a nice starter boat. With "Margaritaville" money piling up,

---

* "... balling a parade of earthy 19-year-olds," Corcoran added, doing nothing to diminish Phil Clark's legend.

Euphoria ceded to *Euphoria II*, the difference being about fifteen feet of yacht, from thirty-three to forty-eight feet in length, and more electronic gadgets—including a bulky video cassette player with a small screen so they could watch *The Wizard of Oz* and *Key Largo* on deck and under the stars. Buffett ordered custom matchbooks, black with silver embossing:

Euphoria II
Key West
"If we weren't all crazy
we'd all go insane"

Writing an early draft of liner notes for the next album, Buffett sat in Nassau Harbor in mid-January 1978 and considered the competing interests of his life. He hadn't touched a guitar since he'd left Florida—save for one night in Bimini, at the Compleat Angler, when he'd jumped up with the band. "I have been a little too occupied changing winches, wiring spreader lights, repairing bilge pumps and numerous other jobs that go hand in hand with the pleasure of being a boat owner," he wrote. There were sweet memories in those chores. Growing up, he'd leave church and help his dad maintain his boat.

From Nassau the *Euphoria II* worked south without interruption. They made it to the far eastern edge of the Bahamas, San Salvador, with Judy Corcoran and Jane along. The women left San Salvador by plane and the guys set out on the 800-plus-mile journey through the Atlantic Ocean to St. Maarten. The ocean decided to flex its muscle and beat the hell out of them for long days and longer nights. When they were finally, mercifully within sight of St. Maarten, they came across two fishermen who'd been blown out to sea from nearby Anguilla. The *Euphoria II* detoured to get them safely back home.

"Not a beautiful luxury cruise," Corcoran says. "When we finally got to the north half of St. Maarten, the French half, the women were there waiting and we all went to dinner and we all fell asleep in our food. We were just toast."

The next day met them with weather fit for a song. They set out for the Dutch side of the island under perfect skies, with perfect seas and perfect wind. "We were getting our reward for the shitty trip across the ocean," Corcoran says.

"Groovy" Gray had hired on as Buffett's captain and, like Azoff on your contracts, Groovy was the guy you wanted on your boat. His father, Gordon L. "Gordo" Gray Jr., had been a navy fighter pilot. In 1955, he set a Fédération Aéronautique International speed record on a five-hundred-kilometer closed circuit, when he flew a pre-production Douglas A-4 Skyhawk an average of almost seven hundred miles per hour. There's a photo of Gordo after the flight, surrounded by Douglas engineers. Gordo's hair was tight, his jaw square, his posture confident. Three years later, Lieutenant Commander Gordon L. Gray Jr. graduated from the Naval War College.

When he retired, he took his kids out of school and they sailed the Caribbean for a year. "That's why Groovy was so good on a sailboat," Corcoran says. Gordo passed along his knowledge, his guts, and some tradition: the Hamburger Award.

On board the aircraft carrier, Gordo's squad had taken a chunk of military grade beef, nailed it to a piece of wood, lacquered the hell out of it, and awarded it to anyone who pulled off the daring or the unexpected. Get laid on leave? "You're a real hamburger." Walk away from a crash. "You're a hamburger, buddy." Each new Hamburger would affix the trophy to the bulkhead of his stateroom until someone else earned the trophy. Gordo carried the spirit home with him and it became a family tradition. Groovy, Corcoran says, took the idea to college and upgraded. He added cheese.

Sailing around St. Maarten that perfect morning, Buffett was at the helm of his boat. The women were sunbathing topless. There were whales surfacing. Passing boats were full of more topless women. They had club sandwiches from a French bakery. "It couldn't have been sweeter," Corcoran says. He and Groovy were on the low side of the *Euphoria II*, balancing beers on their chests when Groovy looked over at Buffett and said, "Bubba,* you're just a cheeseburger in paradise." Buffett's eyes lit up.

"That's where it came from," Corcoran says. "It never came from a restaurant. Jimmy's told dozens of restaurants that he wrote the song about them just so he could get free meals. He told Le Select in St. Barts that he wrote the song about Le Select because he genuinely liked that guy, and I think if there had to be an official restaurant for the cheeseburger in paradise song, it would be Le Select in St. Barts.

"But the fact is, that line came out of Groovy's mouth on that day on that sailboat. Bubba went absolutely batshit." It was going to be the name of the next album. He told Corcoran they could shoot a cover with a big cheeseburger, and Buffett swimming out of it in full scuba gear. He smartly scrapped that idea and settled for a song. The new album would be called *Son of a Son of a Sailor*.

Released in March 1978, the album was announced on its back cover as "Mr. Jimmy Buffett Appearing in the Trials and Temptations of a Son of a Son of a Sailor and Other Recitations Accompanied by His Highly Acclaimed Musical Band." The "Grand Tableau" promised within was set in the hold of a pirate ship, the Coral Reefer Band manning the oars. Commodore Azoff worked the phones with an assist from Bob Liberman. In the foreground, an innocent-looking bellhop stands ready with Perrier, Mount Gay Rum, and Tums for Jimmy and Jane, who look like they got lost on their way to the yacht club. There was a help-wanted ad in the corner: "Able-bodied crew for extended pleasure cruise . . .

---

* Bubba: an all-purpose term of endearment among the locals in the Keys. In 1985, a dozen Key West residents were found guilty of various drug charges in what was known as the Bubba Bust Trial.

Thoughtful captain with 12 years experience. Swingers need not apply."

In June 1978, "Cheeseburger in Paradise"—the only hint of its origin being the final line, "I'm just a cheeseburger in paradise"—peaked at thirty-two on *Billboard*'s Hot 100. So it did okay, but was hardly anyone's definition of a hit. The album reached number ten and went platinum anyway.

To make the record, Buffett again turned to Home at Last for a mansion, a chef, and a maid and to Putnam for production. Instead of Criteria, the bar was set up in Bayshore Recording Studios in Coconut Grove. Finishing touches were applied at Putnam's studio in Nashville.

Buffett cleaned up "Livingston Saturday Night" (a little), and pulled two Keith Sykes songs for the sessions to make up for the one he'd left off *Havana Daydreamin'*. "The Last Line" was about a songwriter's wish to write one great lyric, then walk away, only to realize he can't, and won't. "Coast of Marseilles" was about running away to forget—and how that never works. The past is always right behind you.

In "African Friend," Buffett told the story of two strangers bonding over a hot streak at a craps table in a Haitian casino, one waking up on the steps of a whorehouse with a note from the other pinned to his sleeve: "It was a pleasure and a hell of an evening; it truly was our night to win."

The "Cowboy in the Jungle" was another man out of place, what with his "shrimp-skin boots." He was an adaptable sort, the type to "roll with the punches, play all of his hunches." Intuition had worked well enough. He'd be fine—better than the gaudy tourists puking up rum drinks and lying about the day's fishing, that's for sure.

Time on Tortola and St. Thomas inspired "Mañana" when inspiration was needed, Buffett admitting the new album was old, and he was "fresh out of tunes." He'd find them, as always, in the people he'd meet, the places he'd visit . . . and in the rum he'd drink.

Ever aware of the tide lines of his world, "Fool Button" was a counterpoint—proof he didn't need time off to find a song. It was a strutting rocker about lost rental cars, strange hotel rooms, barroom blues blowouts, and nights gone haywire. And it came with a warning, or maybe a challenge. Go ahead and doubt Buffett and his stories if you like, but "get a bottle of rum and some Eskatrol and watch the same thing happen to you."

"Son of a Son of a Sailor" turned family history into personal myth-building, Buffett reading "dozens of books about heroes and crooks" and taking a little something from each to the far-away "southeast of disorder" where the mango man mingles with a woman from Trinidad.

They were at work on the album when Liberman got another phone call from Buffett. "I got some good news and some bad news," Buffett said. "Meet me at the pool."

The bad news was Mike Wheeler, the tour manager, was leaving. The good news was Liberman had been promoted from Wheeler's assistant to Wheeler's position. He'd barely figured out the first job. "It's not something you go to school to learn," Liberman says, and the new job was growing.

A hit song, a hit record, and Azoff's appearance had tightened protocols—at least for some. "It got to the point where they told Wheeler I need to talk to him to talk to Buffett," says Steve Vaughn, who left shortly before *Son of a Son* was recorded. "They changed everything." It felt like management was trying to separate Buffett from all the people who could be replaced. Before, Vaughn says, it had felt like they were just a bunch of guys on a bus having fun.

Chain-of-command issues aside, the party rolled on. "Fingers one time said I was in the band during the heavy artillery days," says Deborah McColl, who'd joined the tour and broken up the boys' club. "I like to say I was in the band before cocaine was addictive."

They had a bus driver named Grandpa, and one of his rules was he never stopped on an overnight run. One night Buffett

told Liberman he needed his luggage from underneath the bus.
Liberman asked Grandpa to stop. Grandpa said no. Liberman told
Grandpa it was Buffett who needed to stop. Grandpa didn't have
much of a choice. They pulled over on the highway. That's when
the production manager awoke, saw they'd stopped, and decided
to perform another of his duties. It was his job to dump the bus's
holding tanks, and this was usually done on a quiet piece of highway.
What did they hold? Waste. The problem was, they dumped by
the luggage doors—right where Buffett was standing. That's one
way to enrage a benevolent dictator.

The days of bus mishaps, however, were numbered. Soon
enough, Buffett got a plane. A King Air they nicknamed Cheeseburger replaced the Enterprise. "I can't remember the pilot's name,"
Liberman says, "but he always had a cigarette in his mouth, and
you could tell how long the trip was by the pile of ashes in his lap."

Roadies cartooned the previous night's personal destructions.
Taped to the inside of the fuselage, these Coral Reefer comic strips
served two purposes: they were funny, and they helped remind the
band what had happened since they last boarded Cheeseburger.

"We had our own slang, we had our own references," McColl
says. "We were together all the time, and we were apart from the
regular world."

Fingers Taylor's inebriation became a running joke, though it
loses its humor in hindsight, and especially as he fades away, another Alzheimer's victim. But at the time, his one-note harmonica
solos—when he'd stumble forward, hit one note, and fall over into
the microphone—were hilarious. "We were just blind to a lot of that
stuff," McColl says. "We were young and immortal and bulletproof."

Buffett's rules required they be ready to work when they went
onstage, that for two hours a day, they perform (Fingers' act could
be considered performance in that regard). That left twenty-two
hours of not much to do.

"I think I needed some intellectual stimulation, clearly," says

McColl, who's a therapist outside Atlanta now. "I had to turn the wattage down on my brain. It's not that people weren't intelligent, but we didn't have anything to do. We were so catered to."

Buffett wasn't any less catered to, but it was different. What could be seen as management-driven isolation from one point of view might have felt like self-preservation from another. He was detail oriented, driven, and clearly in charge. But every problem couldn't be his problem or else every day would be like standing on the side of the road and having the bus's holding tanks dumped on his head. "And I'd get yelled at a lot," Liberman says. "They'd never go to Jimmy. The whole point of making Jimmy happy is to defuse the situation before it ever gets to Jimmy."

McColl had aspirations for a solo career, and so she pushed that point whenever she got a chance. She wishes now she hadn't. She wishes she'd just been a friend, but everyone wanted something, and Buffett was the guy they thought could give it to them. "Lip balm!" became his call, the bat signal that launched tour manager Liberman into action.

When they hit a break in the tour, Buffett would disappear. He'd heard about Sailing Week in Antigua. They'd done a six-week run of shows, and when it was finished he and Jane hopped a plane and headed first to St. Thomas and then to rendezvous with *Euphoria II* to race and unwind. "I punched the Fool Button," he wrote for the July/August 1978 edition of *Outside*. Corcoran snapped the photos. It was a wild time. Big boats. Fast boats. Gorgeous boats. Big crews. Fast crews. Gorgeous women. They were racing *Euphoria II* when Jane went overboard after part of a bikini she wasn't wearing anyway. When the *Eilean*, a seventy-one-footer from St. Thomas passed them a few minutes later, "there was Jane working on a sail trim adjustment," Buffett wrote. "She had her red bottoms on and seemed quite content."

To get a feel for real racing, Buffett talked himself aboard *Jader*, an eighty-one-footer from Boston that "drives to weather like a freight train," he wrote. Buffett hopped aboard, went to work, and worked hard. When *Jader* crossed the line in first, it was a familiar feeling. It felt like a rock show done well.

"High energy for short periods of time and peaceful elation when the job is done," Buffett wrote. "A million little things could go wrong, but when it all goes right . . ."

After that, it was time to goof off and race the dinghy and fly on a spinnaker, a downwind sail that can be rigged into something resembling a swing. "Spinnaker flying it turns out, lies somewhere between skydiving and Ferris-wheel riding," Buffett wrote. "Unless you're drunk, which I was. Then it's much less dangerous than either."

And far safer than softball. The *Boca Raton News*, May 3, 1978: "Jimmy Buffett, wielding a new set of crutches, hobbled out of Good Samaritan Medical Center in West Palm Beach this morning bound for 'Margaritaville.'"

The culprit: an accident while he'd been visiting Guy de la Valdene. According to the paper, Buffett had tried to get a little softball practice in before flying to Los Angeles to play third base for the Eagles in a game against *Rolling Stone*.

The injury occurred sliding into second base (his team lost) and a hospital spokesman said Buffett arrived around 11 p.m. and spent the next day learning how to walk on crutches. The hospital's staff spent the day fielding phone calls and turning away opportunists.

"We had a guy who brought his guitar and wanted to sing some songs to Buffett to see what he thought," hospital spokesman Ron Errett told the paper. "We had a lot of girls who wanted to pass along how much they love him."

Buffett missed the game and was in a cast when the tour resumed, one more challenge for Liberman. "People think it's glamorous," Liberman says of touring. "You don't see anything. You see the hotel room. You can show me pictures outside of a hotel room and I can tell you what city that is. That's what I'm good at."

Vancouver, British Columbia, is recognizable by its mountains. The gig there was on top of one. Liberman had to transport the show and its stars via gondola, and the rookie tour manager was doing his best. "Why it wasn't at the bottom of the mountain, I don't know," Liberman says, shaking his head.

Buffett had a broken leg and was in a lousy mood. There had been problems with the hotel, where Buffett had pulled Liberman aside and said, "You're doing a great job, but sometimes you need to be more forceful. You need to step in there. Don't let people take advantage of you. You're being too nice."

Duly noted. Up on the mountain, they finished sound check and were waiting for the gondola. And waiting. And waiting longer still. "Jimmy's not really pleased with the environment," Liberman says. "The guy I'm dealing with is a sleazeball. During settlement he tried to pay me with cocaine. I said, 'No, I need cash.'"

The wait for the gondola continued. "He's getting really pissed and I'm noticing," Liberman says, "he" being Buffett, not the sleazeball. "I'm thinking it might be time to step in and do what he told me to do."

Finally, their ride arrived—full of hot dog supplies for the concession stands. Workers unload and the gondola was finally empty and waiting when a group of kids in wheelchairs arrived. "I don't know what they were doing there," Liberman says. "Twelve, fifteen kids in wheelchairs."

Liberman picked that moment to be forceful, to say, "No! I need this gondola." What he remembers saying, actually, was "Ma'am, I've got a rock star with a broken leg. I've got a blind piano player—Jay Spell. Fingers Taylor is drunk all the time. Don't go telling me . . ."

Out of the corner of his eye, he caught Buffett frantically motioning "No, no, please don't for the love of god not now."

"He finally says, 'Let them on, Bob,'" Liberman says.

The kids got on, the gondola moved down the mountain, and Buffett pulled Liberman aside for a second time. "I really appreciate you taking note of what I said," Buffett told him, "but there's a time and a place."

The gondola made its way back to the top of the mountain. Buffett crutched aboard, followed by the Coral Reefer Band and their tour manager. They still had time to shower, change, and rest for the show. Except when they got to the hotel, they couldn't get into their rooms.

Liberman had told the hotel that unless they fixed the issues the band was having—whatever those were all these years later, Liberman doesn't remember—they weren't going to pay. Buffett looked at Liberman like a teacher will look at a student.

"Bobby," he said, "you don't tell 'em you're not going to pay until you're checking out."

Chapter 14

Almost Over the Edge

Son of a Son of a Sailor sold big with limited radio play and no hit single, and Buffett was selling out shows across the country. "Because he's become the Mark Twain of Southern music, you know?" Putnam says. "But I'm getting phone calls every day from the record company." He smiles and slips into an impersonation dialed somewhere between Southern gentleman and Jersey gangster. "Hey! Norbert! When you gonna take Buffett back in? We need another record, ya know, for da third quarter this year."

"Well, I'll call Jimmy," he said.

He mimes calling Buffett.

"Hey, Jimmy. What's going on?"

"Well, I'm out here in Aspen, you know. Really busy."

"Well, what are you doing?" Putnam said.

"Played tennis this morning with Jack Nicholson. And there's a party later at Henley's house, and we all go down to the Jerome every night and stay up until daylight."

"Oh yeah," Putnam said. "Okay. So you're busy. They want another record."

"I can write some stuff," Buffett said. "I've got some stuff in the works."

He had two or three songs. Not a lot to work with, and not much of a surprise. Buffett hadn't been lying when he wrote "Mañana."

He was fresh out of tunes before *Son of a Son*, had scraped together a good record, and now the label wanted more.

Tom Corcoran, meanwhile, was enjoying some downtime camping in Maine. He'd been there a year earlier with Judy and Sebastian when *Rolling Stone* publisher Jann Wenner called trying to track him down because Corcoran was working on a treatment for a screenplay with Hunter Thompson, who had moved into Buffett's Key West apartment after Buffett had moved to Aspen. Buffett had given Thompson Corcoran's name and number to contact when he got to town.

While Buffett was staying out all night at the Hotel Jerome and playing tennis with the stars near Thompson's Owl Farm, Thompson was wrecking boats and learning how to turn himself into a flamethrower with just a match and some 151-proof rum (Chris Robinson taught him that trick). It was quite the cultural-exchange program.

Buffett had "already kind of developed what Hunter had always had, which was a disinclination to hang around with fucked-up people," Corcoran says. "And they were plagued with them, because everyone wanted to show Jimmy what a wild partier they were because he was so famous for being a partier—and he just hated it."

Everyone wanted to get wrecked with Jimmy Buffett and high with Hunter Thompson, to try to out-Gonzo Dr. Gonzo. That never worked. It couldn't be done. It wasn't healthy for anyone—most especially Thompson, because he couldn't turn down the challenge, no matter how much he hated it. He wound up trapped in the character he'd created right to the end.

"Which is why Hunter and I got along so well," Corcoran says. "I had a great taste for beer. I'd tried everything else, at least once, but it wasn't my deal." They could sit down and write and had been doing so. They could hang out. There's a famous photo of Thompson, shirtless, throwing a football. Corcoran's seen it described as being taken in various NFL training camps. It was shot in his backyard. Thompson was throwing a pass to Sebastian.

As surprised as the campground manager might have been to find the publisher of *Rolling Stone* on the phone in 1977, the same guy must have been doubly surprised to hear Buffett on the other end of the line in 1978. He was calling to tell Corcoran they were going to knock out a live album for ABC. He needed his navigator/photographer to hit the road and shoot the artwork. There'd be a plane ticket in Boston.

They began at the Fox Theatre in Atlanta, August 8–10, and then sent the mobile recording rig to Miami for three nights at the Maurice Gusman Cultural Center, August 14–16. Buffett had another broken leg. He'd had to do *Saturday Night Live* with it propped up on boat. "They didn't know what to do with the leg so they said, 'Let's put a boat in the skit,'" Buffett told Johnny Carson in 1981. It was his right leg, his time-keeping leg, and when they went into rehearsals for the tour, Buttrey approached him during a break and said, "Your time is awful." Buffett had to adjust, tapping his left foot and making do. He broke the leg a third time skiing.

"How do you break your leg three times in one year?" Carson asked.

"Very stupidly," Buffett said.

Before the first show in Atlanta, Putnam pulled the Coral Reefer Band aside and asked them to try to keep things straight. Maybe save the drinks and the drugs for after the show. Unlike in the studio, they couldn't go back and fix many mistakes. The band grumbled but did as he asked. "It was the best I ever heard the band play," Putnam says, and he told the Coral Reefers exactly that as soon as they walked offstage.

"I said, 'If this is any indication, it's going to get even better,'" Putnam says. "I should never have said that. They never gave me another note I could use. The entire record is from the first night."

For Buffett, the broken leg was just another source of material.

"This cast is no blast but it's coming off fast and I feel like I'm pulling a trailer," he tacked on to the end of "Son of a Son of a Sailor."

"I broke my leg twice I had to limp on back home," he sang in "Margaritaville" while putting to tape for the first time the song's tourist-sniping "lost" verse. With it in place, "Margaritaville" paired nicely with "Morris' Nightmare," one of two new songs.

Poor Morris. All he wanted was an easy vacation in the sun. He and his wife saved all year to "only see the islands from a tacky cruise ship." They bought all the island trinkets, and when Morris tried to steal a nap—just one lousy nap—his wife yelled, "You can sleep when you get home."

"The cruise ship commandos," Buffett said, offense intended. Give him his "Perrier Blues" instead. It wasn't one of Groovy's favorite songs, if only because Buffett, "riding high atop the main-mast," sweating off a hangover, "asked the boy to lower me slow."

Corcoran recalls Groovy's reaction. "I ain't no boy," he said. The original handwritten lyrics, which Corcoran has, would have been more accurate. In those, Buffett asked "the crew" for a little help. In both, he returned to his favorite topic, the yin and yang of his existence. When the anchor drops "and the sails are all furled," he'd be back on the road. "I don't deny that I miss it," Buffett sang. "I've got this thing for applause."

Corcoran would seed the stage with extra rolls of film so he could reload and keep shooting without being weighed down by supplies. Once, in a stadium in Orlando, opening for the Eagles, he was mistaken for the first band member taking the stage and the crowd erupted.

"I could *feel* it," he says. "It was like a force. A wind just came out of the audience, and any stronger it would have picked me up and moved me back a bit. It was phenomenal. I said, 'Oh, that's what it's all about.'"

The live shows captured, Putnam needed to mix the record, and mix it fast. Corcoran remembers Buffett on the phone and ornery backstage in Atlanta. The record company really did want a new Buffett album in a hurry and sooner than he expected. All production angles were expedited.

Putnam's Nashville studio was booked, and so he came up with the least practical, most entertaining solution: They'd go to London. Not just go to London, but take the luxury ocean liner *Queen Elizabeth 2* (the QE2) across the Atlantic and mix the record at AIR Studios in London. That was George Martin's place. He produced the Beatles. "Our advance is a million bucks," Putnam says. He thought maybe they could fly the Concorde, the new supersonic passenger jet, home.

Artwork was going to have to be finalized as well, which meant Corcoran was going to have to go along. "Judy and Sebastian are at a campground in Maine," he told Buffett.

"Judy can go," Buffett said.

Corcoran found a phone and called the campground, got the same manager Wenner and Buffett had and told him to tell Judy to take Sebastian and the dog to Corcoran's parents' house in Ohio, leave the van, and fly to New York. She could stay at P. J. O'Rourke's. Jane would pick her up and take her shopping. They were sailing for London on Sunday.

"And we didn't have a pot to piss in," Corcoran says. "We were putting clothes for the trip on our American Express. It was just stupid the money we were spending."

But he couldn't say no. Five years earlier, Buffett had been bumming spaghetti. Now he was booking them on a luxury cruise to mix an album with a seven-figure budget. Dan Fogelberg and his girlfriend joined the traveling party and got a suite with a balcony. When *bon voyage* arrived, there was the group, on Fogelberg's balcony, toasting the crowd below, which included P. J. O'Rourke cradling a six-pack on a Sunday morning.

With Fogelberg and his girlfriend along, plus Putnam's wife, that filled one dining room table. Corcoran didn't figure it'd be much fun to sit across the room and watch the rock stars eat and drink, so he booked a second table, for two, in a different dining room. Every lunch and dinner, Putnam sent an expensive bottle of wine. "He knew we couldn't afford anything on the trip," Corcoran says.

While Tom and Judy were enjoying their meals, Putnam and Fogelberg were renaming the album. The working title had been *Almost Over the Edge*. Corcoran had shot Buffett hanging off a wall on the grounds of Vizcaya, industrialist James Deering's early-twentieth-century Coconut Grove estate. Looking at proofs in New York, however, O'Rourke had latched on to a photo of Buffett shot onstage, from behind Buttrey, Buffett's face frozen between a smile, a shout, and a full laugh. "I do magazine covers all the time," Corcoran remembers O'Rourke saying. "That's your cover."

Nothing about the shot suggested *Almost Over the Edge*. Explaining the shows in Atlanta and Miami to Fogelberg, Putnam said, "You really had to be there to understand the energy in the room."

"That's it," Fogelberg said.

They'd call the album *You Had to Be There*, and with that solved, Putnam could turn his attention to wine.

"I said, 'You know, the '61 Bordeauxs have just been released,'" he says. Buffett gave him a quizzical look. "I think he might have thought it was a car or something."

The wine that came from the Bordeaux region in 1961 is that rare perfect vintage. In London, Putnam asked the concierge at their hotel to make dinner reservations each night in a different restaurant with '61 in stock—so he could sample as many as possible.

"And so we're going to dinner, and Jimmy says, 'So this is a good wine?'" Putnam says. "I'd say, 'Jimmy, this is destined to become one of the greatest wines of the century, and so it's a little young. It's a '61.'"

"Oh, so it's old," Buffett said.

"Yeah, but it should be good for a hundred or two hundred years."

"I remember he took a sip of it," Putnam says, "and said, 'Wow. This is okay.'"

By day they'd mix the record, and by night the women would dance until dawn and the men would gamble. Buffett and Putnam gambled, anyway. "Fogelberg and I didn't give a shit," Corcoran says, "So we went to the slot machines and put silver dollars in the slots. I recall standing next to Fogelberg, and he's cranking this thing, putting silver dollars in and singing, 'There's a Place in the World for a Gambler,' and I'm thinking, *This is fucking unreal.*"

Corcoran had to fly to Los Angeles—first class—to meet with ABC's art director. Judy stayed in London and crashed with Bob Mercer, the EMI Records executive who signed Queen, Marc Bolan, and Olivia Newton-John, among many, and his wife, Margie—the former Margie Buffett. They had a place next to Abbey Road and went everywhere by limo. Buffett wrecking Margie's Mercedes in Nashville hadn't totaled the prospects of a long-term friendship.

A week later, Corcoran met up with Judy in Ohio. They picked up Sebastian and drove straight to Key West, arriving in time for Sebastian's first day of a new school year. Putnam went back to Nashville with his wine. Buffett returned to Aspen with a few cases of '61 Bordeaux. *You Had to Be There* was released as a double album and reached number seventy-two on the albums chart just ahead of Buffett's thirty-second birthday, on Christmas Day 1978.

He'd released seven albums in six years that had produced one top-ten single. Not one of those albums had gone past number ten on the albums chart. James Taylor burped more hits in any given week. The Eagles could drop their guitars from their airplane and the wreckage would sneak into the top five. Radio hadn't been able to deny "Margaritaville," but after, it was like radio found the hole in the fence Buffett crawled through and patched it up.

The next career move, then, was obvious—at least if the career's under Irving Azoff's direction, which it was. He put Buffett in a movie about a radio station. When Cameron Crowe visited Azoff for his *Rolling Stone* profile, he accompanied Azoff to a meeting with executives at MCA/Universal Studios. Azoff's job was to strong-arm a May release for *FM*, his first executively produced film. Arriving in a borrowed BMW (Azoff owned a Bentley), he brought along a twenty-minute teaser that included performances by Linda Ronstadt, and Buffett. The assembled vice presidents of this and that were impressed, ecstatic. Then Azoff said he was going to take the film to another studio that would give him a spring release. He got his preferred place on MCA/Universal's calendar and Buffett was back on the big screen playing "Livingston Saturday Night," this time for the fictional QSKY's Save the Whales benefit.

QSKY was a little like WKWF under Corcoran—programmed by music fans for music fans. The fictional QSKY DJs had style and taste and freedom—until the Man, dressed in corporate interests, cracked down in the service of advertisers and a bigger bottom line. In protest, the DJs stage a sit in, listeners rally to the cause, the police are called, all hell breaks loose, and those corporate lackeys, observing the passion of so many dedicated music fans, realize how wrong they were. QSKY is saved. Roll end credits. Nice story.

Sitting in a Nashville studio in 2015, putting the finishing touches on four new songs, Keith Sykes remembers that era of radio, what it was, and what it was about to be. "Margaritaville," he says, came just in time for the fading era of a more freeform medium. "Rock music stations started to really kick in to the middle and late seventies," Sykes says. "They took over that segment, and pop music took over. The pop just played the pop, and the country just played the country."

And there was Jimmy Buffett, still without a genre and nothing like anything on the year-end chart. The Bee Gees had three of 1978's top-six singles, according to *Billboard* ("Night Fever," "Stayin' Alive," "How Deep is Your Love"), Andy Gibb grabbed the number-one and number-eight spots ("Shadow Dancing," "[Love Is] Thicker Than Water"). Debby Boone made the top-ten with

When the tour bus parked, the sails were unfurled. A year after buying the *Euphoria*, and with "Margaritaville" behind him, Buffett upgraded to the *Euphoria II*. At the helm in November 1977—a year after "Popps" and the Coral Reefer Band recorded *Changes in Latitudes, Changes in Attitudes* and changed the game. (© 2017 Tom Corcoran)

Buffett and Mac McAnally, his right hand musician and frequent golf partner, perform at the 2009 memorial service for Buffett's old friend, newsman Walter Cronkite. (Spencer Platt/POOL-CNP-PHOTOlink.net)

A little Texas in his heart. Buffett with Ray Wylie Hubbard, probably playing Hubbard's "Up Against the Wall Redneck Mother," at Mother Blues in Dallas in 1975. (Ronald McKeown)

Like "Margaritaville," the real "Cheeseburger in Paradise" is a state of mind. The 1978 Cheeseburger in Paradise tour, however, was quite real. Backstage at Miami Stadium before a show with Steve Miller and the Little River Band, Buffett (*still on crutches*), mugs with Keith Sykes (*center*) and the guy who started it all, Jerry Jeff Walker. (© 2017 Tom Corcoran)

Taking care of business, and business wasn't bad—even with only one minor hit to his résumé. Buffett checking the count after the show at Mother Blues in 1975. (Ronald McKeown)

Life would be full speed ahead soon enough. Buffett on Staniel Cay in the Bahamas in January 1977, the night he found out "Margaritaville" would be a hit. In a few days' time, he'd hit the road and leave his boat with his pal Larry "Groovy" Gray. (© 2017 Tom Corcoran)

They don't know. Or maybe they do. Buffett and producer Norbert Putnam hard, hard, hard at work on *Volcano* in May 1979 at George Martin's AIR Studios on the island of Montserrat. (© 2017 Tom Corcoran)

He had a thing for applause. Back in the States, the only thing that mattered were those ninety minutes onstage—and they better be right. Buffett, sweaty and hammering into a downbeat, onstage in 1977, a smoking-hot Coral Reefer Band backing him. (© 2017 Tom Corcoran)

Onstage, that cast was no blast, but off, it was just one more thing to laugh about. In a hotel room in San Francisco, 1978, about to turn in a piece on Antigua's Sailing Week to *Outside* magazine. (© 2017 Tom Corcoran)

Back when Jimmy Buffett could still rule his world from a payphone. The original Margaritaville Store, Key West, Florida. A partnership between Buffett and Sunshine Smith, it really was a ramshackle place. (© 2017 Tom Corcoran)

Around the corner from a theater named for Donny and Marie Osmond, and not far from a bar named after gangster Bugsy Siegel, you'll find the Margaritaville Casino, Las Vegas, Nevada. (Author's photo)

If a number one album packed with country stars wasn't enough of a sign Jimmy Buffett had finally conquered Nashville, along came the Margaritaville Café on Broadway. (Author's photo)

The Margaritaville Beach Resort in Hollywood Beach, Florida, rises above the Atlantic Ocean and, with an eye toward every detail, is anything but ramshackle. (Author's photo)

It's not the flip-flop and the pop-top that started it all, but it'll do for a tourist looking for a selfie or two. Hollywood Beach, Florida. (Author's photo)

Hangin' with Allen Toussaint. Buffett sat in with the maestro for his set at the New Orleans Jazz and Heritage Festival in 2011. What'd they play? Toussaint's "I'm Gonna Hang with Jimmy Buffett." (Jason Moore/ZUMAPRESS.com)

Some things never change. The only two people to play on every Jimmy Buffett album since 1973, Buffett and Michael Utley performing after the *Jurassic World* premiere in Los Angeles in 2015. (Matt Sayles/Invision/AP)

the syrupy "You Light Up My Life," and Buffett's old friends the Commodores got there with "Three Times a Lady."

Hard to see how "Cheeseburger in Paradise" finds a spotlight on that dance floor, even if it did inspire the munchies the way Buffett's "little island that's nowhere other than in your mind or the bottom of the Cuervo bottle"—as he put it on *You Had to Be There*—inspired thirst.

A lot of songs make you dance. Buffett's little hit (and "Cheeseburger") popularized the happy hour menu. Corcoran saw it and put it in that piece for *Crawdaddy*. People were drinking margaritas like they'd loved them from the beginning of time—since before Eve ate the apple and became the original woman to blame. They wanted to spend a few minutes—or a few hours, or a three-day vacation—living like they imagined Buffett lived. They weren't alone.

"In a way," Corcoran continued in *Crawdaddy*, "Jimmy Buffett appears to be adapting to his own lyrics."

He wasn't from New York or Los Angeles, and so he wasn't a creation of New York or Los Angeles. He might have moved his business people, but Buffett's sensibilities remained elsewhere.

Outside the power centers, in the towns and cities where Buffett had been making a living for most of the decade, he was . . . relatable, if also enviable. "He represented a lifestyle," Steve Diener says, perhaps with the benefit of hindsight, but maybe not.

Diener, who had replaced Jerry Rubinstein as the head of ABC Records, met Buffett once. After Buffett broke his leg the second time, necessitating surgery in Los Angeles, Diener went by the hospital for a visit. "Quiet, interesting guy," he says. "A real Florida Keys kind of guy . . . He was really an ambassador."

True to Don Light's maxim, Buffett built himself a job, but the need—for a Caribbean poet spinning palm trees and stiff drinks into middle-class fantasy—that was an accidental discovery, like stubbing your toe on a treasure chest left exposed by the tide.

"A lot of the pictures we took were goof-around pictures,"

Corcoran says. "It wasn't formal PR stuff, and that's what made Jimmy's reputation. He was a normal guy who looked like he was fuckin' off in the tropics. He was workin' his head off."

When they packaged *You Had to Be There*, Buffett pushed the work instead of the fantasy. He took himself off the boat and put himself on the road—just as he said he'd do. The list of antics detailed in the liner notes (signed in London) would have killed a lesser operation: Harry Dailey's naked hall meditation, Jay Spell introducing comedian Martin Mull to braille centerfolds, Deborah McColl and Fingers doing their Ike and Tina Turner impersonations in a Montana bar, Buffett helping Fingers rehang a hotel chandelier that had found the bathroom sink. Real rock-star stuff, but so was the view from the album sleeves.

Slid from the gatefold, they revealed hotel room views from sea to shining sea. Some were nice: the photo in New York toward Central Park, or a cove full of boats at anchor in Miami. Others were interesting: the scene in Los Angeles highlighted by billboards for a new Hall & Oates record and for *Hustler* magazine, "For those who think pink." Sometimes, Corcoran would open the curtains and see nothing but another building staring back. He snapped away, the banality as much a part of Buffett's life as *Euphoria II* rocking gently in Gustavia Harbor in St. Barts. *You Had to Be There* was, in its imagery, as authentic a document as *A1A*.

"He was Dad," McColl says. "Throughout all the craziness, Jimmy was the one who would maintain functionality. He could moderate unlike a lot of us, and he kept the ship running."

One afternoon at a hotel on Key Biscayne, Corcoran had a question for Buffett. He padded down the hall, knocked on the door. Buffett opened, but the door was chained.

"Oh, it's you," he said. "You can come in. You can keep your mouth shut."

The door shut and Corcoran heard the chain sliding free.

"And I'm thinking, *What am I going to see in there? Fifteen-*

year-old triplets from Lauderdale?" he says. Nope. "On every horizontal surface there were stacks of receipts and he was doing the paperwork to send to L.A. to Frontline Management. He said, 'This would ruin my reputation entirely,' but he was doing it. The bills got paid. Everything tax wise and all that stuff. He was meticulous, and he said, 'Don't tell anyone you saw this.' And he was seventy-five-percent serious. He knew it sounded ridiculous, but it was true."

Utley laughs when he hears that story. "He still says that when he's exercising," Utley says. "Or when he goes to bed at 9:30." And that happens.

Buffett had hired Marshall Gelfand as an accountant, the same guy Putnam used. Putnam talks about Gelfand being born a hundred years old and how every year he'd make the rounds to see his clients and go line-by-line through the accounting, raising an eyebrow at various and questionable sundries. In the *Son of a Son* liner notes, Buffett thanked Gelfand for "keeping me out of debtors prison," an Old World, semipiratical way of saying he had good people—an eye for talent and the smarts to let them help him be him.

But it's like Don Light said: Buffett knew how to make people think what he wanted them to think. And it wasn't hard to play the part.

When *Rolling Stone's* Chet Flippo called to propose an interview with Buffett in May 1979, Buffett gave him easy directions: "Fly to St. Maarten and charter a boat or a plane to St. Barts. Wait for me at Le Select bar."

Not everything had changed since Light called the Chart Room to find his client. Buffett, however, never materialized at Le Select. Flippo found him harbor side with the Coral Reefer Band at another bar, laughing about the band getting its first suntan and tossing a pile of money on the table for the tab while asking Flippo where he'd been. Buffett saw the plane from St. Maarten land hours before.

They bounced from bar to boat to pizza joint to after-hours disco, encountering horny women, suspicious men, and a population of hippies with "lots of money and no visible means of support," Flippo wrote. He described Buffett as a rake and a rogue and as having been adopted by the locals. "He is *theirs*—he used to run a little marijuana through the islands himself," Flippo wrote, codifying myth as fact° in the pages of America's premier rock magazine. Rock star status was cemented later when Buffett picked up the phone and called Azoff collect to tell him to send someone from Bayshore Recording Studios in Coconut Grove to St. Barts with $2,000 cash and a dozen Ping-Pong balls.

"Tonight we'll be able to play Ping-Pong," he said after he hung up. He and Flippo then headed off for more beer. Aboard the *Euphoria II*, there was a photo of Jimmy and Jimmy (Carter) in the Oval Office, a freshly rolled joint and tape of the album in progress, *Volcano*, which Buffett and the Reefers were taking a break from recording on the nearby island of Montserrat. George Martin had opened a studio there to complement his London operation.

"Next thing I know," Putnam says, "Jimmy's down on his sailboat and he calls me, 'Hey! Norbert! I'm in a helicopter. I'm flying over Montserrat. I just had lunch with George Martin.'"

Putnam called Azoff: "Book Montserrat."

Azoff booked Montserrat—for three weeks.

"We went to St. Croix on a big plane, and from there we took small planes, three or four that he had rented to get us to . . ." Keith Sykes says, trailing off, trying to remember just how they all got to Montserrat.

He's sure his wife arrived near the end of the sessions, because they were going to stay for a few extra days. As he waited for her

---

° So much myth as fact that when Buffett returned to St. Barts after *Rolling Stone* hit newsstands, he was detained by the local authorities. "Me and my big mouth," he told *Time*'s Eric Pooley in 1998. "I had never been a dope dealer; I was just hangin' out in bars, tryin' to be cool."

to arrive, Martin was waiting to depart. "It was me and George Martin and I was cool for about fifteen seconds and then I couldn't do it," Sykes says. "TELL ME EVERYTHING ABOUT THE BEATLES!" he blurted.

But as for how they got to Montserrat, "I know we took small planes from St. Croix to . . . St. Somewhere maybe." It was the time of St. Somewhere, another island Buffett invented, somewhere warm and more inviting than the cold night in Boston, where "Boat Drinks" was written after tossing back a few in Boston Bruins center Derek Sanderson's bar.

Over the years, "boat drink" has become a generic term for anything tropical, and usually frozen. The original? "I think it's rum and Perrier, as Jimmy defined it," McColl says.

If Martin's presence wasn't enough, Beatles engineer Geoff Emerick signed on for the sessions, which gave Putnam a chance to lose *his* cool: "HOW DID YOU ACTUALLY GET THAT PAUL McCARTNEY BASS SOUND?"

"Norbert," Putnam says, this time effecting a distant-but-polite British accent, "Couldn't this possibly wait until we have cocktails later?"

Or after a round at the nine-hole Montserrat Golf Club, the clubhouse raised on stilts and the staff dressed in military uniform. "This was a scene out of a Kipling movie," Putnam says. "It was like something left over from English aristocracy."

Corcoran got the call to get his camera back down to the Caribbean, pick the *Euphoria II* up in St. Barts, and get it to Montserrat. James Taylor and his brothers were coming, and Buffett wanted to show her off. When Corcoran arrived in Montserrat, he joined Buffett and the band for brunch on a cliff overlooking the bay where *Euphoria II* was anchored.

They'd been at work five or six days already and they'd cooked up something Buffett wanted Corcoran to hear. The engineer cued up "Fins." Cowbell filled the studio, followed by Barry Chance's strutting guitar riff chasing Utley's keyboard work around the intro. "I went, 'Oh crap, I'm going to have to pretend to like a rock-and-roll song,'" Corcoran says. "Because I really like Jimmy's ballads—to this day. So I gritted my teeth and I kind of grinned and nodded."

Then he heard a line he recognized about a woman keeping an eye out for sharks lurking in the local bar. "Well shit, he didn't even write that," Corcoran thought. "I've heard that before." As it occurred to him *where* he'd heard it, he looked up and Buffett was flashing ten fingers, as in 10 percent of the song. Corcoran said he'd take it.

They were (partially) Corcoran's lyrics. The story begins in Key West, and the sharks weren't originally sharks. They were Eagles. He was home one night worrying about the bills he was having a hard time paying. He thought about Buffett on his way to millionaire status and figured if his pal could write those songs, he could write those songs.

"The genesis of the song came from Jimmy and Joe Walsh joking about hanging out with Frey and Henley in Coconut Grove," Corcoran says. They'd hit the bar, usually Eagles bassist Timothy B. Schmit would be along as well, and Frey and Henley would be immediately consumed. "Every lovely woman in Miami was hanging there waiting to be anointed," Corcoran says, "and Walsh and Buffett were the ugly guys in the corner."

Corcoran scribbled a few lines at home, and then the phone rang. Whatever it was, it took him away from writing and he forgot about it until Buffett called and told him to pack for Sail Week in Antigua. Corcoran was doing that when he saw the paper, tossed it in his duffle bag, and forgot about it a second time. In the middle of a race from Antigua to Guadalupe, Corcoran was rifling through his bag when he found the lyric and read it to Buffett. Buffett took it and stuffed it in his journal.

Chance must have picked up his writing credit for the guitar riff, and McColl doesn't remember what she contributed. She'd been planning to spend some time with a dive instructor on St. Barts, and so that might have translated to "roll in the sand with a rock and roll man," or, as the lone woman in the operation, she might have been the only girl in town. McColl hadn't come from Cincinnati, as had the woman in the song, but that was as good a city as any to depart for the Caribbean from.

Working on Montserrat was exactly as you'd imagine. They had a pool, and there was the golf club, and another bar was set up in the studio. One of the Taylor brothers took to making pitchers of martinis. "I remember waking up one morning to Fingers and James Taylor walking through my room saying, 'We've lost James's brain. We think it fell in the pool,'" McColl says.

Volcano's title track was written late in what they called recording camp. "One day Keith Sykes came into our house strumming his little Martin, singing the chorus," Buffett wrote in *The Parrot Head Handbook*.

"I don't remember that happening," Sykes says. "What happened to me, my side of it was I had gone to the volcano to see the thing."

He grabbed a golf cart and drove as far as he could up Montserrat's Soufriére Hills volcano, the one responsible for turning the island's beaches black. "I'd never seen that before," he says. He got to the top and his jaw dropped. "There's nothing but this yellow earth with steam screaming out of it," he says. He went back to the studio and told Buffett, who said, "Well, we're going tomorrow."

The next day they went back and played. The steam slashing from vents condensed to form a small river, maybe a foot wide, running off the mountain and down to the ocean. Fifty yards (give or take) from where the river began, they found the water had cooled enough to touch. They built a small dam and splashed at each other. "We went back to the studio smelling like two 150-pound blocks of sulfur," Sykes says. They wrote "Volcano" in about fifteen minutes. They recorded it the next day with a group of local musicians they'd been hanging out with, the Woop-Wap Band, lending a hand. Because the locals played everything in F, Buffett and Sykes wrote their new song in the same key.

"I remember singing, 'I don't know, I don't know,' and Jimmy said, 'Where I'm a gonna go . . .'" Sykes says. "And then we just started trading lines . . . I mean, that's the fastest I've worked on anything. I'm still working on stuff I started in 1968."

"Survive" didn't go back that far, but it went back. Buffett had been listening to Billy Joel and, much the way Corcoran figured he could write a Buffett song, Buffett figured he could write a Billy Joel tune. So he and Utley wrote a pretty piano ballad, and then lost it. Corcoran found it on a demo while cleaning up the boat.

"I plugged it in and I said, 'Well that never got recorded. That's not on *Son of a Sailor*,'" Corcoran says. "So I figure, okay, that's gonna be on the next record, and then it wasn't. It wasn't on the live album. I said, 'Whatever happened to "Survive"? You were working on that for *Son of Sailor*?' And he said, 'I fucking forgot it. Utley! I forgot, "Survive."'"

"Treat Her Like a Lady" was an ode to the ocean, and the respect she deserves, written with Dave Loggins who, according to the liner notes, appeared "courtesy of a bottle of Cristal Champagne."

"Stranded on a Sandbar" sounded a lot like contentment, the self-defined "jester" admitting that while he hadn't found the answers others had by their early thirties, he was "stuck in this fairly nice maze."

"Chanson Pour Les Petits Enfants" translates to "song for little children," the kids in this case being a couple of friends who rowed up to the *Euphoria II* with coffee and croissants the morning after she had arrived in St. Barts. Both the caffeine and the food, Buffett has said often, were most welcome after the previous night's revelry.

The kids, young Mr. Moon and Magnus, soar "through the Milky Way counting the stars, once around Venus, twice around Mars" in what's a sweet little fairy tale—the kind Buffett might play beside the bassinet in Aspen he was trying to figure out how to assemble in "Dreamsicle."

That was a self-portrait, one in which the jester refers to himself as an "overnight sensation" suddenly equipped with "house pets, Lear jets" and a baby on the way. On June 1, 1979, a few weeks after the *Volcano* sessions were complete, Jimmy and Jane welcomed a daughter, Savannah Jane Buffett.

It was possible to see "Survive" as a sequel to "Come Monday," the biggest obstacle between man and woman being distance one more time. Though he gets there. The clouds break and he's looking down on the Rocky Mountains, and it's good to be home. "Let's drink champagne till we break into smiles," Buffett sings.

Jane remained in the background, just beyond the frame—an inspiration for songs, sometimes a cowriter, a pretty-good photographer, and coconspirator (though often unnamed). "Lady I Can't Explain" celebrated her style, and was something of an apology for Buffett's. With "the imagination of a child" fueling the heart of a "hopeless romantic," there was bound to be trouble. But he meant well, and she'd forgive him. "Still you won't let me live some of these episodes down," he sang. And maybe that was what made it work.

When it came time to record "Sending the Old Man Home," a salute to a retiring naval officer, Buffett wanted to sing it with James Taylor. Putnam talked his way in on a bass, because he wanted to be able to say he'd played with Taylor.

Buffett and Corcoran went back up the volcano to shoot some pictures, Buffett taking a seat next to a vent, pointing into the volcano. Then he grabbed the camera and snapped one of Corcoran. When the volcano did indeed blow in 1995, Corcoran thought about that photo and how, in geologic time, it'd only been a second or two since he and Buffett had been goofing off on Soufriére Hills. One more near(ish) miss, and another good story.

The record finished, it was time to go home. Almost. "We're saying good-bye to the kids in the office, I remember one of the girls said, 'Uh, Mr. Putnam and Mr. Buffett, there's just one thing,'" Putnam says. "And we said, 'What's that?'"

"Well, sir," she said. "We're not allowed to charge your bar bill."

"How much is that?"

"That'll be $9,000," she said.

Putnam doesn't remember how they paid. They didn't have $9,000 in cash, and there wasn't time to call management and have more flown in. Buffett's Rolex was in play at some point, but he held onto the watch. Most likely, Putnam says, their savior was American Express.

They took the tapes and flew them off the island. *Volcano* was released in the fall of 1979 and, like all Buffett's recent albums, sold well, pushing to number fourteen. And like all his recent singles, radio wasn't interested. The cover featured a Richard Bibby painting of a lush island marked by a steaming volcano. On the back cover, they used Corcoran's photo of Buffett smiling and pointing toward the venting steam. At the bottom of the shot, three simple words: "Ain't Life Grand."

Not long after the album hit stores, Jimmy Buffett, looking faded as dusk, was found grinning on the cover of *Rolling Stone*.

"Yer all right, Buffett," Flippo said to him in the story. "I understand you're accidentally rich."

Not as accidentally as he made it look, but he wore the lucky beach bum shtick well, and the Coral Reefer Band enjoyed the ride as they went back on the road.

"You had a lobby call at a really nice hotel," Sykes says. "Limos to take you to the private plane that took you to the next limo that took you to the hotel and then took you to the gig. The joke was, 'Gee, I've got to walk all the way from the plane to the limo? Damn!'"

Chapter 15

A Ramshackle Place

As a favor, Kris Kristofferson once asked a talent agent named Bert Block to represent Putnam. Putnam was getting into producing, and producers' deals are easy, but Block had power. Aside from Kristofferson, Block represented Billie Holiday, Miles Davis, Thelonious Monk, Lenny Bruce, Bob Dylan.

Block told Putnam, "I'll help you make your first contracts, but I'm going to set you up with a great attorney, David Braun." Braun represented Dylan, George Harrison, Neil Diamond, and eventually, Michael Jackson.

"So the next day I'm sitting at lunch with the great Braun," Putnam says. "He takes me to a wonderful Japanese restaurant, we're having tempura, and he says, 'Norbert, a couple things I'll pass on to you from my experience now that you're going to be a producer. You're going to meet a lot of talented young people and they're going to have a great song, and a lot of them are going to be what we call one-hit wonders. And you know why? They simply don't have the intellect to deal with becoming a businessman.'"

Here's how the great Braun put it down: A musician works for years on his or her music. He or she will spend 90 percent of the time writing, playing, performing, perfecting. Along comes that coveted record deal and a producer like, say, Norbert Putnam.

They go in the studio and make a hit. The record company pushes the song. The road calls.

"What's he doing?" Braun asked Putnam. "He's doing concerts. He's dealing with his manager, his lawyer, his accountant. He's now a businessman. Music's now ten percent of his life."

How does he handle that? How does she handle that? How would Putnam handle that? "Part of this is I'm evaluating Norbert Putnam," Braun told him. "I want to see if you're a broad, wide guy, or a narrow little music guy."

Braun's point: See what an artist is about. Go to dinner. Talk food. Talk art. Talk film and literature and politics. Talk complicated subjects that have nothing to do with the job on the table. Before Putnam gives too much of his time and his effort, see what's really there. Putnam could help make a hit record, but what would happen next?

"I watched it happen two or three times over the next ten years," Putnam says. "Usually, it was a kid who grew up in a rural environment or the mountains."

Tony Joe White, he says. Tony Joe White had a huge hit with "Polk Salad Annie," and Putnam played bass on it. Tony Joe ended up on *The Johnny Cash Show* and was endearingly awkward as he and Cash sat down to sing. "He didn't really want to make the moves to be a big star," Putnam says.

Dave Loggins was another. Putnam played bass on "Please Come to Boston," the song that (probably) kept "Come Monday" out of the top ten. "Please Come to Boston" was nominated for a Grammy, and Loggins went to Los Angeles and took a seat near Stevie Wonder, and when he came back to Nashville and saw Putnam he said, "I didn't belong there."

"No, David," Putnam remembers saying. "You belonged there."

After that, Loggins went back over to Knoxville, Tennessee and didn't want to tour. The record company didn't want to promote his record. Immensely talented, both Loggins and Tony Joe White have written fantastic songs and had fantastic careers, but they've been under-the-radar, beloved-by-those-who-know-them, "hey, isn't he the guy who did that one song?" careers.

Putnam took Braun seriously. At Quadraphonic, the receptionist—her name was Cookie; they called her Smart Cookie, he says—was instructed to make people wait, to give them a cup of coffee and strike up a conversation about any of those things that weren't music.

When Buffett and Putnam went to dinner at Julian's in 1976 and sat by the fire and talked about working together, Putnam was working out Buffett the way Braun had run Putnam through the drill. He was pretty sure he had Buffett pegged.

"What's that line?" he says, smiling and turning to "Changes in Latitudes, Changes in Attitudes," the song Buffett wrote shortly after their dinner. " 'If it suddenly ended tomorrow, I could somehow adjust to the fall?' "

Putnam doesn't know for sure, but he doesn't think the record company ever again got behind Buffett the way they got behind "Margaritaville." Steve Resnik, who'd been in ABC's promotions department, says it was frustrating for everyone. They were disappointed they were never able to turn any of the follow-ups into hits.

"He was too unique," says Steve Diener, the former president of ABC Records. "He was him. He was that unique. You just gave it up. You gave up comparing him."

The age of singer-songwriters gave way to disco and punk, and then along came the eighties. Ray Wylie Hubbard remembers the impact the 1980 film *Urban Cowboy* had on outlaw country, which was the label the marketing folks finally settled on for what Willie, Waylon, and the boys were up to in Nashville and Texas. Overnight, every yuppie in America had a cowboy hat and boots and knew a line dance. Every bar wanted a mechanical bull. He'd fly into Philadelphia, show up at the club, and the first question was, "Do you play 'Cotton Eyed Joe'?"

"It was about this scene," Hubbard says. "It was like a Hula Hoop or a pet rock. It wasn't about music. It went a little wacky then."

MCA Records bought ABC Records; Diener moved on. New management meant new staffs, and in record business years, Buffett was centuries from the day Don Gant signed him and Don Light said they'd keep to the contract even though Gant couldn't promise much support. Buffett had still made a lot of people money. It wasn't fast or easy, but they'd all done well. He'd built an audience, and that audience couldn't have been genre dependent because he didn't have one, right? Why would a new decade or changing tastes change that?

In September 1980, to follow up *Volcano*, Buffett and the Coral Reefers went north to Alabama and the "Hit Recording Capital of the World," as the sign into Muscle Shoals proclaimed.

The most famous spots are still there. One call from Putnam scores a tour of FAME Recording Studios, where history is a wall of framed photos between Studios A and B. Wilson Pickett standing behind organist Spooner Oldham. Percy Sledge. The Allman Brothers. That's where Aretha Franklin sang, "I Never Loved a Man," and where Pickett put down "Mustang Sally."

Another call from Putnam opens the door to the original Muscle Shoals Sound, at 3614 Jackson Highway, where the Swampers set up shop after leaving FAME, where the Rolling Stones cut "Brown Sugar" and "Wild Horses."

Around FAME, Muscle Shoals has grown into every American city: fast food restaurants and chain drug stores and strip malls galore. There isn't much around Muscle Shoals Sound. There never has been. A few things haven't changed. You still can't get a beer if you hit town on a Sunday night. "Honey," the waitress will say, "it's Sunday in Alabama."

Putnam, standing in the gravel lot next to Muscle Shoals Sound, cicadas singing in surround sound, points to the big mistake. The town never built the amenities the big stars wanted. A lot of people recorded there once, he says. Muscle Shoals Sound was turned into a museum* and the town became, in its way, a one-hit wonder. There were good reasons Putnam and David Briggs went to Nashville.

"We were the first musicians to stay," Swamper David Hood says. "My father was a small businessman and had a tire store and he was expecting me to finish with a degree in marketing and retailing and take over the store and become the tire king of north Alabama."

Instead, like Putnam, Hood picked up the bass. He worked out of FAME. He worked out of 3614 Jackson Highway. He and the Swampers, immortalized in "Sweet Home Alabama," bought a building down by the Tennessee River that had housed a naval reserve training center. Before that, it had been a steam plant powering streetcars. The first time Hood set foot in the place was as a kid, to help his sister hang decorations for a dance. The first time he saw a rock band was in that building. He first saw one of Putnam's bands in that building.

"Built two great studios in there," Hood says. "We were very proud. We'd left this little place we were in." That little place, again, being the original and legendary Muscle Shoals Sound, but when you live history, you're allowed to be casual about history.

Buffett and the Coral Reefers set up in the new Muscle Shoals Sound to make *Coconut Telegraph*. "The first thing, they set up the bar," Hood says. "There was *everything* there. As a rule, none of us drank while we were working, and so it was a *full* bar. We were kind of surprised by that."

The rest of the time, it was a recording session. Buffett wrote again with Loggins ("Island") and J. D. Souther ("The Good Fight," which came dedicated to Muhammad Ali). He dedicated

---

* Though in 2009, the Black Keys resurrected the studio to record *Brothers*, the first album recorded there in thirty years.

"Incommunicado" to John Wayne and John D. MacDonald's aspirational boat bum, Travis McGee.

"Coconut Telegraph" captured the hum of gossip on an island. It was a seven-day news cycle beginning Sunday morning, fading by midweek, and then firing up with another weekend. "Growing Older but Not Up" covered broken legs, manatees, and a lot of wishful thinking.

"Lip balm!" Buffett shouted at the beginning of "The Weather Is Here, Wish You Were Beautiful," engaging the cry that brought tour manager Liberman running. "Jimmy can I open the show in Atlanta, please?" said McColl, echoing what she'd said plenty of times before. "Don't ever start a band," Buffett roared. The song itself was another about running away to the islands and running away from it all.

"Little Miss Magic" was a sweet little song for his little girl—"The Noop," as Buffett had nicknamed Savannah Jane—"constantly amazed by the blades of the fan on the ceiling."

When Juan Thompson was working his memoir, *Stories I Tell Myself*, about growing up as Hunter Thompson's kid, he asked Buffett how that 1977 trip through the Bahamas happened, because even to Juan it was strange his parents would take him from school and send him away on a sailboat for a month with Jimmy Buffett.

"Like all of us back then, we were not that equipped to be responsible parents, and I think that bothered him," Buffett, speaking of Hunter, told Juan. "It bothered me. "

His had been, and would continue to be, a nomadic existence. Savannah Jane's birth certificate was pretty quickly followed with a passport. He'd written "Little Miss Magic" in Le Select on St. Barts, where she'd eventually learn a little French over pinball. That bar, Buffett wrote in *A Pirate Looks at Fifty*, "was our version of daycare."

Savannah Jane saw the world early, and Buffett was probably better tooled than Hunter for the job of Dad. Anyone who can write as innocently as he did in "Chanson Pour Les Petits Enfants" has to have some parental chops. He had to run off on tour, but when he came home, "He was just the pancake guy," Savannah Jane said in 2008, grabbing the microphone while her father spoke and performed for an audience at Google's headquarters in Northern California.

"But it worked, right?" Buffett said, speaking more of the "nomadic existence" than the pancakes, though he takes pride in those, too. His best songs have always been the songs he was closest to, and "Little Miss Magic" counts on that list.

"It's My Job" was written by Mac McAnally, "who reminds me of me seven years ago," Buffett wrote in the dedication. As a writer, anyway. McAnally wasn't ever as dedicated to those certain indecencies as Buffett.

He grew up Baptist, in a small northern Mississippi town called Belmont that's bisected by State Highway 25. One long hot summer years ago, he got a job laying asphalt on that highway. He wore Converse sneakers his first day and they'd melted off his feet by lunch.

"It dawned on me I had a job that sucked," McAnally said in a 2015 interview on Dave Hoekstra's WGN Radio show. "And I started thinking about work, and most people do—most people have jobs that suck to some varying degree. And I thought about that for a while and ended up thinking even though it sucked, I still seemed to pass the time a little quicker if I did my best, if I tried to do my best."

As it happened, McAnally was quite a bit better at music than roadwork. "I met Mac at Wishbone Studios, which was another studio in town," David Hood says. "He had a pair of bib overalls on. Some of the people said, 'You've got to hear this new guy.' Mac sat down and played a couple of songs and just blew everybody away with his singing and his playing and the humor and his songs."

They weren't just any overalls. They were a hand-me-down

pair from his grandfather. Mac was tall, with a helmet of red hair and a bushy red beard almost burying cherubic cheeks. He had then, as now, a quiet manner, a quick wit, a deep Southern timbre, and he went to the studio when Buffett recorded "It's My Job," just as Buffett had gone to see the Glaser Brothers record "Tin Cup Chalice," but it wasn't the first time they met. That was in Philadelphia. McAnally was playing a club. Buffett was playing a basketball arena. "One is basically a pickup truck bed compared to the other," McAnally says.

Choosing songs to record, McAnally says, Buffett looks for things he loves, but maybe couldn't have written—for whatever reason. People pitch him drinking songs all the time. He can write those whenever he wants. "It's My Job" cast the street sweeper beside a bank president beside a rock star, and put them on equal footing.

At Google, Savannah Jane talked about how Buffett's role as Dad, as the Pancake Guy—"and French toast," she added—was humbling. The night before he might have been onstage, worshiped. And that wouldn't matter at all if he burned breakfast.

Buffett had a few lousy jobs, but Mac had stood on that blistering asphalt. Buffett's grandfather passed on fantastic stories from faraway places. Mac's passed down overalls and, one assumes, more than a little wisdom.

When the "imagination of a child" Buffett claimed in "Lady I Can't Explain" takes him to the heavens, McAnally's there to remind him of small towns and Mississippi blacktop. They make a good team.

When *Coconut Telegraph* arrived in early 1981, Buffett stood alone on the cover, not on an island and not in Muscle Shoals. He wasn't anywhere exotic. He was back where he came from, standing in a phone booth at the foot of a pier stretching into Mobile Bay.

Buffett was wearing a sweater, long pants, and loafers. Corcoran shot it in Fairhope, Alabama, on a private estate where Winston Groom was staying in a nearby cottage finishing *Forrest Gump.**

Corcoran got the phone booth from a guy who made decorative phone booths. The guy was also a big Elvis fan. So big he'd once waited forever to get the first tickets to a show in Mobile. To thank him, Elvis summoned him backstage. "Shook his hand and he gave him a ring," Corcoran says. "This enormous, gaudy-ass ring. The guy wanted to thank Elvis by making him a phone booth." It isn't visible on the album cover, but the booth Buffett's standing in features the ring's design etched in glass. Elvis died before it could be delivered.

Coconut Telegraph stalled out at number thirty on *Billboard*'s albums chart. "It's My Job" hit number fifty-seven on the pop chart and number thirty-two on the adult contemporary chart. A year later, in February 1982, *Somewhere Over China*, recorded at Putnam's new studio, the Bennett House, in Franklin, Tennessee, did about the same as *Coconut Telegraph*, rising to number thirty-one.

Buffett offered "late night thanks to the makers of Moët Et Chandon Champagne and Rolaids," and dedicated the album to his *Billboard* mentor, Bill Williams, "who told me a long time ago that he knew that I knew that I could."

The record's best song, "I Heard I Was in Town" came from an overheard conversation about a night he'd spent drinking in Key West with someone he'd never met before in his life. The guy everyone wanted to drink with had become the guy everyone said they'd had a drink with—whether they had or not.

The most interesting song is "Where's the Party," written with Steve Goodman and Bill LaBounty. For the first time in his career, Jimmy Buffett sounded . . . almost tired. Like he'd run out of answers and maybe even lost the line of questioning. Every night

---

* Corcoran shot Groom's author photo for *Forrest Gump*. When Corcoran got his advance copy of the book, he gifted it to Jimmy's mom.

was another night in another town and everybody was looking for the party. "Why should I get all dressed up when there's no place to go?" he wondered.

And then: "Sometimes I wish the radio would learn another song."

Five years (and as many albums) since "Margaritaville," Jimmy Buffett was still the man from "Margaritaville."

Inspired by Sean Penn's forever-stoned surfer, Jeff Spicoli, Buffett contributed, "I Don't Know (Spicoli's Theme)," to the Azoff-produced *Fast Times at Ridgemont High*. He signed a deal with Miller beer and recorded a jingle. At a show in Irvine, California, in the summer of 1982, responding to a request to sing the commercial, Buffett said, "Yeah, we'll do the commercial, yeah! That was the closest thing I've had to a fucking hit in five years! Here you go. You ask for it, you get it."

In the style of a Jimmy Buffett song—bouncy and light—his agent pleading for him to take a meeting because there was a big contract on the table, Buffett sings that he has "no aversion to striking it rich," *but* it was a nice day down by the ocean. He'd think it all over, over a beer.

To his *Somewhere Over China* notes, Buffett appended a quote from an old favorite: "It's young people who put life into ritual by making conventions a living part of life," William Faulkner wrote in *Mosquitoes*. "Only old people destroy life by making it a ritual."

It's possible ritual—or routine—had crept up on Buffett's. He sold the *Euphoria II*, because he couldn't justify the expense. The road called, and the family was waiting at home. "If I could just get it on paper, I might make some sense of it all," he sang. The implication being he couldn't. "Somewhere Over China," set a "seminormal person" in an exceptional situation. With $100,000 from "some silly sweepstakes" he fled to the other side of the world without a thought or a care. But "Somewhere Over China" sounds a lot more like wishing than knowing, a trip to China as likely as the final-verse fantasy of piloting the Space Shuttle.

Aside from wine and art and architecture, Putnam had some literary heroes of his own. He thought *Somewhere Over China* was the best sounding record he and Buffett made. He wasn't as thrilled with the songs. (Here he adds that he's never written a hit in his life.)

Putnam told Buffett he should take a year off and travel. "He said, 'I can't do that; are you kidding?'" Putnam says. He reminded Buffett about W. Somerset Maugham, Putnam's favorite short-story writer. "Maugham had written wonderful stories about the South Pacific.

"I said, 'Buffett, when you write about the real event, no one is better.' I reminded him of 'Margaritaville.' That's the greatest song he ever wrote. And it's all true, right? I said, 'Why don't you be Maugham and go through the South Seas?

"'Norbert, I don't have time for that shit,' Buffett said."

A few weeks later, Buffett called Putnam and said he thought they'd run out of steam together. Putnam agreed, and without a single regret. "You know, I worked with Ray Charles, Elvis Presley, with the Beatles," Putnam says. "I worked during the golden age of American music. So many of us who followed in Sam Phillips's footsteps bumped into the greatest artists of a twenty-, thirty-year period. I couldn't be happier about bumping into Jimmy Buffett."

Between his final albums with Putnam, and after years of threatening, Buffett finally gave up the Waddell Avenue apartment. In Corcoran's 1977 *Crawdaddy* story, Buffett had been ready to pull the trigger then, but after another perfect day in Key West, he wrote the Spottswoods a check for six months' rent. "That damn apartment might tell on me after I was gone, anyway," Buffett told Corcoran.

To make sure *that* didn't happen, he dispatched Corcoran to clean it out, telling him not to worry about the furniture (Jane had sold it), grab anything he wanted as thanks, and then box up everything that wouldn't embarrass him and ship it to his parents in Alabama.

"There was a Waring blender," Corcoran says, "and I said, 'Oh, *the* blender.' Took it home. This is how brilliant I was. Judy plugged it in and got a shock. Did I ever think it could be repaired? No. I threw it away. The original Margaritaville—if anybody ever tries to sell it on eBay, no—I threw the damn thing away because it shocked Judy when she plugged it in. I can still see her doing it."

Corcoran held on to some of the handwritten lyrics he found, including an original draft of "Woman Goin' Crazy on Caroline Street," from *Havana Daydreamin'*, one quite a bit darker than the album version. The woman is desperately dancing with a sailor in the bar when "he winks and holds her dress up high behind her, so the boys can see the blue veins in her thighs." Then comes the fight, and she's left crying, shouting out how they're all sons of bitches.

Corcoran was going to see Buffett in Los Angeles and meant to take it along to have him sign it and then Corcoran would have it framed. He forgot the lyrics, but mentioned them to Buffett, who got a funny look. "Yellow long legal pad?" Buffett said.

"Yes."

"It's not my handwriting," he said.

Corcoran had come across Shel Silverstein's original poem— the reason Silverstein had initially been given a cowriting credit on the song. Silverstein lived in Key West and wrote a number of hilarious Key West songs, "The Great Conch Train Robbery" among them. Corcoran says Buffett took "Woman Goin' Crazy on Caroline Street" to Chicago and played it for Steve Goodman, who loved it but said Buffett couldn't record it. Too dark. Perfect for Shel. Hell, it would have been perfect for McGuane or Harrison. But not Buffett. So Buffett and Goodman went to work revising. When they were done, Silverstein nodded his approval and said it was theirs. "He knew," Corcoran says of Buffett. "He knew he had to please an audience with a lot of women in it. And Goodman was smart enough to know, too."

Darkness—sadness—was one more genre where Buffett didn't fit, and definitely not when women were involved. He had, after all, grown up with Peets breaking office barriers and never backing down from a challenge. He had sisters and a daughter. Jane's influence kept him on track. He was a sentimental romantic, not a boor. He could write "Please Take Your Girlfriend Home," but he didn't put it on the album, and even then, by the end of the song, the girlfriend has the upper hand and he's the butt of the joke.

He knew who he was. What he needed to figure out was where his career was going. Buffett needed a spark, a jolt, an enthusiasm. Even with songs about China and Rio and the adventures of Lester Polyester in the biggest little city of Reno, *Somewhere Over China* felt stationary, as if its geography was pulled from travel books instead of travel.

More than the big drunken party, Buffett's records had always benefited from their worldliness. He needed a change or two. Producer was one. Then he talked Michael Utley into the band full-time.

Utley had continued working with Kristofferson and Rita Coolidge. Coolidge had cut "(Your Love Has Lifted Me) Higher and Higher," the song Jackie Wilson popularized in 1967, and her version had gone to number two in 1977, around the same time "Margaritaville" was everywhere. Kristofferson had gone to Hollywood and was doing more and more acting, which meant less and less touring.

"It wasn't easy to quit Kris, but he was doing so many movies, there wasn't a lot of work," Utley says. Dan Fogelberg had been dangling a job, but he kept pushing off a tour, and Buffett was on the phone asking Utley to not only play, but help produce and help write—to be part of the creative team. It wasn't any easier to call Fogelberg than it had been to call Kristofferson, but the opportunity with Buffett made too much sense.

"As musical careers happen, there's ebbs, there's ups, and downs, for Jimmy and everyone I worked with," Utley says. "You spike and it goes back down and you have to reinvent yourself. That stimulates your career."

Where did they look for inspiration? Well, Putnam's wife called him into the living room one day. Buffett was on television talking about the South Pacific and how many great stories there were scattered in those islands. "I said, 'Fuck you! You son of a bitch!'" Putnam says, breaking into laughter. "No. No. No."

Like Maugham, like Twain in *Following the Equator*, Buffett and Utley set out for Tahiti. "It *is* a long way over there," Buffett told the *Miami Herald*'s Frederick Burger in October 1982. "That's why I like it. I've been to Tahiti for six weeks on two trips this year, and I'm going back in January."

He might not have had the time when Putnam first suggested the far side of the world, but something had changed. Buffett and Jane had separated. "I'd been with Jimmy since I was a child, through the craziest times," she told *Time* in 1998, "and I didn't have a clue who I was. So I left. I got sober."

Buffett would crash in Los Angeles with Liberman, who suggests having Jimmy Buffett as your roommate was a pretty good deal. Then they'd jet to the other side of the world. "We were staying on an island called Moorea, and Jimmy sent me into Tahiti to find Tahitian girls to sing the background," Liberman says. "Once again, I'm thinking, *This is the greatest job in the world.*"

Liberman found the Tahitian singers to accent "One Particular Harbour," the title track of Buffett's 1983 album that included a lasting cover of Van Morrison's "Brown Eyed Girl" and the introduction of two characters to Buffett's world.

The first came from a story the Monkees' Mike Nesmith told Buffett, about a guy he'd encountered in Mexico who would fish all week and then on the weekend power a blender with a generator and a Sears DieHard battery. They'd make margaritas and sing Jimmy Buffett songs. "Twelve Volt Man" was born.

The other character, in the vein of ol' Marvin Gardens, was Francis "Frank" Fitzgerald Bama, listed as president for life in the *One Particular Harbour* credits. Mike Utley's alter ego, Orlando Miguel "Mike" Utel, was credited as vice president and treasurer.

At the hotel on Moorea they encountered a drink called the Boom Boom. "It had rum, vodka, whiskey, one other kind of alcohol, orange juice, something to make it green," Liberman says. "And if you drank four of them you got a free T-shirt." No one got a free T-shirt. One guy tried. He'd arrived on the island with crutches and a broken leg. They found him the next morning in some nearby bushes. Liberman's best guess is he got so drunk he thought he could walk.

Liberman also met his first wife, who was staying at the hotel on a night off from the cruise ship where she worked. When it came time for her to leave the next day—the boat was heading to Bora Bora—Liberman decided to join her.

"Aren't you working?" Buffett said.

True love, Liberman argued. Buffett gave him a sideways glance that proved even the impulsive romantic had a practical side. True love, Liberman continued to argue.

Buffett was the best man at their wedding and, when they eventually divorced, Liberman looked at Buffett and said, "Don't say it."

Told you so.

One Particular Harbour got to number sixty-five on the charts in 1983. "Brown Eyed Girl" and "One Particular Harbour" were both top-twenty-five adult contemporary songs, but didn't chart otherwise.

So that didn't reverse Buffett's course—at least not commercially. Steve Goodman's "California Promises," Arthur Neville's "Why You Wanna Hurt My Heart," and Buffett's "Distantly in Love" all spelled heartbreak, and "Honey Do," written by Utley and Buffett featured a guy out on his own, "dreamin' of your pretty eyes, up in South Carolina."

The same year *One Particular Harbour* was released, Irving Azoff stepped away from his managerial role and took over MCA

Records. He put Jimmy Bowen, who'd produced Frank Sinatra, in charge of the country division.

Aside from his background as a singer and a producer, Bowen brought a degree from the Wharton School of Business and an MBA from Belmont University. He heard the playful sound of change in Chet Atkins's pockets and figured to turn it into the thud of bags of cash landing in the floor of the vault.

"I think he ruined the business," Doyle Grisham says. "The songs started getting bubble gum; they started taking away from the country vein. He didn't like steel guitars and fiddles, and they turned the damn town over to him when it was built on steel guitars and fiddles, musically. I know everything has to change, but it doesn't have to change that drastically."

Putnam remembers Buffett telling him he was going to go work with Bowen and see if he could get on country radio. It was a little more complicated than that. Utley chuckles and says he and Buffett had just recently been talking about what came next.

"We were about to start a new album," Utley says. "We had written the songs, Will Jennings, myself and Jimmy wrote 'em in St. Barts. We're about to go in. He's already in California. Irving calls him and says, 'I want you to do this album with Bowen.'"

Buffett said sure, but he wanted Utley to coproduce, and he wanted Tony Brown, who had played with Elvis and Emmylou Harris and begun producing, to be in on the sessions as well. Azoff and Bowen agreed that'd be fine.

"So it wasn't Jimmy's decision," Utley says. "Well I guess it was. He could have said no, but I don't know what would have happened . . . It's just what happens in the music business sometimes."

Buffett took his turn toward country, and *Riddles in the Sand* barely cracked the top ninety, but country radio was amenable, if not enthusiastic, about a few of the singles. It was 1984 and his split with Jane was all over *Riddles*. "Burn that Bridge," "Love in Decline," "When the Wild Life Betrays Me," Buffett had a hand in writing all of those, and then pulled McAnally's "She's Going Out of My Mind." It turns out Jimmy Buffett could sing sad songs.

"Who's the Blonde Stranger?" was a troubled-relationship song with a sense of humor, the story of a vacationing couple cheating on each other. Though when it came time to shoot the video in Key West, Jane was there, playing the part of the wife. She remained, Buffett wrote in the album's dedication, "the ultimate riddle in the sand," the lady he still couldn't explain.

"Any good artist feels compelled to change, if not doomed to change," Jim Harrison wrote in the liner notes, taking up McGuane's job from a decade earlier and again, in a way, trying to reintroduce Jimmy Buffett. Instead of Xavier Cugat and Hank Williams, the connections were Bob Wills and Bob Marley. Harrison managed *finally* to find a genre for Buffett. Highlighted in yellow were the words Gulf and Western. Wearing a bright yellow shirt on the album cover was Buffett, smiling from under a ten-gallon hat, standing on the beach in blue jeans, holding a guitar and looking the part.

Back in 1982, talking to the *Herald* about Tahiti, Buffett mentioned other projects on his mind. There was a book, for a small publisher in Oxford, Mississippi, tentatively titled *My African Friend and Other Stories*. There was an album, tentatively titled *The Dog Ate My Homework and Other Great Excuses*. That became the much better titled *One Particular Harbour*. He wanted to make a reggae version of the elementary school Christmas program favorite "All I Want for Christmas Is My Two Front Teeth."

His was a restless creativity, and he seemed to have made some small peace with his hit and the idea that it might be his only one, and so he might as well lean on it. He had plans to turn "Margaritaville" into a movie. In 1982, P. J. O'Rourke was writing the script based on an original Buffett story set on Key West in 1971. "It will be a message movie," Buffett told the *Herald*, laughing. "Yeah, it's going to have a moral: Don't take things too seriously. Pure escapism." With a sprinkling of folks fighting developers in an effort to maintain what made the island of Margaritaville special. Production would begin in the summer of 1983.

In September 1983, United Press International reported filming would begin in 1984. "I want a Key West atmosphere, but Key West now is too slick," he told the *Herald* in November 1983.

In January 1985, he told the *Key West Citizen* that they hoped to begin filming in September and he was also at work on a one-man show headed for Broadway called *An Evening in Margaritaville*.

In July 1985, Buffett told the *Boston Globe*, "It's going to happen."

In July 1986, he told Knight-Ridder's Gary Graff the script had gone through seven drafts. Michael Nesmith had signed on to produce and direct. "They tell me the first six years are the toughest," Buffett said.

By October 1987, *Margaritaville: The Movie** had been given the subtitle *A Love Triangle Adrift in the Bermuda Triangle* and carried cowriting credits for Buffett and Terry McDonell, the editor at *Outside* magazine who'd once run the story of Buffett's adventures in Antigua.

The script's synopsis: "Margaritaville is about two guys from different worlds who become great buddies as they; 1) travel from island to island in the Caribbean having adventures and meeting various eccentrics; 2) resolve their comic love triangle with a beautiful girl and; 3) save the Island of Margaritaville and the way of life it symbolizes from the forces of greed and hypocrisy."

The two different guys were James Delaney, a cowboy on the run, and Frank Bama, a hotel owner and former smuggler.

In 1988, the script was sent to Harrison Ford, who'd played a smuggler, and Robert Redford, who'd played cowboys. Both apparently passed.

While Buffett wrote and rewrote the *Margaritaville* script, his

---

* Buffett donated the script, and many other papers, to the Special and Area Studies Collections at the George A. Smathers Libraries at the University of Florida in Gainesville.

lawyers worked a different angle. In 1983, they filed in opposition of the Mexican restaurant chain Chi-Chi's attempt to trademark "Margaritaville."

"It was quite an unusual case," says David Ehrlich, one of Buffett's attorneys for the case. Chi-Chi's was using Margaritaville as a drink special: "From Chi-Chi's own recipe comes a Margarita like you've never tasted," read one table card. Served in a "salt-rimmed goblet" it was available at "special fiesta prices all day Tuesday in our dining rooms or lounge. Come, but be prepared not to waste away!"

So every Tuesday at Chi-Chi's was Margaritaville. Every night of Buffett's work life was Margaritaville—but that doesn't mean you get a trademark. You can't normally trademark a song title. Think of all the songs called "Wrecking Ball."

Ehrlich and the rest of the legal team had to prove Buffett was synonymous with "Margaritaville," inseparable in the eyes of the public and therefore he himself would be infringed upon by Chi-Chi's. That hadn't been done before.

What followed was years of often entertaining legal sniping in filings and counter-filings. The lawyers representing Chi-Chi's attempted to argue there was no such song as "Margaritaville," because the *Changes in Latitudes, Changes in Attitudes* LP sleeve, written in Buffett's hand, read "Wastin' Away Again in Margaritaville."* From a 1985 filing by Chi-Chi's legal team:

> Opposer has taken great pains to allege as its primary case that:
> 1. "Margaritaville" is the name of a song; and
> 2. Jimmy Buffett is a popular singer; and
> 3. That Jimmy Buffett has sold many records with the song "Margaritaville" on it.
> Even if we accept these allegations as fact . . .

---

* It also featured an original Buffett sketch of an old guy in a polka-dot bathing suit, a bottle of tequila and vinyl record with an arrow pointing from the words "Old Champs Record." The Champs' "Tequila" was a number one hit in 1958.

Even if all of that was true, Chi-Chi's attorneys argued: "An equally absurd claim to rights in gross arises from Opposer's claim that restaurant services are somehow a natural field of expansion for entities that publish music. If a nexus exists between songs and restaurants, Opposer could claim an equal nexus between songs and the tangible items of the universe." Opposer could do that, yes. And Opposer was beginning to.

Jim Mazzotta grew up on the Jersey Shore and moved to Fort Myers, Florida, in 1980 to work for the *News-Press* just as its owner, Gannett Co., was figuring out how to make newspapers look less like newspapers. "I came down here and what they basically said to me was we want the pages to bleed color," Mazzotta says. He'd get together with reporters, talk to editors, and brightly illustrate stories that would fill the page. He also did political cartoons. "We had a lot of freedom about what we could draw," he says.

He met a guy named Michael LaTona, another artist, but one with some hustle to his game. LaTona was running a T-shirt business from the trunk of his car. He kept pushing Mazzotta to design a T-shirt, and Mazzotta kept pushing him away. Finally, he gave in. They did some nature prints and a few rock-and-roll things.

Buffett was coming through town, and so LaTona made a run at Florida's favorite rock star. They picked out a few songs, and Mazzotta did for those what he did for the news—he dug into the details and illustrated the story. Buffett's best work had always been his most journalistic. Those T-shirts were no different.

The first, for "Margaritaville," featured a blown-out flip-flop at the start of a road winding toward a sailboat anchored in a cove below a setting sun. On another, a woman in the moonlight affixed a flower to her hair above a lyrically inspired collage: a blender, a glistening margarita touched off with a fresh lime slice, an empty tequila bottle, a salt shaker, and a note, sealed with a lipsticked kiss, saying there's a woman to blame.

Mazzotta and LaTona talked Buffett into coming to a surf expo in Orlando in 1984. The shirts were a hit; Buffett, who'd seen more than enough knockoff and misspelled Jimmy Buffet T-shirts, was impressed. Caribbean Soul was born.

Mazzotta created designs for "Fins," "Cheeseburger in Paradise," "Son of a Son of a Sailor," "A Pirate Looks at Forty," and "One Particular Harbour." He drew a rainbow lizard, the new company's mascot, and hid him in every illustration.

But every time Mazzotta would put a person in the illustration, maybe with a drink in silhouette, or on the deck of a distant sailboat, fans would ask if it was Buffett. They didn't want it to be Buffett. They wanted it to be anyone, and thus everyone. "Everybody can go to the beach and have a drink," Mazzotta says. His solution echoes to this day: "I came up with a parrot holding a drink."

Across the Gulf, the first officially licensed Margaritaville opened in June 1984: J. B.'s Margaritaville in Gulf Shores, Alabama.

Jim Sweet met Buffett and McAnally a few years earlier when they would sneak in and play Judge Roy Beans, the Fairhope, Alabama, bar where Sweet was working. It wasn't far from the house Buffett's parents had moved to on the eastern shore of Mobile Bay.

Sweet had recently finished law school but decided to try the bar business with his brother, Dan. After one false start, they pitched Buffett on licensing the Margaritaville name, a move that wouldn't hurt Buffett's case against Chi-Chi's, which was arguing he'd never used Margaritaville as anything other than a song.

The original J. B.'s Margaritaville wasn't near the water. It was few blocks away. There's a Walgreens there now. It had a nine-hole mini-golf course outside, each hole lined with anchor rope. They called it the Golf of Mexico. "I remember being concerned about leaving all these golf clubs out for people to use when they were drinking," Sweet says. They fitted the walls with small aquariums and framed them with portholes. They stuck a small, motorized diver in one, but it was so small he'd get stuck kicking in place until he wound down.

"I can literally say my earliest memories were of that bar," Jim's son Parker says. "They were hazy . . . remember the tiki torches we had to use? Some drunk ran his car into the sign out front and knocked the lights out and we used tiki torches around the wrecked car to warn people so they wouldn't hit it."

"And to find the bar," Jim says.

Did they sell a lot of margaritas? Yeah, they did. "We bought the machines that are kind of like the ice cream things you'd see, which were a disaster," Jim Sweet says. "Never could get them to work. So we just went to the blenders. It was the constant sound of blenders and bartenders cursing under their breath all night long."

Buffett appeared a couple of times. McAnally would stop in and play. The Neville Brothers took the stage once. Sweet and his brother, feeling the need to improve the plain white office tiles overhead turned one night to spray paint.

"The place was just too bright, so we got the bright idea we were going to make it like the sky," Jim says. "I was up on the scaffold. Dan was pushing me around with the sprayer, spray painting blue up there, and turning blue in the process. Because when you do that, paint comes down your arm."

Did they sell a lot of T-shirts? Of course they did—original to the bar and the new Caribbean Soul line. It was a nice business until the summer of 1985, when a pair of hurricanes threatened the area and scared off late-summer business and the whole thing faded away.

By then, Buffett had moved back to Key West, bought a '64 Ford Falcon, and run into an old friend named Donna Kay "Sunshine" Smith. Like Jane and Larry "Groovy" Gray, Sunshine had come down from South Carolina. She'd married an artist and filmmaker named B. J. Smith, and they'd had a couple of kids and gotten divorced; the bank was foreclosing on her house.

"And Jimmy came to me and said, 'Sunshine Smith, what's happened to you? Let's put up a T-shirt store, put my name on the

roof, and if it makes money, fine. If it doesn't make money, fine,'"
Smith told the Gaming Control Board in Nevada in 2012. "So we
opened a five-hundred-square-foot T-shirt store and it evolved
from there."

It was exactly that simple.

Steve and Cindy Thompson, married by then, returned home
in their RV with their kids after lighting out north and away from
a hurricane. Smith lived across the street.

"We went up to Cocoa Beach," Cindy says. "Sunshine happened
to be out in the yard and she just yelled, 'If you want a job, come
down to Margaritaville. We're hiring, and we have insurance.'

"The reason I went down there was for insurance."

Cindy Thompson is still on the payroll, managing the archives,
and over the years, taking care of the various Key West homes
Buffett has moved in and out of.

The Margaritaville Store opened in Lands End Village on
January 28, 1985, and coincided with what was billed as the First
Annual Margaritaville Film Festival. (It turned out to be the only
Margaritaville Film Festival.) At the Strand Theatre on Duval
Street, Buffett played host to a showing of *Tarpon, Rancho Deluxe*,
the old *Introducing Jimmy Buffett* short he'd shot more than a
decade earlier, and a slide show of Corcoran's best work around
the island. The headline in the *Citizen*: "Buffett comes back to
Margaritaville."

In February 1985, the first edition of a newsletter, the *Coconut
Telegraph*, was published. Its first words: "Margaritaville—a ramshackle place. A rowdy place where for years, rumrunning was the
favorite sport. A place of pirates and parrots and hot, heady tropical
days where there's always 'booze in the blender.' Close to the edge
of paradise, with just a dash of reality thrown in to add flavor."

In June, Buffett released another new album, *Last Mango in
Paris*, featuring a title track about Captain Tony, whom Buffett
helped lose an election for mayor of Key West. Like *Riddles in the*

Sand, Buffett did the bulk of the creative work for *Last Mango* with Utley, Will Jennings, and Marshall Chapman. Tony Brown again coproduced with Utley and Jimmy Bowen, and they worked in Nashville. It did slightly better than Buffett's past few records, but only reached number fifty-three on the charts. "If the Phone Doesn't Ring, It's Me," was perfectly titled for country radio, and country radio responded by kicking it into the top twenty.

The rest of the record had its charms—and a nice guest list. Harrison Ford cracked a bullwhip on "Desperation Samba," about Halloween in Tijuana. Glenn Frey added vocals, guitar, and a co-write on "Gypsies in the Palace," the story of what happens when you go on tour and leave your home in the wrong hands. Buffett's Porsche, for example, ended up in a Colorado creek near his house. Roy Orbison chipped in background vocals on the album-closing ballad, "Beyond the End," and Utley* found himself working with the guy whose single, "Ooby Dooby," lit his passion for music.

The Eagles' Timothy B. Schmit added background vocals on "Jolly Mon Sing," the story of an island-hopping singer who brings happiness wherever he goes. Alone on the seas one night, he's tricked into helping pirates who toss him overboard. He's saved by a dolphin who tells the Jolly Mon, "I've always loved your singing—climb on board and don't let go." Together, they take off for the stars, where they shine on as constellations. He had another song to play to Savannah Jane, and had put another new character into his world. "Jolly Mon" also featured Robert Greenidge, a Trinidad-born steel drum ace who had first appeared on *Riddles in the Sand*, further expanding Buffett's sound.

---

* That was just the start. Also in 1985, Utley and Orbison coproduced all but one of the songs that would appear on 1987's, *In Dreams: The Greatest Hits*. Orbison had decided to rerecord his hits because Monument Records had control of the master tapes. Now Utley was *playing* "Ooby Dooby" with Orbison. "It was so beautiful," Utley says. In 1987, Utley appeared with an all-star cast that included Tom Waits, Bruce Springsteen, k.d. lang, Bonnie Raitt, and T Bone Burnett on the HBO special, *Roy Orbison and Friends: A Black and White Night*.

Hits or not, Buffett and the Coral Reefers did what they'd always done—they hit the road. But something was different. Something was better. "It's funny," Utley says, "during that period is sort of when the Parrot Head phenomenon started happening."

Not long after *Last Mango* arrived in stores, Buffett and the Coral Reefer Band were playing the Timberwolf Amphitheater at Kings Island, an amusement park northeast of Cincinnati. "We were driving in the limo, and there were all kinds of fans partying in the parking lots with crazy costumes and parrots on their heads," Liberman says. Buffett was in the limo. Schmit, who'd joined the Coral Reefer band, looked out the window and marveled at the scene. "These are like your own personal Dead Heads," he told Buffett, then paused. "No, they're Parrot Heads. You've got your Parrot Heads."

"I guess he liked it and kept it," Schmit told VintageRock.com in 2012.

Corcoran's moment of realization was at Chastain Park in Atlanta. He'd moved to Fairhope, Alabama, and wasn't around nearly as much as he'd been in the seventies and early eighties. A friend had the beer and wine concession at the venue and they'd been kicking around backstage, chatting with Buffett and hanging out. At some point, Corcoran got a good view of crowd—the grass skirts and Hawaiian shirts and ornate hats—turned to his friend and said, "What is that? What did I just see?"

"Oh, they've been doing that for a couple of years," his friend said.

The math suggested Buffett's career should be waning. Instead, the crowds were younger, they were more enthusiastic, they were bigger, and they were tropically bedazzled. "We were pinching ourselves," Utley says. "I can remember Jimmy saying, 'I don't know where this is coming from.'"

A month later, back in Key West, treasure hunter Mel Fisher's divers found what they'd been looking years for: the mother lode from the *Nuestra Señora de Atocha*, a Spanish galleon wrecked in a hurricane in 1622. Buffett was nearby shooting art for a greatest-hits album when he got the call on the radio, rendezvoused with Fisher's crew, sat atop a stack of silver ingots plucked fresh from the sea, and sang "A Pirate Looks at Forty" while Fisher drank beer from a champagne flute.

In October, Buffett released that greatest-hits package, *Songs You Know by Heart*, cheekily subtitled *Jimmy Buffett's Greatest Hit(s)*, and hosted some lucky fans at Fantasy Fest in Key West. Included in *Last Mango in Paris* was an entry form for a contest. Winners would receive three all-expenses-paid nights in Key West. Buffett would be their tour guide.

When it came time to pick the winners, the Margaritaville staff dumped 75,000 entries on the floor of the office. "I was going, 'Please, God, don't give me any assholes,'" he told the *Miami Herald*. "But it couldn't have turned out any better, especially when you think of the horror show it could have been. And no, I'm not going to do it again."

Among the perks enjoyed by the five winners (ten people total) was a private concert on Ballast Key. The site of so much bacchanalia in the early seventies, David Wolkowsky purchased the island in the mid-seventies and built a home that even now stands as a testament to engineering. It's solar powered, has a desalinization plant, and is the southernmost private home in the continental United States. Buffett took the winners there on a chartered seventy-four-foot boat and then took requests.

True Parrot Heads, the *Herald* noticed, stick with Buffett regardless of musical fashion. "He writes things we identify with; we're all about the same age," Jim Nichols, a winner from Arlington, Virginia, told the paper. "But he just had the guts to do what we dreamed about. We became bankers . . . So we can live vicariously through him, or through his music anyway."

In the ongoing legal battle over ownership of the word "Margaritaville," things were also going Buffett's way. His attorneys had entered as evidence the licensing agreement with Jim and Dan Sweet for J. B.'s Margaritaville in Gulf Shores, and shown proof of T-shirts and merchandise putting "Margaritaville" to work for Jimmy Buffett.

"These materials provide specific factual support for opposer's allegations that the song 'Margaritaville' and Buffett are well-known and that Buffett has attempted, through his commercial licensing program, publicity, and entertainment services, to associate the term "MARGARITAVILLE" with the public persona of Jimmy Buffett," the Patent Office Trademark Trial and Appeal Board ruled.

Jimmy Buffett was "Margaritaville," and "Margaritaville" was Jimmy Buffett.

A year to the day after the official grand opening of the Margaritaville Store, lawyers on both sides of the case deposed Irving Azoff in Los Angeles. He was asked if, in his professional opinion, Buffett was a "well-known recording artist and public entertainer."

"Jimmy Buffett is a well-known artist and he's also a national figure," Azoff said, "sort of a folk hero."

Azoff said only twice in his career had he been involved with what he called world building. When the Eagles recorded "Life in the Fast Lane," and "Margaritaville."

"I think Jimmy is more entitled to connect himself with 'Margaritaville' than any other artist of any other song that I've ever known," Azoff said. Not Michael Jackson and "Thriller." Not Bruce Springsteen and "Born in the U.S.A."

"And I really believe," Azoff added, "that a chain of restaurants called 'Margaritaville,' for instance, if they were big, neon electronic computerized restaurants, could damage Jimmy's ability to make money, as much money, in the future because it would hurt his image.

"I think that it's very important to Jimmy's continued success to control the name 'Margaritaville.'"

Chapter 16

If You Want to Survive
the Tourist Business

But somehow most of the show seemed but a warm-up for
the climax, "Margaritaville," the 1977 song that catapulted
Buffett from cult figure to pop star. Those were the best
days of his life. No wonder he keeps reliving them.

—Divina Infusino,
San Diego Union-Tribune,
June 1, 1985

That would depend, obviously, on how one draws the borders
of a life. Back in Paris in 1974, during the making of *Tarpon*,
and when Buffett and Jim Harrison weren't peeping the editing
of *Emmanuelle*, Harrison did get to the business of narrating Guy
de la Valdene's documentary.

"Who said we go through life with a diminishing portfolio of
enthusiasms," Harrison said. "So you try to seek out in life moments
that give you this immense jolt of electricity. It's a tranquilizer better than any chemical tranquilizer. So you try to have something
that gives you the electricity and freshens up your feeling about
being alive."

A career is one enthusiasm, sure. But there are others.

With his greatest hit(s) and *Last Mango in Paris* released, with
his ramshackle T-shirt shop humming, Jimmy Buffett could turn
his attention to an impending milestone—his fortieth birthday,
which would arrive at the end of 1986.

The day after his thirty-ninth birthday, Buffett bought a seaplane, a Lake Renegade 250 he named *Strange Bird*. Next, he
hired a flight instructor, an old Chalk's pilot, and they set up class
in Buffett's home in Key West. From there, they set out across
the Gulf to South America and Central America, and then down
into the Caribbean.

He'd signed away the *Euphoria II* in Le Select on St. Barts,
but he'd bought a home there, and then he and Groovy, who'd
bought his own sailboat, purchased a hotel/bar/disco. Autour du
Rocher ("around the rock") sat atop a hill with St. Jean Bay on one
side, and Lorient Bay on the other. "It's the biggest damn financial
nightmare—a great, dumb, stupid, wonderful thing to own," Buffett
wrote in *The Parrot Head Handbook*. "I've yet to see a dime come
out of it, but I bought it truly for no other reason than to be able
to sit on a stool and tell whoever I'm talking to that I own part of
a bar in the Caribbean."

He could slice limes and watch smugglers scheme, imagine spies
exchanging secrets in the shadows, and because it was St. Barts,
look on as the rich and the beautiful chased after the rest of the
rich and the beautiful. Find someone who wouldn't buy something
as great, dumb, stupid, and wonderful as that.

In the fall of 1985, Buffett added Corona Extra to his touring
roster, signing a new endorsement deal with a new beer. He wrote a
jingle, did some posters, hung some signage at his shows. In March
1986, the *Los Angeles Times* profiled Corona under the headline,
"Import's Popularity Baffles Analysts." In that regard, Corona had
hired the perfect spokesman.

Musically, Buffett had given up on Nashville—again. He'd tried
for two albums to walk someone else's middle ground between who

he was and who radio might like him to be. "I never really was a country act," he told Knight-Ridder's Gary Graff. "When they pitched that whole thing to me, I said, 'I'll give you one last shot at thinking radio means that much.' And it didn't work anyway, so I went back to doing what I wanted to do and picking up things I'd been talked out of or compromised on in the past.

"Y'know, I really didn't think I'd live to be forty. Now that I'm here, I've decided they can't tell me to do anything."

Buffett would executive produce the next record. Utley would coproduce. They'd go to Los Angeles, Memphis, and Fort Lauderdale to record. He'd put the legendary Memphis Horns to work, and he'd bring Ralph MacDonald, who'd spent a decade with Harry Belafonte and written classics like "Just the Two of Us" and "Where Is the Love," into the fold. Savannah Jane played mini-congas on the album. Buffett wouldn't worry about genre, but he'd think about audience—his. They liked Jimmy Buffett and so he made them a Jimmy Buffett record.

Floridays, named after poet Don Blanding's 1941 book, put Buffett back among "pale invaders and tan crusaders" at the "corner of Walk and Don't Walk somewhere on U.S. 1." On its cover, Buffett squinted against a fading sun. On the back cover, he posed at the Belize Zoo with his guitar on his lap and a spider monkey named Sparkle Plenty on his head. He went to Rio in "First Look," to the bayou of his past in "Creola," and to Memphis in an attempt to reassemble a relationship ("Meet Me in Memphis") with the help of those horns and an allusion to an old, familiar Otis Redding song.

Buffett took the island ethos of "soon come"—"it means maybe never," Buffett wrote in his 1978 *Outside* story from Antigua—and applied it to the story of one broken airplane and two strangers taking advantage of the situation ("No Plane on Sunday"). "When the Coast Is Clear," his first cowrite with Mac McAnally, could be heard as the antidote to the increasingly crowded island of "Margaritaville." The tourist traps had shut for the season, the hotels were empty, and a guy could sit in peace and quiet and catch up with old friends. "Almost like it used to be, before the circus came to town."

Drummer Matt Betton wrote "If It All Falls Down" like he was Buffett's biographer. "I live the perfect crime," he had Buffett sing, "and crime pays more than it used to."

Ahead of Buffett's fortieth birthday, "Nobody Speaks to the Captain No More" echoed "A Pirate Looks at Forty." The glories of "another place, in another time" have faded into questions: "Hey, what the hell were we fighting for such a long, long time ago?"

One of two songs on the album Buffett wrote alone ("First Look" was the other), it was dedicated to Gabriel García Márquez, Allie Fox, and Phil Clark. Márquez wrote the novella *No One Writes to the Colonel*, about a veteran of the Thousand Days' War. Fox was the anti-consumerism hero of Paul Theroux's novel *The Mosquito Coast*.

Clark was Buffett's old pal, the real pirate who'd once been looking at forty. He'd been found dead on a Northern California beach. Best anyone could tell, he'd been swept overboard from a boat headed somewhere else. In Key West, they took up a collection to fly him home, where, for years, his remains sat above the bar in the Full Moon Saloon.

Floridays charted the way Jimmy Buffett records had come to chart (number sixty-seven), but he took a more natural road to get there. The songs were lived in and comfortable.

"These are exciting times for me," he told USA *Weekend* in August 1986. "I've been doing this for twenty-two years. I'm just a saloon singer who's grown up or at least is making an effort to try to—and I think audiences can relate to this kind of rock-'n'-roll Peter Pan attitude I have."

Asked in that interview about his continued separation from Jane, Buffett shouldered the blame—it was his own damn fault— saying how hard it is to be married to a touring musician and applauding the job Jane had done with Savannah Jane. He said he'd stopped living on the boat because it was hard to order pizza and every tourist wanted him to take a picture with a fish they'd caught. A typical day? "I write, play guitar, eat, read, sing and fish," he said. "I'm like a retired person, only I sometimes have to deal with accountants who call me up and tell me I need to tour soon so our government won't go broke."

He sounded . . . practical. In all things. Including moderation. "I was still feeling pretty bulletproof, but I noticed hangovers were starting to feel like surgical recovery," Buffett said in a commencement address at the University of Miami in 2015. He told a story he said he'd never told before, about a B-I-G T-I-M-E in Denver, "around the time I hit forty," he said.

He and the Reefers played back-to-back nights at Red Rocks Amphitheatre the summer before his big birthday. He still hadn't recovered by the time they hit the stage. "I made it through the show," he said, "but I was mad at myself for not giving the crowd its money's worth. Nobody in the crowd knew, but I sure did. It's not a pretty thing to see talent wasted; it's even sadder to waste it yourself."

His ambition hadn't exactly been sated, his answers and questions weren't locked away, but as Jimmy Buffett moved into middle age, four, five, ten, fifteen years slipped away. Just as they had for the Eddie Balchowsky–inspired gentleman of "He Went to Paris."

He released albums: *Hot Water* (1988), *Off to See the Lizard* (1989), *Feeding Frenzy* (1990), the four-disc box set *Boats, Beaches, Bars & Ballads* (1992), *Fruitcakes* (1994), *Barometer Soup* (1995), *Banana Wind* (1996), *Christmas Island* (1996), *Beach House on the Moon* (1999), *Tuesdays, Thursdays, Saturdays* (1999).

He wrote books: *Tales from Margaritaville: Fictional Facts and Factual Fictions* (1989), *Where Is Joe Merchant?* (1992), *A Pirate Looks at Fifty* (1998).

In 1997 he partnered with Pulitzer Prize–winning novelist Herman Wouk to turn Wouk's 1965 novel *Don't Stop the Carnival*, about the foibles and folly that follow a New York PR guy who runs away to the Caribbean to buy a hotel, into a musical. The book had been at least partly responsible for Buffett's investment in Autour du Rocher (which mysteriously burned down in 1991). When Buffett approached Wouk, he was riding high. *Where Is Joe Merchant?* had spent seven months on the *New York Times* best-seller list. Buffett faxed Wouk's agent his pitch. Wouk faxed back: "Thanks for your interest, but who are you?"[*]

When next they communicated, Wouk had figured it out. "I've checked on you," he said. "You're pretty good at what you do." They didn't make Broadway, but they did okay in Coconut Grove, and Buffett and the Coral Reefers recorded and released the soundtrack in 1998.

Buffett tooled around in that Lake Renegade 250 until he felt the need for more, and replaced it with a Grumman G-44 Widgeon he named *Lady of the Waters*. She'd been a World War II patrol plane and had been found by a friend in Michigan. "Her mission has gone from carrying depth charges to cradling an eight-foot surfboard, a couple of fly rods, a cooler, a bunk, and my Saint Christopher medal," Buffett wrote in *A Pirate Looks at Fifty*.

The medal—and the navy training he'd been required to take to fly a training mission off Key West—came in handy taking off from Nantucket's Madaket Harbor just after 3 p.m. on August 25, 1994. "Just prior to lifting off the water, out of the corner of my left eye, I spotted some contrary water what looked to be to me some kind of swell and decided to pull the power, but before I could do so, the plane veered extremely to the right," Buffett would tell the National Transportation Safety Board. "Attempts to level the plane with opposite aileron was not responsive."

The NTSB report continued: "The pilot stated that he '. . . pulled the power back . . .' and '. . . was able to keep the plane from

---

[*] Buffett recounted the exchange for the March 30, 1997, edition of the *Miami Herald* Sunday magazine *Tropic*.

rolling completely over.' He stated the airplane's left side of the nose impacted the water and the airplane nosed over." The son of a son of a sailor's plane had been flipped by the wake from a boat. Buffett had to fight his way out of the cockpit and onto the wing of the plane, where he was rescued by friends he'd been fishing with moments before.

Barely a year and a half later, Buffett was piloting his newer, ever larger seaplane, a 1954 Grumman HU-16 Albatross named the *Hemisphere Dancer* toward Negril, Jamaica, when authorities, mistaking the Albatross for a drug plane, opened fire. Among the passengers on board were U2 singer Bono and his family, and Island Records president Chris Blackwell.

Not on board was one of Buffett's pilots, his friend Jim Powell. On that flight to Jamaica, Powell told the *Chicago Tribune* a few months later, Buffett's imagination and sense of adventure got the better of him. "What happened in Jamaica was that Jimmy wanted to land on the north coast, and I looked at the weather map and knew the water would be too rough for his seaplane to land and that we'd end up having to make alternate, last-minute arrangements," Powell said. "I didn't have any approval for alternate arrangements." He wasn't especially surprised two days later when he heard what had happened. "To work with Jimmy," Powell told *Time* in 1998, "you've got to be able to think and whistle at the same time."

In 1991, Buffett and Jane finally didn't get divorced. They'd been close, but they couldn't ever bring themselves to finish the paperwork. Promoting *Off to See the Lizard* in 1989, Buffett mentioned to Johnny Carson that he'd taken Jane on a date the night before. They'd gone to the *Batman* premiere.

"You said dating your wife," Carson said. "How long have you been married?"

"Well, I was married about twelve years, but I haven't lived with my wife for six years or so. She wanted some space, so she lives in Malibu and I live in Key West."

"That's a lot of space," Carson said.

It was, but it (and some therapy) worked. They came back around like the "Boomerang Love" described on *Off to See the Lizard*. "Different islands, different worlds," Buffett sang, "but we really are the same."

In 1992, a second daughter, Sarah Delaney, was born. Two years later, the Buffetts welcomed an adopted son, Cameron Marley, and Buffett finally had someone in the house to share in his appreciation of big, slow, noisy, awesome toys like the Albatross. Jane preferred the jets Buffett had also learned to fly.

Hot Water was the first album recorded (in part) at Shrimpboat Sound, a nondescript, unmarked, sun-bleached former seafood warehouse on Key West's waterfront. Thousands of tourists walk by it every day on the way to sunset sails, fishing charters, or a beer at Schooner Wharf or Turtle Kraals. Shrimpboat Sound's only markings remain warnings of 24-hour video surveillance and a sign outlining "Manatee Basics for Boaters."

Shrimpboat wasn't the only new hangout. In October 1987, the Margaritaville Store moved to Duval Street and expanded. The Margaritaville Café was born, a new partnership between Buffett, Sunshine Smith, and Kevin Boucher.

Boucher was born in 1938 and grew up Irish Catholic in Harlem. His dad ran a bar, and so he learned the trade before he could see over the stools. He took those lessons and applied them to 1970s Manhattan, running clubs contemporary of Studio 54, but different. At J. P.'s, it wasn't uncommon for Billy Joel, or Steve Winwood, or Jimmy Buffett to pop in after hours, after a show, and play a few songs.

But Manhattan's nightclub business was getting complicated. Money was pouring in, but so too were the types of people who get interested in fast money. Boucher and his wife, who's Cuban, left for Key West when he turned forty. He didn't hurt for work in a booming tourist town.

In 1987, Boucher was getting ready to go to Miami to capitalize on the rebuilding South Beach scene. He ran into Buffett and mentioned he was leaving town. They'd first met in New York after hours, when Buffett was playing Boucher's club. Boucher knew how to run a business, but he'd also traveled the world, and sprinkles a conversation with stories from the Himalayas, India, Afghanistan, and Greece. He and Buffett got along well. Buffett told him they needed to talk.

The Margaritaville Café and a new Margaritaville Store opened on Duval Street, next to Fast Buck Freddie's in the Kress Building in late 1987. Margaritaville's new offices were connected but wore an address around the corner, 424A Fleming Street. Buffett had new personal stationery printed. David Wolkowsky owned the building and cut Buffett and his team a deal so long as he could keep the rooftop apartment for entertaining friends.

Boucher set the goalposts. They aimed for a middle-class crowd—not too exclusive, but not too cheap. They wouldn't price anyone out, but wouldn't invite the sloppy drunks that fall out of Sloppy Joe's on a Friday night.

They built a small stage in the back of the room—smaller than Buffett would have liked, but they needed the space for tables. Boucher employed his burger recipe—part ground beef, part brisket, other secret ingredients—for the benefit of the Cheeseburger in Paradise.

By the time Margaritaville expanded, it had grown to sixteen employees and was doing $1 million a year in sales, according to a 1988 *Key West Citizen* story. That same story, headlined "Margaritaville Café is a mecca for Jimmy Buffett fans," came with a photo of Buffett playing guitar while Ed Bradley sang and banged on a tambourine. Below the story, an ad for the café asked "What is Margaritaville?" It was more than an attitude, or the staff, or the $20,000 sound system. It was good food, drinks, and music until 4 a.m. "It's a club where you can lift a glass with a friend, and share a candlelit dinner with a date; and maybe run into Steve Winwood, Harrison Ford, Russ Kunkel, James Taylor, Steve Cropper, Michael Utley, Ben and Jerry, Ed Bradley, 'Fingers Taylor,' Jim Stafford, Capt. Dennis Connors, and of course, J. B. himself."

Corcoran did one day. He was in Key West working on a magazine assignment to chronicle all the businesses that had rebranded themselves Kokomo after the Beach Boys' hit.

"That year, you could count the whores, the people who changed their business names to Kokomo this and Kokomo that, even the beach at the Casa Marina hotel was called Kokomo Beach," Corcoran says. Not that the Keys had turned its back on Buffett. The November 1, 1988 *Lakeland Ledger* included an Associated Press story headlined, "Where's Kokomo? Down by Margaritaville" and noted that on Islamorada, the Holiday Isle resort had renamed its pool Kokomo at Margaritaville.

Corcoran stopped at Margaritaville for a beer. "I go in, the place is packed," he says. "And I knew the bartender and I ordered a beer and I'm just standing there." When there was a tap on his shoulder. "It's Jimmy," Corcoran says. Buffett takes a finger, puts it to his lips and says, "Shhhh. Nobody knows I'm here."

He was having lunch with Sunshine Smith. "Nobody, for the entirety of lunch, recognized Jimmy Buffett," Corcoran says. "In Margaritaville."

The concert tours continued apace, the crowds grew, and the shows became ritual. Outside the venues, costumes and cheeseburgers, margaritas and friendship. Inside, Parrot Heads knew when to wave their hands like fins above their heads. They knew all the words to all their favorite songs, and those songs were in the set every night. No exceptions, and not necessarily because those songs came from the best years of Jimmy Buffett's life. He was playing old songs, but he wasn't reliving old glories as much as he was allowing other people to maybe remember theirs for a bit. He had his enthusiasms, and his fans had theirs.

"You have to give the people what they want," Buffett told *Rolling Stone* in 2007. "I'm not out there to make statements. I'm descended from court jesters, not theologians, and I just go out there to entertain. Joseph Campbell said, 'If you have a really great old car, and it keeps running, you may want to change the paint and seat covers, but you don't want to sell the car.'"

His fans were there to escape for a few hours into his world, however they imagined it. "The point is, I lived out a fantasy," he wrote in the *Parrot Head Handbook*. "It may be everyone's fantasy, but I'm sure glad not everyone lives it out . . . I love being the guy who gets to tell people about it." It was "the gospel from the coast," as he'd sung it in "Floridays."

As he watched his audience continue to grow, he recognized a changing demographic. The Parrot Heads were having children and bringing them—the Parakeets—to the shows. As unlikely as it seemed, Jimmy Buffett and the Coral Reefer Band had become family entertainment. Every now and then, "Why don't we get drunk and screw" would turn into "Why don't we get milk in school." Children's books seemed like the next natural outlet for Buffett's colorful whimsy.

In 1988, Buffett and Savannah Jane partnered to expand the story of the *The Jolly Mon*. In 1991, they released *Trouble Dolls*, the story of a girl named Lizzy who, with the help four tiny dolls of Guatemalan legend, sets out in search of her father, an environmentalist who'd crashed his seaplane—a Lake Renegade 250—on his way home from Florida's Everglades. "Children, see what you can see," read the dedication, a simple piece of advice that had worked for generations of Buffetts.

Tales from Margaritaville began with a big idea, and a good one—a "grand idea," Buffett wrote in May 1989 to Bonnie Ingber, his editor at Harcourt Brace Jovanovich. Thinking and whistling, he decided he'd pair his first book with a new album. But he was happy with *Off to See the Lizard*. He thought it might be the best

record he'd made in some time. "The more I think about it, the
book might take a second fiddle to a popular album and all the
hoopla it will create," he wrote Ingber.

"Go ahead and tell me you told me so and I'll take my medicine," he added.

Off to See the Lizard had its charms, particularly "Changing
Channels," an elegant ballad about time passing (cowritten with
McAnally), and "Take Another Road," the story of a cowboy and
his pony making a move down "another road from another time,
like a novel from the five and dime."

But the cowboy's story was better told in *Tales from Margaritaville*. The album went to number fifty-seven when it was released
in the summer of 1989; the collection of short stories topped the
New York Times best-seller list when it arrived in time for the
Christmas season.

In *Tales from Margaritaville*, the cowboy got a name: Tully
Mars. He was on the run from a Wyoming changing faster than
he cared to reckon with. The ranch where Tully worked and lived
(in a tropically adorned Airstream trailer where he slept in a hammock and dreamed of the beach) had been purchased by Thelma
Barston, a "junk-bond queen" who reminded Tully a lot of Cora
Brown, the ex–beauty parlor operator from New York who'd gone
to Livingston, Montana, in *Rancho Deluxe*. Mrs. Barston intended
to turn her new property into a poodle farm.

Tully, then, was left with no choice. He had to punch out her
assistant, who deserved it, if for no other reason than the mink coat
he was wearing. Tully loaded up his horse (Mr. Twain), his Martin
guitar, some Travis McGee paperbacks, a copy of *Following the
Equator* and headed south. "He knew no other person in the world
who had so completely and swiftly ended a long phase of life and
set out to find a better one," Buffett wrote.

As in song, Buffett's fictions were never far from his facts, and
his facts always slightly fictionalized. Corcoran says he and Groovy

used to joke about writing a song titled, "I'm Living a Future Lie," because they'd live one adventure, and then relive a sometimes similar version once Buffett began storytelling.

Like Buffett, Tully Mars had been there for the filming of *Rancho Deluxe* (he'd wanted to get a glimpse of actor Slim Pickens). The New Orleans where Tully danced the night away was Buffett's New Orleans, and Tully was dancing with a woman named Donna Kay he'd met at a diner in Blytheville, Arkansas. Donna Kay is Sunshine Smith's name, and Michael Utley grew up in Blytheville. On the trip to Margaritaville, Tully encounters the Twelve Volt Man making margaritas with his blender (powered by a generator) and listening to *A1A* on cassette. Tully arrives in Margaritaville aboard a shrimp boat named *Caribbean Soul*. Her captain's name: Captain Kirk. Kirk, Tully writes to Donna Kay, will be able to reach him on the *Coconut Telegraph*, should he need to be found. And clearly he hoped there'd be a need, his feelings for Donna Kay echoing Jimmy's for Jane at the time. "Distantly in Love," as the *One Particular Harbour* ballad said.

Buffett took every song he'd sung and every story he'd told and packaged them with a wink for his fans, and a nod to anyone who hadn't paid attention. In the book's opening pages, in a chapter titled "Walkabout," Buffett worked off British travel writer Bruce Chatwin's 1987 book, *The Songlines*. The Aboriginal people of Australia believe the world was sung into existence, and so their songs, passed through the generations, tell the story of the land and map the geography. A song, then, is sacred.

In *Tales from Margaritaville*, "Margaritaville" began its transformation from song to world. Before, it had been a state of mind. After, it had borders and characters and those characters—Tully Mars, Donna Kay, Captain Kirk—rubbed shoulders with faces recognizable from Buffett's other work.

Where is Joe Merchant?, his first novel, was more of the same, filled with asides referencing songs, lyrics, and scraps of Buffett's past—including the near miss with the Gulf tanker en route to the Bahamas before "Margaritaville" became a hit. There's a reference to Ed Bradley, and a Cuban with a pencil-thin mustache; there are squalls out on the Gulf Stream; there's a night spent dancing at the Boca Chica Lounge, and an admonishment not to try to describe the ocean "if you've never seen it," a line straight from "Mañana."

Buffett's seaplane-flying protagonist is Frank Bama, and he first arrived on Key West riding in an old Packard. His on-again-off-again love interest (introduced in a chapter titled "The Lady I Can't Explain") is a woman Bama had met in a phone booth outside the Chart Room. Her name was Trevor Kane, the heir to a hemorrhoid ointment fortune. Joe Merchant was her brother—a fast-moving, fast-living rock star long presumed dead. Buffett was a rock star presumed dead in certain (and especially critical) circles.

And Ms. Kane, upon reading and then balling up and tossing away a story about her brother written by an acidic little tabloid putz named Rudy Breno, says, "They all come down here thinking they're Hemingway. That's what's wrong with the fucking world these days. Nobody wants to put in the time it takes to be legendary. Mythology is not fast food."

No, it isn't, and so Buffett prepared his carefully, setting it in the tropics he knew so well, peppering it with heat-warped characters and just a touch of the profane. He wrote a lone palm with a tire swing hanging from it as the foreground to a seaplane on approach set against a brilliant Caribbean sunset. He wrote mayhem and mysticism. He foreshadowed new songs, casually referenced old ones, and even found a place for the dolphin who saved the Jolly Mon.

"I think I made a D in marketing," he told the *New York Times* in 1993, "but I remember supply and demand." As the one and only Jimmy Buffett, he understood what his fans wanted, and controlled the supply. He mentioned a fan in Chicago who'd reminded him that many Parrot Heads have to wear ties to work. Duly noted, the Margaritaville staff had a tie designed. "It's a real yuppie tie," Buffett said, "but it's got parrots on it."

By then Margaritaville had expanded. Kevin Boucher had moved to New Orleans to facilitate the opening of a location in the French Quarter just around the corner from the Upstairs Alliance's base of operations. Buffett had been eyeing the property for some time. In 1990, the *New Orleans Times-Picayune* reported he was negotiating for what had been the Storyville Jazz Club, where Tully Mars and Donna Kay had danced until dawn. Didn't happen. The building's owners said the highest offer from Margaritaville was still several hundred thousand dollars below what was, at the time, a $1.4 million price tag. Chris Blackwell, the founder of Island Records (who'd be aboard the *Hemisphere Dancer* a few years later when it came under fire), and Taylor Hackford, who directed *An Officer and a Gentleman*, bought the building and opened a comedy club. When that didn't work out, Buffett stepped in and signed a lease.

Buffett's new Margaritaville quickly became a go-to destination for music in the French Quarter. Coco Robicheaux was a regular, as was Rockin' Dopsie Jr., Marva Wright, and the Rebirth Brass Band. Alex McMurray had a band called Royal Fingerbowl that held the 11 a.m. to 2 p.m. slot every Sunday.

"For us it was a Sunday morning, kind of Bloody Mary crowd, and you know, it's a lot of tourists and we were young guys and we were kind of douchebags," McMurray says. "And we had a thing—people wanted to hear the songs they know, and we didn't do any of that." Sometimes they wanted to do "Oh, What a Beautiful Mornin'" from *Oklahoma!*—with a free jazz finish. When the inevitable request for "Margaritaville" arrived—and it was requested every day—they'd play "Margaritaville." But they might sing it in the register of a Norwegian death metal band. "The Cookie Monster voice," McMurray says.

"And the staff loved us, because they were people we knew," he said. "The bartenders thought it was a riot. We didn't just come in and fuck around. What I heard, and I don't know if this is true, Jimmy got wind of our skewering of his tunes and he laid down an edict that nobody could do Jimmy Buffett tunes in the front bar.

"It might be apocryphal."

It might be that Buffett wanted Margaritaville to be what the Bayou Room had been for him—a place to work out your musical chops and get better. He might have wanted local bands to be able to do that without feeling like they had to be a Jimmy Buffett cover band.

Just as Buffett found another reason to spend time in New Orleans, he'd once again worked his way back to Nashville, the city he couldn't quit for long. When he released the career-defining box set *Boats, Beaches, Bars & Ballads* in 1992, it was on Margaritaville Records, an imprint of MCA Records, and it moved more than a million copies.

Margaritaville Records operated out of an office in Nashville, and Buffett turned to a familiar face to run the operation—his ex-wife's husband, Bob Mercer. "What's our philosophy? That pretty much sums it up," Mercer told Cox News Service in 1992. Buffett installed himself as chief talent scout, and gave Michael Utley a similar title.

Buffett signed a couple of New Orleans bands, Evangeline and the Iguanas. He signed Marshall Chapman, who'd lent a hand on the writing of *Last Mango in Paris*. He signed Utley and fellow Coral Reefer Robert Greenidge as the instrumental group Club Trini. Buffett tried to sign Amy Lee, the Coral Reefer's saxophone player and leader of the horn section. But he wanted her to sign an eight-record deal, and she'd once been warned about signing multi-record deals—by Buffett. "Jimmy wasn't very happy with me," she says, "but I had a good teacher."*

---

* Buffett's word, however, was good. Lee remembers one night on the plane, after a show, when Buffett broke out his new signature Martin acoustic and she joked that everyone in the band should get one. He agreed, but then checked his watch. The official rule was anything he said after midnight didn't count. It was a few minutes before midnight. When she got home from tour, a box arrived, and it was a guitar.

Buffett was more successful signing Todd Snider, a sharp-witted singer-songwriter originally from Portland, Oregon, who'd bounced around Texas and landed in Memphis, where his father was working in construction. "My dad was in a bar in Memphis and he met a guy who knew where Keith Sykes lived," Snider says.

He set about politely stalking Sykes, who, by then, had stopped performing and gone full-time into the publishing business. Armed with an address, Snider began mailing Sykes songs. "I called him up and said, 'I like your songs,'" Sykes says. "Next thing I know, he's standing at the door." Almost before Sykes could hang up the phone, like a Looney Tune.

Snider had a standing gig at a bar called the Daily Planet. Typical bar crowd. The kind of place built for happy hours and to dispirit a singer alone onstage with only a guitar as defense. Sykes braced for a slaughter. "He starts singing songs and people started singing along with him and I thought, *Damn, how did that happen?*" Sykes says. "He just had this magic thing where people connected immediately."

He had what Buffett had, for better or worse. In New York and Los Angeles, Snider was too country. In Nashville, he wasn't country enough. It took three years of hard work, but Sykes finally helped Snider land a six-month development deal at Capitol Records. "And I was worse then at being me than I am now," Snider says. "So I fucking *exploded* that thing."

Recollections differ on what happened next. Sykes remembers going to the Margaritaville Records offices when Buffett was in Nashville and playing him Snider's stuff. Buffett dug it; Bob Mercer *really* dug it, and they invited Snider for a meeting. As Snider tells the story—and Snider tells remarkable stories, some of which are even mostly true—he and Sykes were on their way to have lunch with Jimmy Bowen when Sykes saw Buffett's car, honked, and waved hello.

"Bob Mercer just sort of took over from there," Snider says. "Bob saw me, and called Jimmy from Memphis." Buffett had Mercer send Snider to California to open a show. "That was my audition," Snider says. "When I got done playing that show, I came off and he asked me if I wanted to make an album for him."

Utley, in his Margaritaville Records role, caught Snider in Nashville. "It was like hearing a young Jimmy, a young Kris, although I didn't know Kris when he was young," Utley says. "The freshness of the songs, the honesty."

Margaritaville released *Songs for the Daily Planet* in 1994. Utley coproduced with Tony Brown, and it did well for a debut. Snider moved more than 100,000 copies of a record that was funny, heartbreaking, and often both at the same time. "My Generation (Part 2)" was Snider's answer to his father's Woodstock generation saying Snider's generation, "raised up in the hallowed halls of half a million shopping malls," wasn't good for anything. So Snider made a list of things they were good for: hair gel, hanging out at health spas, condom sense, drum machines, forty-dollar tie-dye T-shirts, and living off dad as long they could. "Oh my generation should be proud," he sang.

But the song that got Snider the most attention barely made the record and didn't make the track list. It was hidden at the end of the album, tacked on to "Joe's Blues." A nod to Bob Dylan's talking blues takes on Woody Guthrie's talking blues songs, "Talkin' Seattle Grunge Rock Blues" was about a band that moved to Seattle to capitalize on the grunge craze. They bought flannel shirts, they cranked up their amps, but that wasn't enough. They needed a gimmick. They landed on silence. They'd be "the only band that didn't play a note—under any circumstances." And they didn't. Not even when they were asked to play MTV's *Unplugged*—where they refused to play acoustic versions of the electric songs they hadn't recorded. "Then we smashed our shit," Snider said.

"That song was undeniably great," Sykes says.

The label wanted to push the song. VH1 wanted a video. They

were practically *begging* for a video so they could make the song a hit. "And I could just see the K-tel commercial and balked," Snider says. He had a song about a band willing to do anything for success, and he wasn't willing to do anything for success. "And now I think what if I woke up in the middle of the night and saw myself on the K-tel commercial and I'd be like, 'Oh, kick *ass*.' But when I was twenty-eight I thought no way do I want to wake up at fifty and see myself on that."

It was that resistance to opportunity that led Buffett to dispatch his bodyguards to summon Snider to a dressing room in a stadium in Miami. Upon arrival, Buffett pelted Snider with fruit. "Why fruit?" Snider wrote in his book *I Never Met a Story I Didn't Like*. "Because it was Jimmy Buffett's dressing room . . . Fruit was handy."

Buffett, seen through the lens of his mythology, was the easiest-going guy in America, Captain Laid-back. But he couldn't under-stand—or abide—a willfully missed opportunity. He had to fight to get Snider to play the song in his set; fans—paying customers—wanted to hear the song. Play the damn song.

There was a night in New Orleans that Snider wrote about in his book. They were at the Margaritaville Café and had just fin-ished their set when Buffett, Hunter Thompson, and Ed Bradley materialized backstage. Thompson didn't as much request as *challenge* Snider to play a song. Snider told him the guitar was already packed away. Hunter shoved him. "Menacingly," Snider wrote. Then laughed as he and Buffett and Bradley charged out into the French Quarter, leaving Snider behind. Maybe he could have joined them, but he didn't feel he belonged. There was aggressiveness, an assuredness of purpose and ability he didn't possess. They were from the sixties and the seventies and success meant something different to them than it did to Snider. It meant more.

"I see it as a positive thing that he had that I didn't have and don't," Snider says. "It was this thing that's kind of gone from America, and it's not Trump-y; it's swashbuckling. It was a different time, I have to think. And those guys had that confidence that didn't seem bullshit . . . I kind of think that character is gone in our culture, to a degree."

And with that success and that confidence came power— conferred, not requested or required. "He couldn't escape it," Snider says. "It was like, 'Can we get him a better table? No? Then build him one.' And he's like, 'Fuck it, man. I want to go swimming.'"

Jimmy Buffett had attained his stardom, his wealth, his power by taking advantage of the opportunities he'd had, and unapologetically. He appreciated people who could and would do the same. Enter a different kind of swashbuckling character.

John Cohlan grew up in New York, went to college in New Jersey (Princeton) and law school at Georgetown, and then made what he considers a smart decision. "I never practiced law," he says. Instead, he went into private equity, what was then known as the leveraged buyout business, in New York's financial district. In the mid-nineties, he was working for a company called Triarc, which purchased a conglomerate known as DWG. They owned Arby's and RC Cola. "We actually bought Snapple at some point," Cohlan says.

The head of the company, Nelson Peltz, had a home in Palm Beach and, like millions before him, thought it'd be nice to move to Florida. So he moved his business to Florida. "I was thirty-six, thirty-seven," Cohlan says. "I was single. The last place I wanted to go was Palm Beach." He called a friend, Michael Fuchs, who was running HBO. "Look," Fuchs told him, "there can't be much of a social life in Palm Beach, but I have a good friend, Jane Buffett, if there's any social life down there, she'll know about it."

Cohlan called Jane and met Jimmy. What he knew of Buffett he'd learned in college. When spring came to New Jersey in the late-seventies, the women would pack away the sweaters, dig out the halter-tops, and play Jimmy Buffett songs. "He invited me to be his guest at something I'd never heard of growing up in New York," Cohlan says.

Quint Davis runs the New Orleans Jazz & Heritage Festival, and his friendship with Buffett is equal to Buffett's friendship with the city and the festival, which has grown to encompass seven days of music over two weeks at the Fair Grounds Race Course. It maintains a liberal definition of "heritage." Bon Jovi has headlined.

In the sixties, Davis ran a head shop called the Love Shop when Buffett was playing the Bayou Room. He later spent time on the road with Professor Longhair, B.B. King, and Chuck Berry. He can sometimes be seen on the sideline at New Orleans Saints home games, standing next to Buffett.

Buffett played to a massive audience at the 1998 Jazz Fest, opening with the hometown boogie-woogie of "Saxophones" and even sneaking the not-often-enough-played "Biloxi" into the set. "And I'm standing there at the side of the stage," Cohlan says, "looking at *all* those people."

Triarc was a holding company. He wasn't operating any of the companies they controlled. Once a month, executives managing the day-to-day would arrive for reviews. "Among other things, they'd talk about their brands and what was going on with their brands," Cohlan says. "I kind of looked out at these 100,000 people and I said, 'Oh my God. *This* is a brand.'" Forget RC Cola. It's a beverage, but what's it stand for? Refreshment? There's nothing uncommon about that. Margaritaville had an ethos.

Triarc's Florida experiment didn't last, but Cohlan's friendship with Jimmy and Jane did—and despite his initial misgivings about what the move to Florida might do to his social life, he met the woman he'd eventually marry while he was living there. He moved back to New York, but was a regular visitor to South Florida and emailed often with Buffett. One day, Buffett called.

Edgar Bronfman Jr. had called Buffett with an offer. Bronfman led Seagram Co., the liquor giant that had purchased MCA and

Universal Studios. That made him the owner of theme parks *and* Buffett's record label. He wanted to license Margaritaville and build a restaurant outside the park in Orlando.

Buffett had toyed with an Orlando theme park at least twice before. In a 1998 profile in *Playboy*, he said Disney approached him in 1989 with an offer to put a Margaritaville in its park. Buffett turned to his father, who pointed out that he had enough money to do anything he wanted. Why do anything he was uncomfortable doing? Buffett thought about it and made Disney a ludicrous counteroffer. "I asked for a percentage of the gate on nights I played," he told writer David Standish. "I told them I work on eighty-twenty splits most of the time doing concerts, so I want twenty percent of the whole gate on nights I work." After Disney's execs stopped spinning, they said no. Fine. "In Margaritaville, you expect to see dope dealers, various riffraff—and Disney World is too clean," Buffett said.

For *Where is Joe Merchant?*, Buffett invented Cat World—a park across the street from Disney where parents could engage in catharsis by feeding mice dressed like Mickey Mouse to hungry cats.

By 1998, however, with a growing business, Buffett didn't say "No," or wildly counter. He called Cohlan. "Jimmy is one of the more intuitive people you'll meet," Cohlan says. Buffett was interested, but he wasn't sure he wanted to license his name. "So he called me up and said, 'Look, you sort of talked about this like a brand . . . if you come and do this with me, it could be fun.'"

It could also have failed miserably, and Cohlan was making a lot of money on Wall Street. But Bear Stearns & Co. had taken Planet Hollywood public in 2006. "So I kind of knew there *could* be a business in the big box restaurant," Cohlan says. "I did two things."

He had a friend, a banker, who was from Mississippi and well versed in all things Buffett. Cohlan asked his friend to ask *his* friends how far they thought Margaritaville could go. "Because, between you and me, being in front of a theme park didn't strike me as the most logical place for a Margaritaville, right?" Cohlan says.

The report he got back was it would work as long as it was "high quality, clever and fun." A model for that existed—in Key West and New Orleans. Boucher had figured much the same thing.

"The other thing I did," Cohlan says, "I figured, well, if I'm going to do this, do one of these big things in Orlando, you gotta do one in Las Vegas."

He'd never been to Las Vegas, but he had a friend—another banker—whose clients included Vegas casino mogul Steve Wynn, who, it turns out, is a big Jimmy Buffett fan. Cohlan asked his friend if he'd ask Wynn if the idea of a Margaritaville in Las Vegas made any sense. Word came back early the next morning that Wynn would do a deal like that tomorrow, if he could.

Cohlan left Wall Street, and he and Buffett started Margaritaville Holdings. "And it was really started with the Universal Orlando restaurant," Cohlan says. "It was real entrepreneurial. Jimmy was like, 'Come be my partner, but it's not Wall Street. We gotta figure it out.' And we did figure it out."

They even got Seagram's to pick up the $12 million construction tab and then hand over the keys. Cohlan went and found Dan Leonard to run the restaurant and the McBride Company to design it. McBride continues to design Margaritaville properties. Leonard is now president of Margaritaville's hospitality division.

The Margaritaville Café at Universal CityWalk opened in 1999. Buffett played there in March of that year. "I think we did in that first year, $18 million," Cohlan says.

Everyone—Boucher, Cindy Thompson, Michael Utley—*everyone* who was around before, marks Orlando as the after. "If you want to learn how to survive in the jungle, you train in Belize," Archibald "Archie" Mercer, an ex-soldier running a Central American wildlife preserve in Buffett's 2004 novel *A Salty Piece of Land* said. "If you want to learn how to survive in the tourist business, you train in Orlando."

The *Hemisphere Dancer*, keeping watch on the diners
and the drinkers outside the Margaritaville Café at Universal
CityWalk, Orlando.

Archie's training had come in a reboot of the Cat World concept from Buffett's first novel. Buffett, meanwhile, kept right on touring. The schedule had eased. They'd work on Tuesdays, Thursdays, and Saturdays, and only for a couple of weeks. Then they'd break and he'd travel or write, surf, fish, or sail. Then they'd fire up the machine—and it had become an efficient touring machine—and return to the road. "If angst is your diet and serious thought is your idea of recreation, then PLEASE DON'T BUY THIS RECORD," Buffett wrote in the liner notes of 1999's live *Tuesdays, Thursdays, Saturdays*. "But, if you like the beach, need some escapism and like to laugh, stomp and dance, then you have come to the right spot."

Just how it all had grown stunned an old friend who had gotten his first look at the expanding world of Margaritaville on the same tour where Buffett captured the live record. After working on *Havana Daydreamin'* in 1975, Doyle Grisham didn't play on another Jimmy Buffett album until 1982, when Buffett returned to Tennessee to make *Somewhere Over China*, and then not again until 1999.

Grisham always figured Buffett would move on and fill out his sound with other musicians, and, by 1976, he figured it was time for him to do something like "Margaritaville." Grisham absolutely noticed when it hit, and then went back about his life, playing on albums by Randy Travis, George Jones, and anyone else in need of a lonesome sound.

"After that, I didn't keep up with him much," Grisham says. "He moved into another different area of music, and I didn't notice as much airplay. But I didn't notice a lot of people. I was spending ten to twelve hours a day in the studio. You kind of lose track of things, if you don't keep track of them on your own. So I was very surprised when I saw 25,000 people. Country acts weren't drawing that at that time."

Mac McAnally bought an old house in Muscle Shoals that had belonged to one of the town's prominent doctors. (Swampers bassist David Hood's Sunday school teacher once lived next door.) McAnally had turned it into a studio, La La Land. In 1999, Buffett and the Coral Reefers went there to record a chunk of what would become *Beach House on the Moon*. Grisham was called in to play and then asked to join the tour. They kicked off at the end of May in Charleston, South Carolina, playing a sold-out arena that didn't quite fit 25,000 but must have felt like it to someone sitting on Buffett's stage for the first time.

"It was such a well-known secret, how popular he was," Grisham says. He looked out across the Parrot Heads and arrived at a reasonable question: "I wonder how long this is going to last?"

"Little did I know," he says.

Chapter 17

What Would Jimmy Buffett Do?

"I would write with people, and there was this one guy I was writing with, he was really, really talented and really young and dumb and he didn't know any better," Don Rollins says, prefacing why it's sometimes good to be young and dumb and not know any better. "He had a ten-year-old Honda Civic and two hundred bucks and he went to Nashville."

For every famous face on the wall of Tootsie's Orchid Lounge, the Bluegrass Inn, or any other old time haunt on lower Broadway in Nashville, there are a million stories that start with an old car and $200 and end with an old car, an empty tank, and no cash to fill it. But within six months, D. Vincent Williams had a record contract and a publishing deal with Warner/Chappell Music, which, after taking a look at the writing credits on Williams's work, offered Rollins a deal as well.

Unlike Williams, Rollins couldn't just run off to Nashville. He was teaching saxophone and directing the jazz band at Lamar University, his alma mater, in Beaumont, Texas—where he'd grown up. For a few years, Rollins taught during the school year, concentrated more effort on songwriting in the summer, and balanced his jobs. In 2000, he made Warner/Chappell an offer: If they'd pay him a little more, he'd move to Nashville and take a run at writing full-time. At the end of the 2000–1 school year, he moved to Nashville and into the glamorous world of songwriting, where his job was to sit in a room and churn out ideas—one song a day, five a week. "Most of what you get is a pile of rejection slips," Rollins says.

He met Jim "Moose" Brown in a recording studio. Brown's done plenty of touring, including with Bob Seger's Silver Bullet Band, but around Nashville his reputation was made in the studios. "A really fabulous session player," Rollins says. Some things are the same as they were back when Buzz Cason opened Creative Workshop and Tompall Glaser assembled the Hillbilly Central crew. Songwriters write, session guys record, managers and publishers pitch. That's how Rollins met Brown.

In February 2003, they sat down together to write a song for a singer named Colt Prather, who was looking for "a Jimmy Buffett song, something with that groove," Rollins says. He had two lines ready to go. The first was something he'd heard a colleague in Texas say whenever he wanted an early beer: "It's five o'clock somewhere." The second acknowledged their starting line head-on: "What would Jimmy Buffett do?" The rest fell into place. They finished the song before lunch, demoed it in March, and pitched it to Prather's producer. When it was rejected, Rollins went right on writing songs. That was the job.

"Then I get a call that Alan Jackson has it on hold," Rollins says. "I didn't think anything then, either, because you get songs on hold all the time." Rollins didn't think the song was country enough for Jackson. But when he heard Jackson wanted to do the song with Buffett, then things got interesting.

"Alan recorded it April 15," Rollins says. Barely two months after he and Brown had completed the song. "And that is, like, light speed for Nashville. Traditionally when you hear a song on the radio out of Nashville, it was written three to seven years ago."

"It's Five O'Clock Somewhere" tapped the impatience of every hourly worker who feels they're "getting older by the minute." It was for every office drone pushed a little too far by a boss for too little in return. It was for everyone who punches a clock, watches the clock, and can't understand why the damn clock isn't moving any faster. It was in the great and lasting tradition of Johnny Paycheck's cover of David Allan Coe's "Take This Job and Shove It," but with the added appeal of a Jamaican vacation.

It was about, as Mac McAnally (playing the part of Jackson onstage) likes to say, the theory of drunkativity. He worked up a lab experiment, also shared with the Parrot Heads. "You take your watch off, you throw it in the punch bowl and you slosh beer all over it," McAnally said in Austin in 2013. "You can dance around it if you want. It's not really important. Turns out time quits mattering."

Well, some time matters.

"I just want to thank Alan for the thirty-four seconds I spent in the studio," Buffett said. "It turned out really good."

Buffett spent more than thirty-four seconds in the studio and the song, but not much more. After Rollins and Brown sent their work-a-day Joe to the bar for a liquid lunch, he pours himself into a cab to get back to the office by two. "At a moment like this, I can't help but wonder," Jackson sang, "What would Jimmy Buffett do?"

He'd pour a drink and engage in topical banter with Jackson as the song fades out.

"It's always on five in Margaritaville," Buffett said.

"I've been to Margaritaville a few times," Jackson replied.

Jackson affixed "It's Five O'Clock Somewhere" to *Greatest Hits II*, and ended up with the first song for his next greatest hits record.* "It was a steamroller," Rollins says. It cracked the top twenty on *Billboard*'s Hot 100 singles chart and spent eight weeks in the summer of 2003 at number one on the country chart. "A lot of it was because Buffett hadn't been on the charts," Rollins says. "He hadn't been on the radio much in forever and people loved Buffett. They never forgot about him."

---

* He put it on 2012's *Playlist: The Very Best of Alan Jackson.*

Rollins and Brown won the 2004 Grammy Award for Best Country Song. Buffett and Jackson won a Country Music Association award for vocal event of the year, and Academy of Country Music awards for single of the year and video of the year.

Three decades after Jimmy Buffett arrived in Nashville from Mobile, he was an overnight country music sensation. And after twenty years of saying from stages some version of "I don't need awards when I have fans like Parrot Heads," he had a little hardware. "I thought I'd make it through with a clean slate," he told *60 Minutes'* Steve Kroft in 2004. "I was at the point where it'd be cool not to get anything."

The 2003 CMA Awards featured a performance by Jackson, Buffett, and their combined bands. More than any other genre, country music likes to salute itself, and the CMAs are one of the biggest parties of the year. "All the kids were there," Buffett told Kroft. Toby Keith. Kenny Chesney. Martina McBride. Everyone who might maybe want to sing on, say, a new Jimmy Buffett record.

"I had this idea to do this project, and you always have to have a Plan B and I thought, well, if nobody comes to the party, I have a perfectly great band, and perfectly great singers and we'll do it that way," Buffett said. "But I'm gonna ask 'em, because all they can say is no."

So he made his pitch: come to Key West, work a little, play a bunch. He told George Strait he could bring his boat. Everyone was interested. "The other thing is, I think it's probably true and I can admit to the fact, is I don't take this stuff as serious as everybody else," Buffett told Kroft. "I'm not a go-to-the-studio-and-shake-every-note kind of person. I'm a go-capture-the-magic guy."

The record he wanted to make with all his new friends made as much sense as any he'd recorded since *Changes in Latitudes, Changes in Attitudes*, when Norbert Putnam led Buffett to the sea.

It hadn't been a fluke that Don Rollins and "Moose" Brown had come across a singer looking for a Buffett-styled beach/drinking song. As awkward as Buffett might have looked in 1984, on the beach in his jeans and his cowboy hat on the cover of *Riddles in the Sand*, he was ahead of the curve—or, in that bright yellow shirt, lighting the way. By the time "It's Five O'Clock Somewhere" hit, Buffett had become a bigger influence on Music Row than Willie, Waylon, or any of the boys.

In 1996, Chesney recorded one of Mac McAnally's best songs, "Back Where I Come From." It's about pride in a place as charming and warm, humble and funny as McAnally and the people he grew up with. Where, in Sunday school, they teach you who made the sun shine—for everyone already knows who made the moonshine. Those little towns off interstates where time passes with "Amazing Grace." It's a perfect little dirt-road country song, and Chesney, who grew up in Knoxville, Tennessee, wore it well.

In 1999, Chesney was still that guy, projecting farmhouse cool in a white T-shirt and brown cowboy hat on the cover of *Everywhere We Go*, an album that featured the hit, "She Thinks My Tractor's Sexy."

That was before he got a yacht. Three years later, when Chesney released his next studio album, he'd shed the sleeves on the T-shirt (now black) and was standing on the cover in a Caribbean paradise, peaks rising from blue waters behind him. *No Shoes, No Shirt, No Problems* was his new promise. He moved four million copies of that album.

"When I really think about it, would I have been the next Jimmy Buffett? I think even then I thought that wasn't a great idea," Todd Snider says. "Then I saw Kenny Chesney do it and I thought, 'Damn, it was there to do.' In my mind I was thinking the world's not going to let that happen."

Chesney followed up *No Shoes* with a Christmas album, *All I Want for Christmas Is a Real Good Tan*. In 2004, he released *When the Sun Goes Down* and followed that up with *Be As You Are*, which included "Guitars and Tiki Bars," and "Old Blue Chair"—his "Tin Cup Chalice."

Online, there's a video of Chesney sitting by the beach wishing he could bottle everything he's seen in the islands, all the fun he's had, and the "heart and the energy and the passion my friends bring to the show." If he could bottle all of that . . . well, he did bottle all of that. It's called Blue Chair Bay Rum.

In 1998, Buffett solved his radio problem when he launched Radio Margaritaville online. In 2005, it was added to Sirius's satellite lineup (while remaining free online). "It's like the old pirate radio stations that sat offshore and played what they want," Buffett told the Associated Press in 2001. What he wanted was some Jimmy Buffett music, but also old soul, New Orleans R&B, reggae, world music, live broadcasts of Buffett shows, and a couple of times a week, old shows—also available on demand.

In 2016, SiriusXM and Chesney launched No Shoes Radio for his No Shoes Nation—the name of his fan club. No Shoes Nation flies pirate colors from their tailgates to the tops of the football stadiums Chesney packs every summer.

If Buffett's analogy is the Grateful Dead, Kenny Chesney is his Phish.

Chesney's full turn to surf from turf was a natural conclusion. Someone was going to see Buffett's touring revenue, see the pageantry and loyalty of the Parrot Heads—see the *brand*—and recognize an opportunity. Toes had been dipped in those waters for years.

In 1995, Clint Black took to the beach (in a wetsuit) for the video for "Summer's Coming." Garth Brooks took "Two Piña Coladas" to the top of the country chart in 1998. The cover of the single featured Brooks in all black, smiling between two illustrated palm trees. Phil Vassar's 2001 top-ten country song "Six-Pack Summer" made a good-time checklist that included "the sunblock, a blanket and the best of Jimmy Buffett."

In 2004, Blake Shelton's "Some Beach" opened with some poor schmuck driving down a highway, thirty minutes late to wherever and singing "Margaritaville" as a coping mechanism. The same year, Toby Keith could be found lounging in a hammock with a couple of women singing about Steve and Gina, a margarita-inspired couple-for-the-night who met at Sammy Hagar's Cabo Wabo Cantina. Soon enough, Keith would have his own mescal label; Hagar already had Cabo Wabo Tequila and a little club in Mexico that had come out of Van Halen's 1988 song "Cabo Wabo." Hagar has built Cabo Wabo into a Margaritaville with louder guitars.

Buffett had once been too country for New York and Los Angeles, and not country enough for Nashville. He'd tried to be something other than himself, and then given up and given his energies to the Parrot Heads. And then he became a genre unto himself. The industry finally came around.

While Music Row was booking beach vacations, Buffett was busying himself being Buffett. He was, for example, wandering the narrow side streets of Corsica with his son, Cameron, in search of a dagger, "a shipboard promise for good behavior," Buffett wrote in the liner notes of 2002's *Far Side of the World*. They found a shop, open but with a chain preventing their entrance. "Inside, a large man with steely eyes and a long beard sat sharpening the blade of an ominous-looking knife," Buffett wrote.

An hour later, they left with the knife, some smiles, and a few more stories from another mysterious corner of the world unlocked. "In *Innocents Abroad*, my old hero Mark Twain said, 'I flit and flit—for I am ever on the wing—but I avoid the herd,'" Buffett wrote aboard his *MV Continental Drifter*.

Far Side of the World was full of songs from Africa (the title track) and memories from St. Barts ("Autour Du Rocher"). There was a cover of Louisiana slide-guitar hero Sonny Landreth's "USS Zydecoldsmobile"—and an inconsequential bumper sticker song, "What If the Hokey-Pokey Is All It Really Is About?" that seemed better suited for merchandise than set lists. But it was fun, and his fans liked fun songs.

Buffett had been across the northern Sahara, to the Nile, and on to Tanzania. He'd been in St. Barts and South Florida and at his summer home on Long Island. His influence wasn't his worry.

McAnally, who'd made Music Row a second home, hipped Buffett to his hard-won victory in the battle of Nashville. Then came Alan Jackson's call, a big hit, a few awards, way more laughs about how they'd finally made it, and a trip to Key West to make an album built on a collection of duets with the biggest names in country music.

"If you haven't already guessed by the title, this album will have a solid barefooted base in what we have always done, but with a toe or two leaning in the direction of today's country market," Buffett wrote in an email to all involved in what was originally titled *Conky Tonk*. "Let's face it. This is not a big stretch for me."

Clint Black, Chesney, Keith, Jackson, and Strait joined Buffett on Hank Williams's "Hey, Good Lookin'." Buffett and Jackson combined forces on Guy Clark's "Boats to Build." Chesney joined Buffett again on "License to Chill," another lots of work and the boss is a jerk song. With Martina McBride, Buffett sang a birthday song, "Trip Around the Sun," and he recruited Nanci Griffith for "Someone I Used to Love."

The most incongruous—and surprising—guest on the album was Bill Withers, who appeared on his own "Playin' the Loser Again" and added a cowriting credit with Buffett on "Simply Complicated."

"Bill Withers is the closest thing black people have to Bruce Springsteen," the drummer for the Roots, Questlove, told *Rolling Stone*'s Andy Greene in 2015. Withers essentially retired in 1985 and hadn't released any music—until Jimmy Buffett called.

With Toby Keith, Buffett worked up a Will Kimbrough song, "Piece of Work." Some months earlier, Buffett had gone to dinner with his niece Melanie and asked her what had ever happened to Kimbrough, a guitarist from Mobile who'd played with Todd Snider. Melanie dropped Kimbrough a line and told him he should send her uncle some songs. Kimbrough packaged up all his work and sent it FedEx.

Kimbrough remembers his first encounter with Buffett well. In February 1995, Kimbrough was backstage at Tipitina's in New Orleans. "The backstage at Tipitina's is like three or four broom closets opened up into a space, with mops and buckets and a giant ice chest with hot water and hot beer floating in it," Kimbrough says. "It's nasty. But everybody wanted to be back there."

Jerry Jeff Walker might have been there that night. Kimbrough *knows* Buffett was, because at one point, jammed up against a wall by the mass of people, he looked over and realized he was standing next to Buffett.

"Hi," Kimbrough said.

That was the first time he and Buffett met, but being from Mobile, he and Buffett went back. "Everyone had the records," he says. "Like anyone who's that big, a cultural icon, their hometown absolutely loves them and desperately needs them to come back and *tell* them he loves them."

Jammed into the closet-like backstage at Tipatina's, when Buffett found out Kimbrough was from Mobile he said, "Oh, you're another escapee." Kimbrough loves Mobile. Still has family in Mobile. Plays Mobile all the time. "To me Mobile's a place that's wonderful to go back to when you're older, because it doesn't change that much," he says. "But when you're eighteen, a place that doesn't change that much—some people just thrive and some people just feel like they're stuffed in a box."

After Snider's Nervous Wrecks disbanded in the late-nineties, Kimbrough went to work producing, recording, and touring, working still with Snider from time to time, but also with Rodney Crowell, Emmylou Harris, Guy Clark, Rosanne Cash, and a roster of heavy-hitting *artists*.

He also made his own records, including *Home Away*, which Kimbrough released in 2002 and included in his shipment to

Buffett. Time passed before he got a call from Buffett's people saying Jimmy wanted to cover two songs: "Piece of Work" and "Champion of the World."*

"Is that okay?" they said.

"It's great," Kimbrough replied.

"Piece of Work" was written in the hospital one night after his second daughter was born. She'd had to stay a few extra days, but the night before she was scheduled to go home, the whole family—Kimbrough, his wife, and their oldest daughter—spent the night. Kimbrough couldn't sleep, and so he got up and sat in the bathroom reading when a song popped in his head. He grabbed a paper towel and jotted down a collection of contradictions: iron and lace, angel and fiend, lavender and gasoline. "I'm the CEO of the mailroom clerks," he wrote. "Lord have mercy what a piece of work."

Minus any guest stars, Buffett threw in a Grateful Dead song ("Scarlet Begonias") and another tune from Tom Corcoran's *Greatest Hits of the Lesser Antilles* mix, Leon Russell's "Back to the Island."

Buffett and McAnally wrote "Coast of Carolina," a sequel to "Come Monday" capturing all those many nights since Jimmy and Jane first connected in the phone booth outside the Chart Room. It's a celebration of longevity, and so it's a celebration of perseverance and compromise. "The walls that won't come down, we can decorate or climb or find some way to get around," Buffett sings. True in life, in love, and even in Nashville.

License to Chill, as the album was eventually titled, was released in July 2004 and debuted at number one on *Billboard*'s albums chart—Buffett's first number one. All it took was thirty years from the summer "Come Monday" gave him a shot at a career. Jimmy

---

* "Champion of the World" didn't get cut for Buffett's record, but Little Feat's Bill Payne was playing keyboards in the sessions and Little Feat would record the song with Buffett for its 2008 duets record, *Join the Band*.

Buffett was, finally, a brand-new country star—with a chain of restaurants instead of bowling alleys. No wonder the art inside the CD featured him looking back over his shoulder, laughing.

"Hiram Hank Williams worked at the Alabama Dry Dock and Shipbuilding Company from 1942 to 1944," Buffett wrote in the liner notes, signed from Buenos Aires. "In his own handwriting, he scribbled his occupation on his job application as 'welder/musician.' I know this because I read the file after my mother discovered it when she worked at the shipyard. She thought it was something I would be interested in. She was right."

Buffett reached back to Thomas McGuane's words from *A White Sport Coat and a Pink Crustacean*, to the "curious hinterland where Hank Williams and Xavier Cugat meet." Buffett admitted he wasn't sure what that meant in 1973. "Now I do."

"I've always had a love-hate relationship with Nashville," Buffett told *60 Minutes*, breaking into a grin. "Right now it's love."

Zac Brown called up Buffett to lend a hand on 2010's infectious hit, "Knee Deep" and then CMT paired the two for an episode of *Crossroads*. They shot it outside Nashville, and Kimbrough took the solo on Brown's down-home "Chicken Fried," and they all put down "Nobody from Nowhere." Written by Kimbrough and Tommy Womack, it had been the lead track on Buffett's 2009 *Buffet Hotel*, an album that took its name from a West African hotel Buffett encountered on a journey to get his passport stamped in Timbuktu.

Buffett and Zac Brown mashed up the latter's "Free" with Van Morrison's "Into the Mystic," and soon Buffett was playing that, "Knee Deep," and sometimes even Brown's "Where the Boat Leaves From" in *his* shows. He didn't have anything to do with "Where the Boat Leaves From" (other than to set the template and inspire the spirit), but Buffett knew it was exactly the kind of song Parrot Heads wanted to hear.

Toby Keith and Buffett continued their mutual admiration society. In July 2013, Keith hosted a benefit concert in his native

Oklahoma to lend a hand after a devastating tornado. Sammy Hagar came and played and mentioned he'd done a duet album and cut "a laid-back version of 'Margaritaville,'" Keith says, as if the song wasn't born laid-back enough. Keith sang a few verses, and Hagar included "Margaritaville," set to an "Under the Boardwalk" beat, on his 2013 record *Sammy Hagar & Friends*.

A year earlier, Buffett had pulled Keith in on "Too Drunk to Karaoke," for Buffett's *Songs from St. Somewhere*. He'd sheepishly asked Keith to lend his voice after Buffett had turned down Keith's offer to join in on his 2011 top-ten hit "Red Solo Cup," a song about red Solo cups. "You can tell me no, because I deserve to be told no," Keith recalls Buffett saying. In 2015, Toby Keith enlisted the Coral Reefer Band for "Rum is the Reason"—"pirates never ruled the world." Buffett helped Keith out on "Sailboat for Sale."

After *License to Chill*, Will Kimbrough got a call to join Buffett in St. Barts for a writing session. They'd get going at 10 a.m. Buffett would usually be on his way up from the beach. He's got a duplex on the harbor. "Nice little place," Kimbrough says.

They worked on a song Kimbrough brought called "Bodysurfing in a Hurricane." It quickly became "Surfing in a Hurricane." Much of the song Parrot Heads would hear on 2006's *Take the Weather with You* was cut in Buffett's living room. "He had the cheapest little Pro Tools interface and a Shure SM58 microphone, and we put the microphone on a paperback book in front of the amp and recorded surf guitar," Kimbrough says.

Sometimes, as was the case with "Wings," from *Buffet Hotel*, Kimbrough sent a work in progress and Buffett's interest was piqued. Other times Buffett might have words, but would need music. He's still engaged in songs and songwriting. Sometimes he needs a push. "I think he gets inspired and then he wants someone to spark the fire back up and get it finished," Kimbrough says. "Get him excited."

Kimbrough eventually earned honorary Coral Reefer status, a

thrill for a guy who grew up with Buffett's songs. "A Pirate Looks at Forty," "Son of a Son of a Sailor," "He Went to Paris," those were his favorites. Buffett jokes that Kimbrough got new living room furniture out of the deal, but he got a lot more than some nice checks in the mail.

Kimbrough's played with most of Nashville. He's in demand as a guitarist and a producer. He makes his own solo records, and has a band called Willie Sugarcapps with a group of Gulf Coast friends. They play swampy Americana. Will Kimbrough is anyone's definition of an ace.

But when Buffett—who's long championed underappreciated writers like Jesse Winchester and Bruce Cockburn, and who introduced Todd Snider to an audience he maintains to this day—cut "Piece of Work," it made Kimbrough see himself as a more serious songwriter. It made him work a little harder.

"The ball's always in his court," Kimbrough says. "I'm here doing my thing: making my records, playing on people's records, touring, writing songs, producing records. I'm busy, because that's just the life, if you're lucky enough to get it.

"But the main thing I've ever gotten out of it is the experience of getting to write with him and record. It's a joyous thing, about ninety-nine percent of the time and I think all of the great songwriters I've ever been around take joy out of it."

Chapter 18

A Salty Piece of Land

In Margaritaville, as Jimmy Buffett once said, you expect a few dope dealers and ne'er-do-wells. So in 1978, the *Euphoria II* was in San Salvador, anchored in a postcard cove with only one other boat nearby. Buffett was up the mainmast sweating out the previous night's misbehavior when he called down, "You should see what's coming our way."

It was a Cigarette boat—the brand *Miami Vice* would introduce to the rest of the United States soon enough—sleek, powerful, and expensive. It pulled up alongside *Euphoria II* with a request.

"What would it take to use your radar?"

"What would it take to drive your boat?" Buffett said.

Easy trade, and after a wild ride in the speedboat, everyone went on with their day. Evening fell, and the cast of the *Euphoria II* invited the folks aboard the other sailboat for dinner. After dinner and revelry, Buffett decided he wasn't ready to call it a night. He hopped into his dinghy, bumped it playfully into the hull of the other boat, tied up, and kept the party going until he fell asleep—in the dinghy. And that wouldn't have been a problem, but his knot didn't hold and he drifted to sea. When he awoke, he saw nothing but water in every direction—with no idea which direction would take him to the safety and comfort of *Euphoria II*.

That's when, for the second time in as many days, the Cigarette appeared. Over the horizon came another boat—the mother ship, loaded with product. The guys who'd been so friendly the day before weren't as happy to see Jimmy Buffett in his dinghy. Tensely, they pointed him in the direction home.

"If it hadn't been me," Tom Corcoran remembers Buffett saying, "I'd have been dead." The exchange felt dangerous. That was new.

Key West grew. The storefronts on Duval Street filled. The sunset celebration at Mallory Square got a little more professional and managed as space shrunk and more artists, musicians, and vaudevillians came to compete for an increasing pile of tourism dollars. Hotels were remodeled. Bed and breakfasts opened. Captain Tony finally won a term as mayor, from 1989–91, and was named Mayor Emeritus after that.

In 1977, Corcoran saw something he hadn't seen before: college kids. On spring break. In 1978, it was cars full of nearly identical-looking young gay men. By 1979, families had arrived. "I went, Oh crap," Corcoran says. "This was before Jimmy could make this happen. Now surely, everyone who's a fan of Jimmy Buffett wants to see Key West at least once. But the same can be said of Hemingway, or fishing. There are all these draws. The romance of the islands, and all that stuff."

When historian Tom Hambright, who was stationed in Key West after enlisting in the navy in 1960, gives talks about the island, he asserts "Margaritaville" and Buffett brought far more tourists to town than any billboard. His is anecdotal evidence, but he has a lot of anecdotes.*

---

* He also has a file of Buffett-related clippings, mostly old newspaper stories, magazine features, and the first edition of the *Coconut Telegraph*. Then there's the photocopy of a note from Buffett: "When I first moved to Key West and spent summers in town this library was a place to pass the days browsing and reading about the old days on this island for songs I'd eventually write—and it was air conditioned. If you ever need assistance to keep the air flowing, I'd be happy to help. Thanks for keeping me cool in those happy summers not so long ago and being my office before I could afford one." He signed it October 22, 1987. Hambright said only once have they almost called in the favor.

Chris Robinson, Buffett's old downstairs neighbor, remembers a toga party Phil Tenney, the owner of Louie's Backyard, threw. This was probably 1979 and, to be specific, it was a combination toga/costume party. Robinson topped his bedsheet toga off with a colander wrapped in tinfoil. He was the Lost Shaker of Salt. Nobody guessed. When the cruise ships let out these days—as they do more regularly than ever—passengers pack the Margaritaville Store to buy Lost Shakers of Salt.

Among the old gang, there were breakups and crackups and people calmed down, little by little. Robinson lives about twenty miles from Key West now, working as a fishing guide on Sugarloaf Key. "Some have become successful," Robinson says. "Some are starving fishing guides. But it's a nice office out there."

He keeps the big picture in focus. The old timers on the island when he arrived, they told him he should have seen Key West ten years earlier. Someone's always been anywhere first, and it was better then. It'll always be that way, everywhere.

"It's Margaritaville for a younger group now," Robinson says. "They come down here, and they're from the Midwest, and they've never seen anything like this. I try not to take it for granted, and of course things are a lot more serious. DUI and the police, and the property values have gone up so much. I paid two hundred dollars to live on the water and now it'd be five thousand dollars, but it's still fun. I do miss living here at times."

The kids come down now, and nobody knows of a time when the bars didn't serve margaritas and you could park anywhere on Duval and have the sheriff let you drive him home.

It was early November 2015 as he sat chatting by the beach. The afternoon was sticky—Corcoran says the old rule in Key West was to try to smell like today, not yesterday—but a breeze had kicked up from offshore. Dark clouds were piling in the direction of Cuba. It looked like rain. Robinson turned his eyes to the sky and shook his head no. Fishing guides know what's going on out in the office.

Lunch had been by the beach and the next stop was the Casa Marina, a Waldorf Astoria resort. Before the Casa Marina was a Waldorf property it was a Hilton. It began as another of Henry Flagler's dreams, a place for his railcar passengers to relax in style at the end of the tracks, which would become the end of the road. When the hotel was expanded in 1978, Robinson and Hunter Thompson sat on their backyard beach behind the Waddell apartment and drank beer while they watched the construction workers wrestle with wheelbarrows on an awkward shoreline.

From that same beach today, you could still throw a flip-flop and hit the Casa Marina's property. A throw in the opposite direction might knock over a drink at Louie's Afterdeck. A group on a bicycle tour paused in front of Louie's Backyard, its guide pointing to the white building next door. "That's where Jimmy Buffett lived."

It's sacred ground now, all of it, and that's why Parrot Heads from around the country were beginning to arrive for the annual Meeting of the Minds. In the bars and restaurants of Key West, Meeting of the Minds is known as "the Parrot Head thing." It is not necessarily a term of endearment. Among the service industry veterans, Parrot Heads have something of a lousy reputation when it comes to tipping. Corcoran figures this is probably true for some and made up for by the generosity of others. In total, the good-bad customer ratio can't be any different than the population at large. And coming in November, on the heels of the annual Fantasy Fest parade and party, it's another kick to the local economy after the summer lull and hurricane season.

Still, you hear it all over town. In the Green Parrot Bar: "Oh, it's the Parrot Head thing this week." Over at Captain Tony's: "This week's the Parrot Head thing, isn't it?" Down at the Chart Room: "We're bracing for the Parrot Head thing."

The Parrot Head thing: In 1989, Scott Nickerson had a flash of inspiration. He was a musician living in Atlanta and he'd go see Buffett, who, at the time, was playing three- to five-night stands in a market that had been good to him since the Bistro days. Nickerson would see the same people every night, and then not see them again until Buffett came back the next year. He thought he could form a club without making it explicitly a Jimmy Buffett Fan Club.

Almost a decade earlier, Buffett had teamed up with Senator Bob Graham to form the Save the Manatee Club, a group dedicated to protecting Florida's loveable, and endangered, sea cows. In that spirit, Nickerson thought he could toss some community service into the mix and then they'd all retire to a backyard for barbecue, a beer, and some music.

He took out an ad in *Creative Loafing*, an entertainment-themed paper in Atlanta. It was a little ad, free he thinks, and filed under miscellaneous. "About as big as your little finger," Nickerson says. "Whatever I put there, it was enough to get phone calls. And I got a few." He got one from a woman in his apartment complex. Others came from around the city. On April 1, 1989 (no joke) they met in the parking lot at Chastain Park, where Buffett often played, threw Frisbees, and had a few laughs. For anyone who stopped and asked what they were up to, they had flyers. That perfectly casual afternoon was the first meeting of the world's first Parrot Head Club. "I can't tell you how many people that was," Nickerson says. "It was under twenty."

He made a call to the Margaritaville office in Key West to make sure what they were doing was okay. That set in motion a loose affiliation that continues today. Buffett's lawyers indemnified their client, and Margaritaville was generous with the use of their trademarks. "Sunshine Smith was with us on the whole thing," Nickerson says.

The *Coconut Telegraph* wrote about the club and passed along Nickerson's number. "And then my phone rang off the wall," he says. He worked with Margaritaville to develop a few guidelines, a template, and by the end of 1992 there were Parrot Head Clubs in Texas, New York City, Orlando, Detroit, and New Orleans. In December of that year, another musician, Jerry Diaz, organized the first Meeting of the Minds—in New Orleans. About eighty people showed up. A year later, attendance doubled. By then there were nineteen Parrot Head Clubs.

Helped along by the Internet, the numbers kept growing. In 1995, George Stevenson, the kid who'd discovered Buffett pounding on the door of the Euphoria Tavern, cofounded a Parrot Head Club in Oregon. In 1998, Meeting of the Minds made the logical move to Key West. As of 2015, there were 216 Parrot Head Clubs in the United States, 1 virtual Parrot Head Club for fans who don't live where there's a chapter, 11 clubs in Canada, and 1 in Australia.

Between 2002 and 2015, Parrot Head Clubs donated more than $41.3 million and 3.6 million volunteer hours to local charities. Nickerson's idea was a good one.

The 2015 Meeting of the Minds was the twenty-fourth annual. Its theme: A Salty Piece of Land. In the 2004 novel of the same name, Buffett returned to the story of Tully Mars, his cowboy in the jungle.

"Like most tribal celebrations, the myths, cultures, and historical events that originally sparked them still present a slight attraction to the attendees, but it is more of an excuse to throw a wild party," Mars says of a stop in Cheyenne, Wyoming, for Frontier Days, "during which time the local chambers of commerce and religious leaders tend to cast a blind eye toward the debauchery because of the business it brings to town."

There's no reason to cast an eye, blind or otherwise to the more than 3,500 that now travel to Key West and book every room in the Casa Marina and many more around town. The Key West Police Department sells T-shirts—featuring, in 2015 anyway, a parrot wearing a hat and badge—to raise money for the Police Athletic League. A map in the back of the convention guide offers an official, "Welcome to Beautiful Key West, Florida."

The cover of the guide matched the back of the official T-shirt, both of which echoed Jim Mazzotta's early Caribbean Soul designs. Buffett's *Hemisphere Dancer* cuts through a splash of margarita and over palm trees lining the beach in front of the Casa Marina.

Inside, Parrot Heads were greeted by ads for the Margaritaville Beach Resort in Hollywood Beach, Florida; Margaritaville Foods ("Escape to Paradise Tonight!"); Margaritaville Tequila ("Paradise Is Just a Sip Away"); and a lineup of sponsors that included Margaritaville Premium Spirits, LandShark Lager, Magaritaville Travel Adventures, the Margaritaville Vacation Club by Wyndham, and Radio Margaritaville. A two-page centerpiece photo of two empty chairs on a beach near a lone palm invited an "Escape to Margaritaville" where you can dine, stay, and shop.

The welcome bag included a coupon for 20-percent off any one item (and free shipping) from Margaritaville Cargo (home to the line of Frozen Concoction Makers), a coupon for fifty cents off one box of Margaritaville Freezer Bars (flavors: margarita, piña colada, and strawberry daiquiri), a coupon for one dollar off any two bottles of Margaritaville sauces or rubs, an actual bottle of Jimmy Buffett's Island Tea (peach mango), and one box of strawberry-daiquiri-flavored Margaritaville gelatin.

When Cohlan partnered with Buffett and they got Seagram's to build them the Margaritaville Café in Orlando, Cohlan made one more move—a stone-cold Wall Street shuffle. He told Seagram's Margaritaville wouldn't serve Seagram's spirits.

Seagram's had recently introduced Parrot Bay Rum, which Cohlan and Buffett felt cut a little too close to Buffett's Parrot Head branding. "Nobody had the courtesy to call," Cohlan says. And remember, Seagram's wasn't just Buffett's restaurant partner at the time. It also owned his record label. Seagram's begged ignorance, asked forgiveness, and requested a meeting to make things right. Their peace offering: a line of Margaritaville spirits for the Orlando restaurant. Cohlan, however, had done more research—

research that, unsurprisingly, showed a high correlation between Margaritaville, Jimmy Buffett, and tequila.

Cohlan didn't see any reason to limit distribution to the three Margaritaville Cafés in existence at the time. Why not go far and wide with a Margaritaville Tequila? "This," Cohlan says, "is when I realized what the potential for this could be."

Liquor led to beer and a partnership with Anheuser-Busch, who developed a Lone Palm Lager for Margaritaville. They pulled the name from a song on *Fruitcakes* inspired by a couple of beach chairs Buffett spied while having lunch on St. Barts, a Larry McMurtry novel, and something Art Neville said.

The Neville Brothers were opening for Buffett in Cincinnati, and Buffett stopped to see Art in the hotel: "And I walked into Art's room and he showed me the view from his room, which was a demolition site," Buffett said onstage in Sag Harbor, New York, in 1999. "And he looked back and he said, 'Hey, Bubba, not even a bird would fly by this window.'"

"Lone Palm" isn't that lonely a song. There's a garden full of tropical fruit, a couple sitting in those chairs, and they stare contentedly out at the ocean. It's an admission of love's complications ("we sailed from the Port of Indecision"), but it's a nice, peaceful place.

People liked the beer, but when Margaritaville test-marketed the name, however, people connected it with drinking alone, which is sad. They turned next to an old standard, "Fins," and Land-Shark Lager* was born. The world Buffett had been building in his books—one expanded from his songs and the stories he could tell—began to populate the Margaritaville brand.

The real live Jimmy Buffett recognized what was happening. He introduced a new character in *A Salty Piece of Land*, an old

---

* In 2006, when Buffett turned his tour sponsorship over to Margaritaville Tequila and LandShark Lager, Corona turned to . . . Kenny Chesney.

rock star named Willie Singer. "Unlike most entertainers, Willie Singer became more popular the older he got," Buffett wrote, "but he didn't care that much for the fame. Though he was still making great music, it was his other exploits that kept him in the headlines and made him a fortune."

Fictional facts, and factual fictions. Art imitating life, packaged and sold and neatly displayed in the pages of a convention guide. Corcoran had no idea there was Margaritaville gelatin. But he got a kick out of it when he saw it included in the Meeting of the Minds welcome kit.

About a month before the gathering, convention director Andrew Talbert sent an email to registrants. It wasn't subtle: "I have just been advised that JIMMY BUFFETT is coming to play FOR YOU on Thursday of Meeting of the Minds and this is only for YOU at the CASA MARINA!!!"

Also: "I was asked by the management to keep this show private for the Parrot Heads at MOTM!!!"

Mac McAnally had been scheduled to headline the first official night of the convention behind his recently released album *AKA Nobody*. Buffett hijacked the slot because he could and because he needed to be in Cuba a few nights later to play for the marines. Anticipation was high. Security would be tight.

If Meeting of the Minds is anything, it's a music festival. There's a shop—the Mini Mart—and a street fair on Duval in front of Margaritaville. There's lounging poolside and lots of drinking, but all of these activities are accompanied by music. Much of it is trop rock. Buffett is considered the pop of trop.

The Trop Rock Music Association began as the Margarita M.A.F.I.A,* but there are an awful lot of songs about rum, drinking rum, drinking rum on beaches, and throwing away careers to drink rum on beaches.

---

* M.A.F.I.A.: Musicians, Artists and Fans In Alliance

John Frinzi isn't exactly trop rock, but trop rock fans love him. He's a Florida-based singer-songwriter with a sense of melody to match his sense of humor, and he's always going to look like he's about twenty-eight—even when he's sixty-eight.

He's the biggest star around the Casa Marina who isn't a Coral Reefer. While the rest of the trop rock world fans out across the island, Frinzi was signed exclusively to the Casa Marina's stage. He'd secured a pass for Chris Robinson, who was looking to get his hands on that before Buffett hit town and access tightened up.

The Casa Marina opened on New Year's Eve in 1920. President Warren G. Harding stayed there before it was a week old. Henry Flagler never saw it open. He died in 1913; construction began in 1918. To honor his memory, architects Thomas Hastings and John M. Carrère, who'd designed the New York Metropolitan Opera House, the New York Public Library, and the office buildings of the Senate and the House of Representatives kept careful eye over every detail. A $43-million renovation was completed in 2007. The Casa Marina carries a classic elegance, its two pools surrounded by lush vegetation, its sidewalks lined with palm trees and reflecting pools. Its private beach is the biggest on the island. A pier reaches into the Atlantic.

In the middle of opulence, Robinson stood in fishing clothes, his white hair past his shoulders and his mustache catching the breeze, an original pirate hanging happily with his old friend's flock.

The main stage was set over on the beach, its back to the Waddell apartment. Palm trees had been candy striped in yellow caution tape: LandShark Sighting. Robinson didn't see Frinzi, but Thom Shepherd was on the second stage, set up at the foot of the pier, near a sand sculpture of a lighthouse and a setting sun. Shepherd was working up to a song that had become inescapable on Radio Margaritaville.

He wrote "Always Saturday Night" about landing in Key West on a Sunday night only to discover, much like when it's "Five O'Clock

Somewhere," that time is irrelevant in certain situations. As an added touch, at the end of the song, Shepherd threw in the five most familiar notes from "Margaritaville."

Shepherd's producer talked him into that. "I said, 'There's a strong likelihood this is going to get played on Radio Margaritaville; it could be a bad thing,'" Shepherd says. "I have found that apparently they really like it. And the crowds love it, too."

The crowd was doing just that when a woman in a bikini walked by and complimented Robinson on his mustache.

"Rides are affordable," he said. Timing being everything in comedy, she blushed and laughed and they began talking—her husband included. They were from Colorado. Their Parrot Head Club had been trying to get Buffett to play Red Rocks for years, carrying signs to various shows. The sign for Thursday night's set was already drawn up.

Corcoran, smiling and nodding toward Robinson like old friends do, strolled casually into the scene. Corcoran's a Parrot Head magnet. Everyone knows him and his history with Buffett, and at six-foot-five, he's easy to spot.*

The next to arrive was Roger Bartlett, fresh from rehearsal with Frinzi's band. Key West can still collect some characters. It was Bartlett's first Meeting of the Minds, and he was nervous. His 2013 album *Manhattan* was a blues record. Superimposed on the cover against the Midtown skyline, he was wearing a skull and cross-swords T-shirt, but his island wasn't tropical, and it wasn't relaxed. They honk a lot of horns up in the city.

Despite his foundational place in Buffett's—in Margaritaville's— musical history, Bartlett hadn't worked the Parrot Head circuit.†

---

* Somehow, Corcoran is sometimes mistaken for Buffett. "I'm six-five!" he says, retelling one story. Buffett is not.

† Though he did make a 2001 Coral Reefer Band reunion in South Carolina. Among other highlights, Keith Sykes did "Jimmy Bob," his impersonation of Bob Dylan singing "Margaritaville."

He'd be playing with Frinzi's band, and as good as Frinzi's band is, it was still a pickup band with one rehearsal. He wanted to impress.

He had, however, arrived to a pleasant surprise. His pass was all access, all the time. For a few years after Bartlett left the Coral Reefer Band, he'd drop in on shows, maybe sit in for a few songs. Sometimes, if they needed a guitar player for a short run, he'd get a call. Those calls stopped, the drop-ins stopped, and he lost touch with Buffett. Bartlett didn't figure he'd be allowed anywhere near Buffett's backstage. His pass said otherwise. He was interested to see what would happen the next day.

The Casa Marina on the first official day of Meeting of the Minds—the day Buffett was coming—wasn't as casual as the day before. Security—both volunteer and courtesy of Key West's finest—had taken up positions at the door, scanning credentials to keep the non-initiated out. The registration line moved efficiently. The woman passing out T-shirts warned, "Do not bring it back and say it's dirty. That's how the collar looks."

The stilt walkers were out, followed closely by their boss, Tim Glancey, who calls them "the kids." Glancey's a magician. He was living in Orlando in 1989 when the NBA came to town and named its new franchise the Magic. Glancey saw an opportunity. He told the Magic they should work together, what with all they had in common. "We don't do magic," they said.

"Neither do I," he said. "I do sports magic."

"What's that?"

"Give me a day."

He became in-game entertainment and patented an expandable backpack basket he could run around the arena as fans lobbed shots from their seats. Within five years, Sports Magic Team Inc. employed sixty and was making more than $1 million a year, in part because of something that happened in 1992. The NBA All-Star Game came to Orlando.

Glancey was doing card tricks for high rollers in a luxury suite when someone tapped him on the shoulder and said, "Jimmy wants to see you."

Glancey spent the next fifteen years on the road with Buffett as something resembling an opening act and assisting with the more vaudevillian pieces of the stage show.

On the Havana Daydreamin' Tour in 1997, they came up with El Stumpo the Bando as a way to open the second half of the show. A couple of fans would be called to the stage to put Buffett on the spot with a request. "As a rule, we weren't allowed to tell Jimmy what songs were requested," Glancey says. Buffett spent the tour carrying around an eight-inch-thick book of lyrics, studying. Sometimes he'd flash Glancey a look that said, "Where the hell did you find this one?" Sometimes he'd call on Utley for an assist. But he was always game for the challenge. With the foundation of the set list the same night after night, it was a way to build fun and spontaneity into the set—as much for the band as the fans. "That's probably why he is the success he continues to be," Glancey says. "Because he's not set in his ways."

At the Casa Marina, the kids on stilts were smiling and posing for pictures. The bars around the property were open and busy. Cheeseburgers were available. The Mini Mart was humming. Inside, Corcoran was entertaining questions about Jimmy this and Buffett that and doing fast business with his recently finished novel, *Crime Almost Pays*—a break from the Alex Rutledge mystery series he set in Key West and began with 1998's *The Mango Opera*. Next to Corcoran, J. D. Spradlin's Radio Margaritaville equipment was ready and waiting his broadcast.

Bartlett was still nervous a few minutes before his set. Needlessly so. "Brings back such memories," he said from the stage. "Especially since I don't remember them." He played "Dallas," his contribution to *A1A*, after opening with "Let the Good Times Roll." Utley joined him onstage for a few songs and smiles.

Author's photo

Roger Bartlett, playing the blues for the Parrot Heads
at the Meeting of the Minds, Key West, 2015.

Backstage, Buffett arrived, looked at Corcoran, and said, "Are you still alive?" Buffett looked at Bartlett and didn't say anything, at least not at first. Bartlett didn't think Buffett recognized him. "I have lost thirty pounds since he last saw me," Bartlett says. They had a quick chat, but a welcome one after all those years.

Well before he landed in Key West, Bartlett had been practical about the different paths their careers had taken. He'd read an online estimate that Buffett was worth $400 million.* "I'm not," he says. The people who are worth that much—and Buffett's likely worth far more—tend to hang out together. Still, it was nice to see his old road-trip partner, who took the stage with the smile he's been smiling since *A White Sport Coat and a Pink Crustacean* reintroduced him to the world. That smile's never changed.

---

* In December 2016, *Forbes* estimated Buffett's net worth at $550 million, ranking him thirteenth on its list of America's Wealthiest Celebrities, just ahead of Bruce Springsteen and Howard Stern and $10 million behind Madonna. "As long as people enjoy being drunk on a beach," *Forbes* wrote, "expect the Margaritaville empire to expand."

"Good evening, everybody," Buffett said, adjusting a turquoise Fender Stratocaster while the Coral Reefer Band filled in behind him. When you're Buffett, and when shorts and T-shirts are your work attire, it's a fine line between business and business casual. But the baseball hat, the faded shorts, and what appeared to be whatever T-shirt he'd walked off his plane in suggested a more-casual-than-usual Jimmy Buffett.

"Oh, look," Buffett said, motioning to his right. "It's *eight-time* CMA musician of the year." The night before, in Nashville, McAnally had indeed won his eighth musician of the year award.

"Thank you, Bubba," he said.

"How big is that statue?" Buffett said.

"It's . . ." McAnally began, before being interrupted.

"It's large," Buffett said.

"It's a pretty good size, yeah."

"And you have eight of them?" Buffett said.

"Yeah, there's eight."

"Are they in the back of your Suburban? Where do you keep them?"

"There's four in the mantel in Muscle Shoals and there's four on the mantel in Nashville," McAnally said. "They're getting a little crowded, but that's a good problem."

Buffett paused.

"I wouldn't know," he said. "We better play."

Buffett and the Coral Reefer Band shifted into "Great Filling Station Holdup," eventually found the right gear (after someone began playing "Cuban Crime of Passion"), and then segued at the end into the Allman Brothers Band's "Midnight Rider," a regular event in the big rooms they play on tour.

"Let's face it, you've heard this stuff for a long, long time," Buffett said. "So, what are we going to do to kind of get excited? How many quarters can you put in a Magic Fingers until it's dull?"

He'd decided they would play *A White Sport Coat and a Pink*

Crustacean in its entirety—though out of order—and unrehearsed. For a night, he'd be the Jimmy Buffett on Waddell, the guy who'd arrived in the Flying Lady as opposed to the guy flying one of his toys. It was a short walk and a lot of years from those first days to the Casa Marina stage.

"I saw Tom Corcoran, my friend who some of you know, who was down here taking pictures when nobody knew who we were," Buffett said. "The first time the Coral Reefer Band was ever together was in the filling station on the corner of Simonton and Fleming where he had a hat shop at that time.

"That college degree and that naval education served him well in that *hat shop*. I was glad he was there because he let us have the garage next door, and that's where the Coral Reefer Band first rehearsed. And we played, it's not there, many things are not here anymore . . ."

Not Logan's Lobster House, where the Coral Reefers played their first show. Not F. T. Sebastian's Leather Shop. It's a Chinese restaurant. Not Howie's Lounge. It's the redundantly branded $5 Dollar Store. The Old Anchor Inn lives on only as a plaque near the door to the Red Garter Saloon, the self-proclaimed number one strip club on the island and home to what they advertise as Husband Day Care. Fast Buck Freddie's is now a CVS drugstore. They no longer unload bales of marijuana in the middle of the day at the shrimp docks. The Downtown '76 revitalization project is memorialized on a faded plaque on a sidewalk corner along Duval Street.

Fausto's Food Palace is still there on Fleming and is still the place to go for a remedy on those mornings when your head hurts, your feet stink, and your relationship with the Lord has been called into question. But rather than a burned-down Jimmy Buffett pushing wearily through the doors, the day before found Buffett on the front page of the *Key West Citizen*. "Buffett: Build Amphitheater" read the headline striped across A1.

He'd put his name behind a proposed $4-million performance venue at a park planned for land the navy handed to the city in 2002. "I applaud your efforts and look forward to the amphitheater becoming reality," Buffett wrote in a letter to Mayor Craig Cates.

There to here. Here to there. It had been a long time since those early mornings in the Boca Chica, "which stayed open until 5 a.m.," Buffett said onstage, "and then you could go to the airport bar that opened at five. There was a logic to this place that defies description."

Forty feet from the stage, Robinson shook his head. "The Boca Chica was open twenty-four hours," he said. When Buffett announced his arrival as November 1972, Robinson shook his head again and said, "1971." Farther back on the beach, Corcoran did the same, and when Buffett finished *A White Sport Coat* and played "Woman Goin' Crazy on Caroline Street," Corcoran told a few nearby friends about the Shel Silverstein connection.

Introducing "Why Don't We Get Drunk," Buffett turned the story to Atlanta, where he overheard those late-night negotiations and where, decades later, the first Parrot Head Club would form. When they'd run through *White Sport Coat* and moved on to "Margaritaville," he invited Nickerson onstage to play drums. Nickerson nailed his part.

It was a special set, and most everyone appreciated it for what it was—a trip back through the years with the guy who was there when the island was untamed. Most everyone, anyway. A woman in the crowd drinking rum from a water bottle lost patience during one story and shouted, "Oh stop talking already."

He hardly played any of the have-to songs, and so, for once, he got to sing a few of the want-to tunes. Introducing "Death of an Unpopular Poet," he said, "I don't get to play this song enough. I love this song. I really do."

He makes the set lists. He could play it more, but then maybe he can't. What's worse, after all, not playing a song you love, or watching a basketball arena get up and go for more beer while you play the song you love?

"It's the tailgate party," Utley says. "Jimmy laughs at it; we're music for their party. And it's true. Management doesn't like to hear that, but it's true. It's the experience that's important to the people now, and so it does overshadow the songwriting."

For a night, however, Jimmy Buffett was able to step out of the character of Jimmy Buffett and play the guy the brand was built on—himself. He introduced "A Pirate Looks at Forty" first by remembering the day he got a call from a friend who said Bob Dylan had played the song the night before,* and then by remembering Phil Clark.

"It wasn't about me, it was about him, and he truly was the pirate looking at forty in those days," Buffett said. "And it's great to play the song in the place where I wrote it about the person who was the inspiration."

Down at the Chart Room, where Clark worked when Jerry Jeff brought Buffett to town, the Thursday night crowd—including Steve and Cindy Thompson—listened live on Radio Margaritaville. "So Phil, wherever you are," Buffett said. "Actually, his ashes are in the bar downtown that used to be the Full Moon Saloon. So you can go say hi to Phil if you want. I might stop by. I don't know."

As Buffett sang "A Pirate Looks at Forty," Chris Robinson, who'd replaced Clark at the Chart Room, sang quietly along.

Buffett finished the set with "We Are the People Our Parents Warned Us About," said goodnight, and was off to Cuba the next morning. The Parrot Heads moved to the beach, or over to Louie's—where the Afterdeck filled up—or out onto Duval Street for as late as they could go. Corcoran pulled up on a lawn chair next to friends. Doyle Grisham stopped by for a drink. Thom Shepherd

---

* That happened. In Pasadena, California, in 1982. With Joan Baez.

returned to the second stage and pulled Aaron Scherz up for a late-Thursday-night rendition of "It's Always Saturday Night."

In 1986, writer Phillip Lopate crafted a fantastically grumpy essay, "Against Joie de Vivre": "All the people sitting around a pool drinking margaritas, they're not really happy, they're depressed," Lopate wrote. "Drunk, sunbaked, stretched out in a beach-chair, I am unable to ward off the sensation of being utterly alone, unconnected, cut off from others."

If that's not the exact sentiment "Margaritaville" captured, it's only off by its disdain. "Margaritaville" wasn't born a happy song. Its narrator—Buffett, mostly—is falling apart, frustrated, dispirited, and disillusioned. Why had he stayed so long? What was the point and what was he accomplishing? Not much.

"If you just read it off the paper, it doesn't read as the positive force it is," McAnally says. "If you just say the words of 'Margaritaville' it's not necessarily a positive thing. It's only when you put that song together with Jimmy's ridiculously positive personality that it becomes this *thing*."

This big, beloved *thing* that lifts people up from what is and sets them down in what was, or what could be—even if only for a day (or hour) or two. And, yes, sometimes they drink.

If the Day One mood had been anticipatory, Day Two dawned (sometime after noon) hungover. The crowd around the Casa Marina pools was subdued. Naps were in progress. There was a street party on Duval, and it would fill up, but not fast. Whenever. Soon come.

A stage had been erected outside the Margaritaville Café. From the company's first office,* above the CVS (which is down the street from another CVS), people threw Mardi Gras beads. Across the street, the balcony above Banana Republic had been adorned with banners for Margaritaville Spirits and the Margaritaville Vacation

---

* The corporate headquarters is now in Orlando.

Club. LandShark necklaces and Margaritaville-branded beach balls were everywhere—dozens of inflatable indicators of the size of the empire. Under this corporate umbrella, the people danced.

Parrot Heads get a bum rap, and not just as tippers. If they're considered at all, they're considered a cultural problem rather than a symptom. *VICE* once let a writer loose in Margaritaville's Bossier City, Louisiana, casino and hotel complex. He took a look around and characterized Buffett as "money-hungry and creatively bankrupt—a songwriter peddling bland, unobjectionable good-time tunes to over-the-hill office workers who fantasize about being burnouts."

Go behind the VIP lines at the Coachella Valley Music and Arts Festival sometime. Watch Usher wait for a wood-fired pizza while dozens of impeccably primped Southern California cool kids pretend to be too cool to take photos of Usher waiting for pizza. Watch them sneak those photos and catch what's become known as festival fashion. The costumes aren't any less ridiculous at Coachella than they are in front of Buffett's stage. They're just on (often) younger and (sometimes) fitter bodies.

The only difference between a Coachella-associated pool party at the Ace Hotel in Palm Springs and the Casa Marina scene is a more earnest brand of singer-songwriter, and Snapchat.

No one fantasizes about being a burnout, because being a burnout is easy. A lack of effort is paramount to the job description. But burnouts miss their kids' soccer games. No one wants that. The Meeting of the Minds crowd is full of people holding jobs—often very good jobs—and caring for families. Once a year they like to blow off a little steam with people they know, like, and have something in common with. The world's full of stress and worry and overtime demands. What's wrong with a little fun?

"The great thing about Parrot Head Clubs is they're organized," Thom Shepherd says. Shepherd once wrote a hit called "Redneck Yacht Club," and it's become as close as he's gotten to a "Margaritaville" of his own. Craig Morgan took it to number two on the country chart. There's a bar in Oklahoma that licenses the name from him.

He wrestled a little with whether or not he wanted to be perceived as a guy who played Parrot Head parties. Would that hurt him in the broader musical world? But he also wrote a song called "Parrot Head" with a punch line about waking up with feathers in his bed and realizing he "flocked a Parrot Head." It's on an album called *Tropicalifragilisticexpialidocious*, and that's *exactly* the kind of linguistic trick that'll get you invited to festivals like Feeding Phrenzy (Panama City, Florida), One Particular Phlocking (Breinigsville, Pennsylvania), or C-U in the Prairibbean (Champaign, Illinois).

It's not exactly the tour schedule Shepherd first imagined, but it's a good career. When he flies to play a show and he calls to tell the organizers when he'll arrive and where he'll stay, most often they say, "We'll pick you up, and you'll stay with us." And no one expects him to be a Jimmy Buffett cover band—though plenty of those exist. Nickerson was in a popular one called A1A.

Shepherd likens the experience to playing the Bluebird in Nashville, the listening room where Utley first heard Todd Snider and where so many great, great, great writers have gone to work out material. "Playing for the Parrot Heads is like playing for a Bluebird crowd in Hawaiian shirts," he says. "They like originals. I've even done Parrot Head gigs where they say, 'Please do not play any Jimmy Buffett songs.'"

After the street fair, Frinzi was booked to play some Jimmy Buffett songs back at the Casa Marina. But he wasn't going to just play Buffett songs. He saw Keith Sykes and started finger picking "Coast of Marseilles" as a way of coaxing Sykes onstage and then he handed over the guitar so Sykes could play a new song, "Come As You Are Beach Bar," part of the four-song EP he'd been recording in Nashville. Another of the songs, "Best Day," was based (loosely) on that long ago day off Key West when they lost their sangria and had to scrape together enough booze to get loaded in the sun.

With a nod to Corcoran, who'd given Frinzi a copy of *Greatest Hits of the Lesser Antilles* and was called to the stage for the moment, Frinzi played Tom Waits's "Shiver Me Timbers." Later, he played "Shoreline"—a poem Corcoran wrote in 1967 and Frinzi put to music.

By then Grisham and Utley were sitting in and after a short break, Frinzi reemerged as the Shrimper Dan Band, named after the man Billy Voltaire kills in "Cuban Crime of Passion." Each year they pick an album to play in its entirety, and *A1A* was the winner.

Bartlett was called on for "Dallas." Aaron Scherz took an emotional vocal on "A Pirate Looks at Forty." The Shrimper Dan Band walked the line between reverence to source material and reliance on Buffett's belief he descended from court jesters and not theologians. As the mistakes piled up, so too did the laughs.

Coral Reefers came and went and when Frinzi and his band were done, they handed the stage to Bill Wharton, the Sauce Boss. He makes gumbo during his set. Buffett immortalized him in the song "I Will Play for Gumbo."

Saturday brought the Coral Reefer Band playing some Buffett songs, some Ralph MacDonald* songs, and some of their own songs. When they were finished, the Trop Rock Music Association Awards Show took center stage. James "Sunny Jim" White picked up male vocalist of the year. He's the Mac McAnally of trop rock. He wins every year. Sunny Jim lives near Venice, Florida, though his musical address is Laid-back Lane, and once a month will play a show at the train station the circus used to leave from. The massive sliding doors were for the elephants to walk through.

Sunny Jim earned his beach cred playing the Hyatt on Grand Cayman. He worked his way into *The Firm*, the Tom Cruise flick

---

* MacDonald died of cancer in 2011.

based on the John Grisham book, and onto the soundtrack with a song called "Blame It on the Rum." He worked his way into Buffett's *A Pirate Looks at Fifty* by sneaking off to the Grand Cayman airport to try to say hello when Buffett landed the *Hemisphere Dancer*. When Buffett's ride didn't arrive in a timely manner, White offered a ride. When Jimmy and Jane needed a babysitter so they could go to dinner, White and his wife, who had twins about the same age as Sarah Delaney and Cameron, offered. Buffett returned the favor by sending Radio Margaritaville to the island to broadcast some live Sunny Jim music.

Howard Livingston & Mile Marker 24's set included a brightly costumed dance number and a gag where he makes a margarita onstage, mixing it with a 1952 Johnson outboard and then auctioning the finished product off for charity. There's a companion song about how it takes a while to get his Johnson going.

Out over the Atlantic, lightning flashed as a breeze picked up and carried Livingston's song out past the Casa Marina and into the night. There were seats to be had at the poolside bars, and the hotel lobby was quiet. Around the corner, past the Waddell apartment that never did have a front porch swing, Louie's Backyard (which did) was open and the Afterdeck was alive. "It's the Parrot Head thing," a waitress told a group looking for a table. While off in a corner, Chris Robinson and Keith Sykes caught up on the years, and remembered what used to be.

Chapter 19

Searching for Margaritaville

He does these huge shows and people are passionately committed to the shows. In essence, I'm only interested in thinking about him as someone who wrote some really great songs. "Margaritaville" is a nice song. People will put something down because it gets so popular. If he recorded that now, and it came out, people would really, really like it. It's a nice story and there's nothing in it that's dated. It's got this wistful feel. It's like a party song that's not a party song.

—Dave Rawlings,
singer-songwriter-guitarist

So we return to once upon a time, to sleepy little Hollywood, Florida, and a scrappy lot across the street from low-slung, coral-colored motels with names like the Riptide, the Neptune, and the Marlin. Old Florida.

A Sunoco station opened on that lot in 1959 and then closed in the early seventies, a victim of the oil crisis. Pinched between A1A and the Intracoastal Waterway, a man named Russell T. Kouth bought the property in 1974.

Originally from Pennsylvania, Kouth made his money as a pilot flying Coppertone banners over South Florida beaches. On a dare from a restaurant owner, Kouth built a bar and restaurant by hand on the lot, opening Le Tub in 1975, but fully assembling it over four years from scrap and debris he found jogging daily on the beach.

Washed up boogie boards and frayed ropes, water skis and glass floats hang from the walls and ceilings. Outside, along A1A, he marked his place with bright yellow toilets and bathtubs he turned into planters. A yellow toilet seat near the entrance says "Seat Yourself." The floor is uneven, the ceiling low in some places, high in others—as if Kouth had been waiting for a level to wash ashore and then gave up.

Le Tub was there in 1976 when Jimmy Buffett and Tom Corcoran guided the *Euphoria* down the Intracoastal on her maiden voyage to Coconut Grove, where she'd live while Buffett set to work making *Changes in Latitudes, Changes in Attitudes.*

And Le Tub is still there today, across the street from a 17-story, 349-room, nearly $200 million beachfront testament to the allure of an ever-expanding Margaritaville: the Margaritaville Beach Resort.

John Cohlan's official title is CEO of Margaritaville Holdings, but in keeping with company ideology, he'd prefer a more casual approach. He's Buffett's friend and business partner for twenty years. Buffett once bought him an antique dime, had it framed, and included a note that said while it wasn't the first dime *they'd* made, it might be the first dime ever made.

Cohlan and Buffett share an office in Palm Beach. The day Anheuser-Busch sent a team with mockups of LandShark Lager's packaging, Buffett happened to be around. Cohlan told the group they should take the designs and the bottle in to show Buffett, who signed the bottle before the beer guys got in the car and went to the airport.

A few months later, they were on the phone to work over marketing. "Normally our history had been, with corporate partners, it took them a while to really get the DNA of the way to talk about this brand," Cohlan says. "They call me up and they say here's our idea, it's 'Let the Fin Begin.'"

Cohlan loved it. "I said, 'I gotta tell you something. We've been doing this a while, we've been doing this for ten years, that's about as good as anybody's ever come back with,'" Cohlan says.

On the other end of the line, Dave Peacock, the president of Anheuser-Busch laughed. "He says, 'John, don't you know the derivation of that?'" Cohlan says.

He did not.

When Buffett signed the bottle, he signed it, "Let the Fin Begin—Jimmy Buffett." The Anheuser-Busch team got in the car, looked at the bottle, and said, "There's the tagline."

When Cohlan called Buffett to tell him about the ad campaign, Buffett said, "That's good. That's really good."

"And I said, 'Jimmy, it is good. You know why it's good?'"

He did not.

He didn't remember. He'd just scratched it on the bottle and didn't think twice. He'd been doing that all his life, from the earliest days of his career. Four decades on, there's still nobody who understands who Jimmy Buffett is and what Jimmy Buffett does better than Jimmy Buffett.

In 2009, when the Miami Dolphins renamed their stadium LandShark Stadium for a year, there were Buffett and the Coral Reefer Band playing "Margaritaville" and a rewritten "Fins" ("you're at the only game in town") for fans and season-ticket holders in front of a banner that read . . . Let the Fin Begin.

"It was little details about dealing with vendors, dealing with promoters," Corcoran says. "Dealing with different concert halls. Dealing with sound systems. And when he got somebody who was good, he hung onto them, and if they started to screw up, which happened when they were partying too much and they took it for granted, he knew. He was very detail oriented, and so it was a growth thing. He just paid attention to shit. And that's the way he was on the boat."

By any reliable measure of pop stardom, Buffett shouldn't have the career he's had. "Margaritaville" was the fourteenth-biggest hit of 1977 according to *Billboard*, and that's about all he got. He should be going on at 3 p.m. in the middle of a state fair opening for whatever Mike Love is passing off as the Beach Boys.

Or he should have scaled down, written more carefully detailed ballads, and played the theaters John Prine and Todd Snider play. "Most people like Jimmy Buffett have lives like mine," Snider says. "He's really an exception. His is a major exception to the troubadour rule—especially the one-man troubadour just trying get the job of guy-who-doesn't-have-another-job and sings songs."

In the early days of the Internet, a number of sites built *by* Parrot Heads *for* Parrot Heads emerged. One, the Church of Buffett, Orthodox, announced Buffett as "chief poet, insofar as he has best espoused a philosophy of cheerful hedonism." *A White Sport Coat and a Pink Crustacean*, *Living and Dying in ¾ Time*, *A1A*, and *Havana Daydreamin'* constituted the "spiritual core" of the "holy canon." *Changes in Latitudes, Changes in Attitudes* was problematic because it held the "apostasy" of "Margaritaville." Less than enamored with "the real time Jimmy" for his turn toward commercialism, they anointed Snider "the rightful heir to the title of Chief Poet, Cheerful Hedonism division."

"If I ever had to defend myself to the Church of Buffett," Buffett told *Time* in 1998, "I would only say that the bitterest artists I know are those who had the chance to jump through the hoop and chose not to take it. They stayed on as coffeehouse singers. But I jumped through not knowing what was on the other side. And when I got there, I had to deal with it. It wasn't 'happily ever after.' I was just getting started."

Since 1990, Buffett's played to more than 10 million fans and grossed more than $400 million touring. Between 2000 and 2009, he was the tenth-highest-grossing act in the country, putting him in the company of Bruce Springsteen, the Rolling Stones, U2, and Elton John.

They all enjoy their money, but there's no Thunder Roadside Inn. It's not Bruce's style, but even if it were, what would that brand be? How do you capture the complications of finding your way into a meaningful adult life while struggling with unresolved issues resulting from a conflicted relationship with your father? What's *that* hotel room look like?

Margaritaville looks good on a cruise ship and in shopping malls and on the Home Shopping Network. Margaritaville plays. It's a 305-acre resort on the western edge of Walt Disney World; a hotel and casino in Tulsa, Oklahoma; and an escape in Tennessee's Great Smoky Mountains. Margaritaville is a $130 throw pillow; a $300 Margaritaville Key West Frozen Concoction Maker; a $12 bottle of tequila. It's bicycles, hammocks, bedding, luggage, candle scents, scratch-off lottery tickets, online games, and dozens of other products. Cohlan says they move more than three million cases of LandShark a year—and not just to people who remember when. There's a college ambassador program taking the brand on to campuses around the country.

Margaritaville.com has become a one-stop lifestyle warehouse where travel stories mix with drink recipes and Buffett's tour dates. In 2015, when Buffett decided to play the small theater inside the San Carlos Institute on Duval Street, fans were asked to go to Margaritaville.com and vote on the set list. In 2016, Buffett had a list of songs the band hadn't played in a decade compiled, and fans could vote on which of *those* they'd like to hear. In both cases, Margaritaville expanded its database of potential customers.

The Margaritaville Café in Las Vegas is one of the highest-grossing restaurants in Sin City. The Margaritaville Café in Orlando is one of the highest-grossing restaurants in America's family destination. Margaritaville has opened in the Mall of America and in a mall in Syracuse, New York, called Destiny USA.

There are hats and shoes and T-shirts, sunglasses (featuring Margaritaville Polarized Technology), and yes, flip-flops. There are vacation packages to Bimini and the Gulf Coast, and if you're wondering what to wear, the Margaritaville Apparel Collection announces itself as "The Authentic Expression of the Casual Lifestyle." The hat, with a bottle opener screwed under the brim says, "Chill: Est. 1977."

Take a little Margaritaville home, Margaritaville Store,
Hollywood, Florida.

"I often say, even though we don't have an airline, what Margaritaville is with all these different businesses we're in, is we're a travel company," Cohlan says. "Because everything we do is sort of about taking you away, in one form or another. Transporting you."

From wherever you are, to wherever you dream of being. By late 2016, Margaritaville was approaching $2 billion of capital investment. Fifteen million people a year visit the restaurants, hotels, casinos, and timeshare resorts. They're doing $1.5 billion a year in sales, and Cohlan sees nothing but clear skies, full blenders, and continued growth.

Why?

Because of Jimmy Buffett.

"Who he is and what he stands for," Cohlan says. "There is no Tommy Bahama. There really is a person behind this whole idea of Margaritaville."

And as that guy approached his seventieth birthday, in 2016, he was as active as ever. He was in and out of Cuba, including a quick set strummed for U.S. Embassy employees before heading out to see the Rolling Stones. He played some songs in Augusta, Georgia, during the Masters and hit golf balls barefoot into some undisclosed bay. NFL star J. J. Watt sat in with the band on percussion one night in Texas. Jerry Jeff Walker opened for him outside Dallas, and when he played "Mr. Bojangles," and the party crowd grew restless with a ballad, Jerry Jeff promised it'd be the last of those in the set.

Buffett flew to Tahiti and then to Easter Island. He played the Ryman Auditorium for the first time—sitting in with Jenny Lewis on a Traveling Wilburys' song. He took Roy Orbison's part and had a bedazzled marijuana-leaf sport coat made for the occasion.

He readied a musical, *Escape to Margaritaville*, for a 2017 debut in San Diego with eyes on New York and Broadway in 2018. He recorded a new Christmas album, *'Tis the SeaSon*, to celebrate his birthday. It included, finally, that cover of "All I Want for Christmas Is My Two Front Teeth," he'd talked about so long ago. They rewrote "The Twelve Days of Christmas" for the Parrot Heads: "2 tattoos and a purple parrot in a palm tree."

He sailed and surfed and fished and wrote touching tributes to friends Glenn Frey and Jim Harrison—after each passed away. "Margaritaville" was inducted into the Grammy Hall of Fame and cited by the 11th U.S. Circuit Court of Appeals in a case regarding the regulation of tattoo parlors in Key West. Wrote the court:

"But the singer in 'Margaritaville'—seemingly far from suffering embarrassment over his tattoo—considers it 'a real beauty.'"

Buffett played big shows, and he played little shows just for fun. He recruited his old friend from *Rancho Deluxe*, Jeff Bridges, to reprise his most famous role, the Dude, and appear onstage as the animated Clairvoyant Coconut. Far-out, man.

Buffett celebrated his thirty-ninth wedding anniversary, and played with Paul McCartney at a Hamptons fund-raiser for Hillary Clinton. He hurt his leg surfing, and he went to Paris—again. He went to Japan to play a few shows on military bases, and posted photos to Facebook from the cockpit of his plane as he descended into Alaska to refuel on the way. On the way home, he stopped in Hawaii to step back into his role as Frank Bama on the television series *Hawaii Five-0*. A few weeks later, he was fishing in the Bahamas.

He and Jane made their annual appearance at *Vanity Fair's* Oscar party, and hosted a few fund-raisers that made society columns. Jane mostly stays out of the spotlight, as do their two youngest, Sarah Delaney and Cameron. Savannah Jane followed her dad into the lifestyle business, working on travel documentaries, spinning tunes, and generally seeming to have a good time, all the time.

In some ways, 2016 wasn't any different for Buffett than 1974, when the sum of his destinations and adventures seemed impossible to fit into a single calendar year.

And just as that calendar flipped, there was Buffett on St. Barts, singing "Auld Lang Syne" with McCartney at a party hosted by Russian billionaire Roman Abramovich. A few weeks later, Buffett was peddling his bike around Key West as the news broke that the Westin Key West Resort and Marina, just a few blocks from the Chart Room, would soon become the Margaritaville Key West Resort and Marina.

Ever forward, ever toward that "Ever Elusive Future"—to steal the title of the song he wrote for *Jurassic World*. That was in 2015, when sixty-eight-year-old Jimmy Buffett became a meme, the guy swooping in to save the margaritas from a table outside Isla Nublar's Margaritaville Café as dinosaurs were swooping in for the kill.

That *Jurassic World* was, aside from a vehicle for Chris Pratt's biceps and charms, a lesson in the dangers of soulless corporatism didn't matter. Margaritaville might be corporate, but can it ever be soulless when Jimmy Buffett's at the helm? People still like Jimmy Buffett—always have.

He continues to "flit and flit," as Twain wrote and Buffett quoted not that long ago. He continues to smile a smile that hasn't changed in decades, a smile that says "Can you believe I got away with this?" Mac McAnally calls what they do each night on a stage a "rolling ball of goodwill," and Buffett and John Cohlan have figured out how to spin that into something people will pay for time and again.

It's a funny thing, because if you're looking for Jimmy Buffett, you won't often find him in a Margaritaville Café. "Ever on the wing," to quote Twain once more, you'll find him far from the herd, possibly riding BUFIT ONE, the air corridor south from Palm Beach International Airport, and then banking toward some remote piece of beach.

He's a daydream, Jimmy Buffett. He gets you through the workday, through that job you took so you can buy the house, the one that needs a little work. Maybe a new deck for the grill. He's a dream in place of the dream you set aside because the house was the smart play, the safe play. And the backyard's nice. You can host your friends, fire up the Frozen Concoction Maker, have a few laughs. Maybe at night, after the kids are asleep, you sneak a joint out there and stare at the stars and imagine what's beyond the Bed, Bath & Beyond. There must be something beyond the Bed, Bath & Beyond.

Jimmy Buffett's out there. Turn on Radio Margaritaville and exhale.

Has there been a cost for Buffett? Sure. Well, maybe.

"I don't think it's taken away from Jimmy as an artist, or making really great music, but it has commercialized it," Utley says. "And that's what it is. Musicians don't do it as often; actors do it all the time."

It's harder to play the ballads—the songs that mean the most. In Las Vegas in 2013, "Colour of the Sun," a pretty little song about the things that endure, from *Songs from St. Somewhere*, was treated as a bathroom and beer break. If Buffett noticed, he didn't say anything other than "You throw a great party. We're glad to be your band."

Remember what Jim Harrison said in *Tarpon*? About seeking out those jolts of electricity that make you feel alive. They live in the future, but they connect to the past.

In September 2015, the city of Pascagoula dedicated a bridge to Jimmy Buffett. It's a small bridge on Beach Boulevard, but it's a bridge.

On a blistering afternoon, the shore filled with boats, the beach filled with fans, the cheeseburgers were cheap, the T-shirts custom, and the LandShark cold. Buffett piloted his seaplane over the scene, landed on a nearby lake, and got a police escort to the stage. "I loved riding behind the police," Buffett joked. "It used to be the other way."

He and McAnally played a few songs inspired by Buffett's youth. They played "Margaritaville." And just when it seemed they were done, Buffett ran back onstage for one more. Alone, he played "The Captain and the Kid," a song that almost never makes the set list at the big shows, and he got to play it next to a bridge that crossed Baptiste Bayou, which runs right up to his grandparents' old backyard and the ghost of a crab pier and a long-ago moment between grandfather and grandson.

After he left, fans took pictures next to the mural on the bridge Buffett had stopped to sign. "Start Here," he wrote. It's worth looking back sometimes. "Let's just say, the odds were long," Buffett said of his career.

When Bob Dylan was asked in 2009 who his favorite songwriters were, he said Jimmy Buffett (citing "Death of an Unpopular Poet" and "He Went to Paris," specifically) and sent the world scrambling to figure out if Dylan was joking or not because 1) he's Bob Dylan and 2) *Margaritaville candle scents*. But why wouldn't Bob Dylan like Buffett? Song-and-dance men recognize each other.

"Waylon, when he was still alive, I saw him out at a studio and he talked about 'He Went to Paris,'" Utley says, "how he loved that song. Most people, most of the acts never recorded his songs, it's just they listened to him, and they liked what they heard."

Ben Jaffe, of the Preservation Hall and the Preservation Hall Jazz Band, was standing in the audience when Buffett and the Reefers played a fund-raiser in New Orleans in 2016. He was standing next to a rock star the world would expect to cite David Bowie, Springsteen, or a thousand other musicians before even thinking about Jimmy Buffett. Jaffe says Win Butler, of the Arcade Fire, turned to him and said, "He tells personal stories without being overly complicated."

Which is a hell of a lot harder than it looks.

McAnally once did a songwriting seminar with Jesse Winchester and someone asked Winchester the key to writing great songs. "You just try to say what matters," Winchester said, "and try not to say anything else."

In the middle of the lobby of the Margaritaville Beach Resort in Hollywood Beach, there's a towering electric-blue flip-flop. Inspired by Jeff Koons's three-ton sculpture *Tulips*,* it stands on end. Its strap has broken free. It's blown out. There's a pop-top next to it and the sculpture quickly became a popular stop for family vacation photos and selfies.

---

* Parrot Head Steve Wynn purchased *Tulips* for $33.7 million and put it on one of his Las Vegas properties.

At one end of the lobby sits JWB Prime Steak & Seafood, Buffett's first fine-dining option. At the other end, the corporate mantra—"No Passport Required"—welcomes guests to the front desk. Seating alcoves are crowned by lyrics from "Margaritaville." The Margaritaville Coffee Shop offers an "Escape from the Daily Grind."

The body pillow on the bed reads "Changes in Attitude" or "Changes in Latitude"; parrots are faintly embossed on the comforters. An old photo of Tom Corcoran's, of a sailboat at sea, is on the cover of the hotel guide. The stationery features a map of the Caribbean and the pencils read, "Mother, Mother Ocean." The "Do Not Disturb" sign says, "License to Chill." The ice bucket is Margaritaville branded ("Destination Relaxation") and the minibar is set to "Island Provisions." The "Nibblin' on Sponge Cake" snack pack is $50. The "Wastin' Away Again in Margaritaville" drink pack is $110 and includes your choice of one bottle of Margaritaville Tequila or rum (with a choice of flavors), twelve LandShark Lagers, and mixers.

In Las Vegas, the 5 O'Clock Somewhere Bar sits in the middle of a casino lit by overhead fixtures built to resemble sliced limes. In Nashville, that old half-sunken shrimp boat from the cover of *Living and Dying in ¾ Time*, the *Good Luck*, has been resurrected and floats happily in a painting on a wall. You can order a Cheeseburger in Paradise or the Volcano nachos. The *Euphoria*, once Buffett's prize possession, his insurance policy against an unstable world, is now a daiquiri. "One Particular Harbour" built with all the beauty and peace Tahiti had to offer Buffett in the tumultuous early-eighties, is also a bank of slot machines.

When he sings that song—and he sings it every night of his working life just the same as "Margaritaville"—and he reaches the lyric about how he'll one day disappear, he pauses for a slight beat and says, "But not *yet*."

Onstage in Las Vegas in 2013, Buffett talked about Willie Nelson coming to play a little surf bar in Montauk, New York. Buffett jumped onstage with Willie for a song, and they hung out on Willie's bus.

"Did you inhale?" Utley said.

"Why wouldn't I?"

But the point of the story was this: Willie told Buffett his band had been worried. Willie had turned eighty and they were wondering what would happen when he retired. "And Willie went, 'Retire? From what?'" Buffett said.

Good point, but nothing lasts forever. Jimmy Buffett has taken a little song he wrote in a few minutes, carried it around the world, and then turned it into a world of its own.

He's played it in football stadiums and basketball arenas, and he's played it on beaches and in bars and on boats. In 2015, "Margaritaville," and the rest of a set from Houston, was beamed to the International Space Station.

Buffett's found verses and lost verses and written entirely new verses. After he fell off the stage in Australia in 2011, he added one that left him recovering in Hawaii with some sake, some yoga, and a little weed.

For forty years, Jimmy Buffett has played "Margaritaville" for anyone who's wanted to hear it because it's allowed him to be a version of himself he could only ever have dreamed of—the person millions themselves dream of being. It's bought him everything he's ever wanted and allowed him to move with style around the globe in much the same way Hemingway did after his myth-defining years in Key West.

But maybe one day Jimmy Buffett will get to the end of "One Particular Harbour" and let the song fade out with no "but not *yet*," no promise of another show. Maybe he'll even end the set there, walk off stage, and that'll be that. There'll be rumors. The *Coconut Telegraph*, digital and faster than ever, might catch a glimpse of him back in Moorea, or in Le Select. Maybe he'll grow a big David

Letterman beard and tell stories at the end of some bar he owns but hasn't put his name on.

He can always play Baz Bar on St. Barts, where photos from earlier performances are taped behind the bar and where, when he sits in with the band, word travels fast and the waterfront fills with locals and tourists alike.

Seems unlikely, but it could happen.

A few years ago, in Portland, he played "He Went to Paris," and it was special. Not every song is when you've been playing them as long as Buffett has. The wear and tear of all those years can show on a song. But the pros, the really good ones, they find a way to get to what made a song great.

Buffett got there that night and held an arena quiet while he unfolded a story that moves closer to his own with each passing year. As he reached the conclusion—"But I've had a good life all the way"—the arena's silence broke into applause, and then cheers. He laughed a little.

"Thanks," he said.

Epilogue

I was staying at the Margaritaville Beach Resort in Hollywood, Florida, when the news broke that Allen Toussaint had died in Spain. I grabbed my iPod, got a cup of coffee from the Margaritaville Coffee Shop, and went for a walk on the beach listening to *The Bright Mississippi*.

A few months earlier, I'd met Mr. Toussaint in the lobby of a hotel in downtown Portland. I'd been instructed to call his drummer and son-in-law, and he'd put me in touch with Mr. Toussaint, who emerged from the elevator in a resplendent blue suit and said, "How can I help?"

I wanted to talk about New Orleans and his long friendship with Buffett. When BP's Deepwater Horizon well spilled into the Gulf of Mexico in 2010, Buffett organized a show. CMT broadcast from the beach in Gulf Shores, Alabama. Among his guests, he brought Will Kimbrough, Toussaint, and Jesse Winchester, who danced quite the jig while singing "Rhumba Man."

After the television broadcast, Buffett and the band returned to the stage and ripped into Kimbrough's "Piece of Work." They did "Biloxi" with Winchester. And Toussaint returned to play a song he'd written called "I'm Gonna Hang with Jimmy Buffett."

"It seems like I've been on him forever," Toussaint told me when I asked how long he'd been friends with Buffett, "but that's not so. He has such a bright spirit. By the time I got to know Jimmy, 'Margaritaville,' was already making the world happy."

Toussaint wrote and produced pages of the American songbook. He wrote "Yes We Can Can." He produced the Meters. He wrote "Everything I Do Gonna Be Funky (From Now On)." Find a cooler song than that. I dare you.

Toussaint was responsible for so many of those hits drifting from New Orleans to Buffett's grandparents' house in Pascagoula. As Toussaint's website still says, if Professor Longhair was New Orleans's Bach, Toussaint was its Mozart. He'd made the world happy a few hundred songs over and had the license plate on his Bentley to prove it: SONGS. How had he come to write one about Buffett?

"I was looking at TV one day, and the news, as news is so many times, the people were hustling and bustling, and things were not coming all together," he said. "There were so many conflicting things going on, and I thought about Jimmy Buffett and the persona he presents, not fake at all. He lives his heart. His heart is out there and he shares it with the people. I was thinking, rather than all this stuff, I was going to hang with Jimmy Buffett."

He tapped a rhythm on his knee as he began to recite the lyrics, his recitation more musical than most albums. Toussaint could blink an earworm. "Grinding at the grinding stone grinding away," Toussaint said. "Gotta make another buck no time to play."

Ah, but he saw some birds flying south and pointing the way to where they serve the blues beater, "that famous margarita."

At Toussaint's memorial service, among New Orleans legends, Buffett got up dressed in black and played "Fortune Teller" one more time, just as he'd played it on street corners in the French Quarter when no one knew who he was, or cared.

Toussaint embodied the spirit of New Orleans the way Buffett grabbed that brief period of time in Key West's history. Listen to "Southern Nights"—not Glen Campbell's hokey hit, but Toussaint's, the way it dances across the bayou in the moonlight and plays hide-and-seek in the Spanish moss.

As the sun rose over what Hollywood Beach calls its Broadwalk, the morning filled with coffee drinkers, joggers, and bicyclists. In my earbuds, Toussaint's piano glistened like the Atlantic and I remembered the way he smiled when I asked if he'd ever considered expanding his reach beyond music into the food or style of his Louisiana.

"Never, never," he said. "I'd rather go hang with Jimmy Buffett."

Acknowledgments

Growing up in Ann Arbor, Michigan, Florida was our vacation. My uncle Bill lived in Tampa and the four of us—Mom and Dad, my brother Andy and I—would make the drive down I-75. Two days down, two days back. In between, we'd hit fish shacks and amusement parks and waste days at the beach. Dad liked to walk. Slowly down the beach by himself, shedding at least some of the weight of what always seemed through my eyes to be overwhelming responsibilities. I'd watch him wander off, staring at the horizon.

I was sitting at the bar in the Margaritaville Casino in Las Vegas one day when I called and asked what he thought about on those walks. "Jimmy Buffett, I guess," he said, possibly for my benefit, but probably not. That exhale from the real world, that mental break—that's the service Jimmy Buffett has been providing for decades.

I first saw Buffett when I was in college. It was in Columbus, Ohio, on July 16, 1994. Not long ago, I found the ticket stub tucked in a copy of *Fruitcakes* (on CD). I visited Key West for the first time the next year. Both Buffett (or the idea of Buffett) and the island he made famous have danced in and out of my life since. Buffett's songs have been especially welcome in uneasy times. Whenever anyone asked me what this book was about, my one word answer was always this: change.

Buffett, and his little island, began as outsiders. Now they're defining features of suburban middle class. But then, I can buy a Nirvana T-shirt at Target. That's what happens around here. Our outlaws become kings. Most everyone has to settle down and figure out how best to work through the world. Even Jimmy Buffett.

I first began thinking about this book in 2010, not long after my daughter was born. Three years later, the day after leaving a newspaper job I'd had (and loved) for nearly sixteen years, I went to the beach. On an unusually warm day, with the rest of the house napping, I poured a drink and went for a walk listening to *Changes in Latitudes, Changes in Attitudes*. I decided then to see if I couldn't make this real.

The book I imagined while wading in the Pacific Ocean is far different than the one you hold in your hands. A great many are owed thanks for that.

My friend Peter Ames Carlin read the earliest drafts of the proposal (and there were many), told me where I was wrong, and insisted I could be right. My agent, Zachary Schisgal, was more confident than I was while I wrestled that proposal, and then knew what to do with it when it finally was finished.

Matthew Benjamin believed in the initial idea and then gently and smartly nudged me toward better ideas as the days and months moved along. He and the team at Touchstone deserve more than the Lost Shaker of Salt I sent from Nashville.

There are more than 104,000 words in front of this paragraph and I'd need at least 104,000 more to begin to adequately thank Tom Corcoran. He didn't have to respond to my email, much less let me come to Lakeland, Florida; take me to dinner; let me into his home; and tell me story, after story, after amazing story. And then he sent a collection of mix tapes. Thank you, Tom. Again and again.

Roger Bartlett took my call and then kept taking them. He connected me with his old friends and helped connect countless dots. Norbert Putnam showed me Muscle Shoals, showed off a couple of adorable dogs, and told me all about playing with Ray Charles on *Hee Haw*. That was a good day.

Poor John Cohlan. Well, not poor. He's done quite well for himself, but he was checking into the Margaritaville Beach Resort in Hollywood, Florida, when I recognized him and felt the need to introduce myself. He was gracious (and on brand in a pair of Margaritaville flip-flops). When I ran into him at the coffee shop the next morning, he had a few smart follow-ups about the project and allowed me to keep in touch. I thank him for his time and assistance in getting the business end of things as right as I could make it.

Michael Utley took time out from a morning off in New York to talk about his long and amazing career. Mac McAnally fit me in while waiting for his car to be returned from an auto shop in Nashville. Doyle Grisham picked up breakfast in Key West—an unnecessary but welcome gesture. I owe you one, Doyle.

Peter Cooper didn't have to dig into his archives and pull out a lengthy interview with Buffett's first manager, Don Light, but Peter did. And then he sneaked me into the Country Music Hall of Fame for a look around. Check out Peter's records. Look for his books.

In the interest of time and space—but with the understanding I could go on like this about everyone—thank you to: Will Kimbrough, Todd Snider (and Brian Kincaid), Keith Sykes, Deborah McColl, Phillip Fajardo, Amy Lee, Bob Liberman, Steve Vaughn, Clint Gilbert, Tim Glancey, Ray Wylie Hubbard, Judy Hubbard, Gary P. Nunn, Jeff Ragsdale, Ben Jaffe, Dave Rawlings (who I shanghaied while discussing his last excellent record), David Hood, Patterson Hood, Steve Diener, Jerry Rubinstein, Steve Resnik, Chris Robinson, Steve and Cindy Thompson, Vaughn Cochran, Cydall Cochran, Larry Schmidt, Doug Beveridge, Cindy O'Dare, Buzz Cason, Travis Turk, Milton Brown, Mike Shepherd, Kevin Boucher, Joe Nuzzo, David Ehrlich, Jim Sweet, Parker Sweet, Judi Gulledge and everyone at the Mobile Carnival Association (check out their museum),

Steve Joynt, Jim Mazzotta, Scott Nickerson, Thom Shepherd, John Patti, Andrew Talbert and the Parrot Heads in Paradise, George Stevenson and the Key Northwest Parrot Head Club, James "Sunny Jim" White, Hugo Duarte (RIP), Alex McMurray, Davis Rogan, Allen Toussaint (RIP) and his family, David April, Mike Davis, Douglas Roll (and family), Joe Thornhill (thanks for the rum), Tom Hambright and his staff at the Monroe County Public Library in Key West, Elizabeth Theris at the Mobile Public Library, Jacqulyn Kirkland at the Alabama Historical Commission, and everyone at the Special and Area Studies Collections at the George A. Smathers Library at the University of Florida. It's weird entertainment to walk into such a stately academic setting and ask for the Jimmy Buffett Papers. I felt like I should have brought a cooler.

Visit Stuart Jennison and the folks at Jennison & Shultz P.C. for all your United States Patent and Trademark Office needs. (Seriously, I could never have gotten my hands on the Margaritaville case file without them, and their prices are reasonable.) The Gaming Control Board in Nevada let me sit in their records room and scroll through the transcript of Buffett's appearance.

I sent an email to the Los Angeles Parrot Head Club, hoping to find someone who had been at the Roxy in 1976. Frank Bellino replied that he was there, and had a recording of the show. He sent me "Margaritaville," one of the first performances, and I sent it to Roger Bartlett to prove to him he'd played on the song. It's a funny world.

On that front, thank you to all who have taped shows over the years and put them online. Thanks to Radio Margaritaville for broadcasting nearly every show live. Thanks to Bing and Bong for their preshow banter. There's good stuff in there.

Two blissful Internet-free weeks were spent in the Oregon outback courtesy of Playa, a nonprofit that provides residencies for artists and writers. It's pretty country and a wonderful program. Apply if you can.

To Jimmy: Thanks for being the best and only Jimmy Buffett we've got.

Thanks for beers, thanks for guidance, thanks for listening and lending encouragement along the way: Patrick Green, Helen Jung, Brett and Jessica Hamilton, Andy Dworkin, Sarina Saturn, Rachel Bachman, Mona Qureshi-Hart, Michael and Erin Rosenberg, T. J. and Rachel Lentner (double thanks for getting married in Key West), Alison Fensterstock, Courtenay Hameister, Stacy Bolt, Scott Poole, Jake Buff, Chelsea Cain.

Mom and Dad, you're still the best.

Then there was the November day April Baer called to tell me we had a mouse in the house. I told her I couldn't help, because I was at the beach in Florida and had possibly been drinking for a few hours. She didn't change the locks before I got home. She never did anything but tell me I could do this. Thank you. I love you. And I promise the next book will be *Rust Belt Steel Mills in February*.

And to Stella, yes, finally, the book is done.

Index

Note: Page numbers in *italics* refer to illustrations. Songs and albums are by Jimmy Buffett unless otherwise noted.

About the Author

The author of *Springsteen: Album by Album*, Ryan White has twice been named one of the top feature writers in the country by the Society for Features Journalism. He spent sixteen years at the *Oregonian* covering sports, music, and culture. He's written for the *Wall Street Journal*, *Sports Illustrated*, the *Sacramento Bee*, the *Dallas Morning News*, and *Portland Monthly* magazine. He writes "Daddy Issues," a parenting column for *Metro Parent* magazine. Born in Ann Arbor, Michigan, he lives in Portland, Oregon, with his wife and daughter. He is a perfectly okay beer-league hockey player.